Creating a Christian Lifestyle

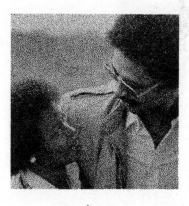

**Saint Mary's Press
Christian Brothers Publications
Winona, Minnesota**

Creating a Christian Lifestyle

by Carl Koch, FSC

To my mother and father, who
taught with their lives what is
written in this book

Nihil Obstat: Rev. Msgr. Roy E. Literski
Censor Deputatus
1 February 1988
Imprimatur: † John Vlazny, DD
Bishop of Winona
1 February 1988

The publishing team included Barbara Allaire,
development editor; Stephan Nagel and Rev.
Robert Stamschror, consulting editors; Susan
Baranczyk, production and manuscript editor
and indexer; and Carolyn St. George, designer.

The acknowledgments continue on page 362.

Printed in the United States of America

Printing: 6 5 4 3 2 1

Year: 1994 93 92 91 90 89 88

ISBN 0-88489-184-4

Contents

Foreword

A foreword is a short section that introduces a book. *Foreword* sounds like *forward*, and *forward* is a good word with which to begin this book about lifestyles, vocations, and callings. Much of your senior year will be spent looking forward to graduation, then to college or technical school or a job, to having your own place to live, perhaps eventually to marriage—in short, to beginning a life that is truly of your own making.

Your senior year is a time of looking forward, and it is also a time of making decisions that will help you to go forward. Though many decisions can be reshaped, most of the decisions you are making now have more concrete consequences for your whole future than the decisions you made even one or two years ago. Most seniors feel the weight of these decisions, but there is a real temptation to hold off serious considerations about the future and to simply enjoy the status of being a senior.

However, moving on is inevitable, and it can be wonderfully exciting if you have done some realistic dreaming before you hear the command to march forward to receive your diploma. Indeed, "forward" is the order given to get the troops moving. Seniors who leave high school without some plans and strategies are like a troop of soldiers all wearing blindfolds. They might be lucky enough to reach the next hill, but then again, they might march over a cliff. Reflecting about the future and making some tentative decisions will not guarantee perfect happiness and complete success—there will always be snags to trip over and holes to fall into—but at least the chances of living a fuller life are far better.

Moving on can be exciting if you have done some realistic dreaming.

Four Seniors

Here are four stories to consider, each of which reflects a senior's situation.

Marisa

Marisa finishes the last bit of her calculus homework. She smiles contentedly because she likes mathematics and, just as importantly, is very good at it. Tossing her books and papers into her book bag, she takes out the catalog from the university she wants to attend and flips to the section on electrical engineering. Scanning the list of courses, she remembers what a graduate from last year told her about each of the classes she will be taking. Although she knows that electrical engineering is a tough major, she feels excited about it.

Unfortunately, two clouds hover over Marisa's plans to study at the university next year. One problem is the discouragement she feels when some of her friends say things like, "You'll probably be the only woman in the whole engineering school," or "Don't you think that psychology or social work is better for a woman?" She hates it when people tell her that women shouldn't be engineers, yet she is concerned about being able to fit into a profession dominated by men.

The other problem is money. Marisa is sure she can get a loan. Her parents can give her some help, but she needs a well-paying summer job if she is going to make ends meet next year. What if she cannot earn enough money? With the tight job market, finding any summer work could be tough.

Joe

Joe sits at the dinner table, staring out of the window into the night sky.

"Well, Joe, what do you think? Have you decided yet?" his father asks.

"I don't know. I just don't know yet," Joe answers, irritated.

His father's look is not unkind, but he adds, "You have to make up your mind one of these days, Joe."

"Yeah, I know."

After supper, Joe returns to his room, puts on his headphones, and cranks up his stereo. He opens the drawer that holds his catalogs—catalogs for the Navy, a local community college, and an area technical school. Each brochure makes promises for a full, successful future.

However, Joe's thoughts always take him in a different direction. He imagines himself having his own apartment, a car that he really wants, and enough time to hunt, ski, and fish. Further schooling and a stint in the Navy only seem to be more delays.

Mary

Mary is thrilled by the offer of a basketball scholarship from the university. The scholarship solves a big problem because her parents cannot afford to send her to school there. The university has a great program in women's athletics.

The only remaining problem is that Mary has not been studying very hard. She simply cannot get very interested in her subjects. Her grades are okay for high school, but she knows from friends at the university that the academic regulations for athletes have recently been raised. A few top-notch players from last year are now on academic probation.

Mary wonders if she can meet the academic standards and still have time to play basketball. On the other hand, if she cannot play basketball, she cannot afford to go to the university.

Terry

Terry surprises everybody but himself when he announces that he has always wanted to be an artist—a sculptor. Even his art teacher tells him that he will not make it. His parents are so disappointed that they refuse to pay for his college education unless he studies something that they consider at least remotely useful. His father's opinion is that if Terry wants to major in art, he can fritter away his time at the junior college with his own money: "When you come to your senses, we'll talk about helping you." His friends just think he is goofy: "You'll snap out of it."

Few people to whom Terry has shown his artwork think that his sculpture shows much promise. Nevertheless, Terry is determined. He works more hours at his job, saves money, and looks forward—although with dampened enthusiasm—to college art classes.

Each of the decisions and dilemmas facing these imaginary seniors has many implications for them and for the people in relationships with them: their parents, friends, brothers and sisters, co-workers, and so on.

Each decision and dilemma has many implications.

- Marisa, by becoming an engineer, someday may have to choose between her career and starting a family. As a woman in a male-dominated field, she may have to be much more assertive than she is prepared to be. Perhaps this will be good for Marisa and she will rise to the occasion, or perhaps she will feel crushed.

- If Joe chooses to go to technical school, he will have to decide to view the experience either as a chance to grow, become more competent, and meet new people or as an unhappy delay of his freedom to do what he wants.

- If Mary accepts the basketball scholarship, she will need to shape up her study habits before showing up for practice. At the university, she will certainly feel the tension of constantly weighing and sorting out her values and priorities: study, friends, basketball, and social life.

- Even college art courses probably will not help Terry to become a sculptor if he does not have the necessary talent. Without accurately assessing his chances of success before he leaves high school, Terry is setting up himself and his family for disappointment.

Your situation is certainly different from those of the four seniors described in these examples. After all, you are unique, one of a kind. Even so, the decisions you are making now are important and do require asking some of the serious questions involved in the cases above. Your decisions will largely shape your life.

How many times have you heard the cliché, Not to decide is to decide? Clichés remain popular because they contain more than a little truth. The truth behind this cliché can be stated this way: if we do not reflect on a life plan, our fate easily can be determined by other people, circumstances, ignorance, whim, or lack of courage. We must consider such issues as the following:
- what we expect from the future
- what we need to learn
- the place of work in our life
- how much money we need to be satisfied
- whether the single life, marriage, religious life, or ordained life is right for us

What This Course Is About

This course is intended to help you make forward-looking, health-promoting decisions about your future. Planning for the future first requires that you know what you want or what your dream is. Chapter 1 discusses the identification of your dream and the transitional period of your life that is confronting you immediately. Having a reasonably clear sense of your dream is an important starting point for planning, but to fulfill your dream you need to have a strong sense of who you are and what you are capable of being and doing. Chapter 2 should help you to clarify your sense of who you are and what it means to direct your own life.

Each of us needs to ask, What gives my life focus? On what basis do I make decisions? The main point of chapter 3 is that loving is the central value that can guide a person to full life and salvation. Love is not simple. Consequently, this chapter outlines the qualities, benefits, and types of love, along with ways of building intimacy. Closely related to love is communication, and chapter 4 provides some helpful ideas about communicating positively, handling conflict, and giving and receiving feedback.

Chapter 5 focuses on sexuality as a great gift, a gift from God. Regrettably, our understanding of sexuality is often limited by popular myths and fallacies that float over the airwaves of television and radio or are relayed by well-meaning but often ill-informed friends. Sexuality can be appreciated only when it is

Planning for the future first requires that you know what you want or what your dream is.

understood in the context of whole personhood. One of the main developmental goals of young adulthood is to integrate sexuality into a whole way of life.

Chapters 6, 7, 8, and 9 discuss lifelong learning, work, money and possessions, and leisure. These four facets of living need to be examined in a course on lifestyles because whether you are single, married, a religious, or a priest, you need to learn, work, deal with money and possessions, and have time for leisure.

Lifelong learning, work, money, values, and leisure must be considered when planning a way of life.

These four topics often are ignored when planning a future way of life. Consequently, many difficulties in relationships arise from problems that relate to these topics: For instance, in a relationship one person may learn and grow more than the other, or one person may never have time to spend with the other due to overwork. Many marriages have been damaged because of arguments about money. Right now you might be anxious to discuss some of the later topics in this book—single life, courting, or marriage—but please give serious thought to how and why you should be a lifelong learner, what work means to you, the role of money and possessions in your lifestyle, and how you use leisure time. The better informed you are about these topics, the better you will understand chapters 10 through 15, which examine specific life paths.

Most of us will live alone for some period of time, and an ever-increasing percentage of people are choosing to remain single indefinitely. Chapter 10 examines the single life and how being single can be a fulfilling lifestyle.

Chapters 11, 12, and 13 concern marriage. In chapter 11, dating and courting are outlined. Research and common sense indicate that time, patience, and careful building of a relationship before marriage will best ensure its success. Chapter 12 explains the steps immediately preceding marriage, the meaning of the Sacrament of Marriage, and the marriage ritual. Then, in chapter 13 you will have a chance to consider the many facets of married and family life. A marriage only *begins* with the ceremony; it is *built* over the lifetime of a couple. Chapter 13 examines how a marriage can continue to be an adventure in growth.

The lifestyle of members of religious orders needs to be examined and considered as an option in lifestyle decisions. Religious life has had a grand tradition for centuries and has fostered great people, even saints. Chapter 14 introduces you to the rich potential for a full life that is found in religious communities. Next, in chapter 15, the ordained ministry is examined. Bishops, priests, and deacons are called to a unique role in the church. The ordained ministry is part of the Catholic heritage and, like religious life, is perhaps too often overlooked when people are considering the options they have for shaping their lives.

In the treatment of all of the topics in this course, the wisdom of the Bible and church tradition will be used. Specifically, Jesus came into the world to lead all people to full life. Throughout the last two thousand years, the Christian community has developed a body of teachings by which all Christians can guide their lives. So a Christian perspective will permeate our discussions of all topics in this course.

Your teacher will have explicit requirements for you in this course, but openness, serious thought, and a willingness to question are imperative if you are to create your lifestyle—which is, after all, the goal of this course. As a senior, you are at the threshold of an important transitional period in your life. The period between the ages of seventeen and twenty-two can be one of the most exciting and engaging times in a person's life.

So, forward.

As a senior, you are at the threshold of an important transitional period in your life.

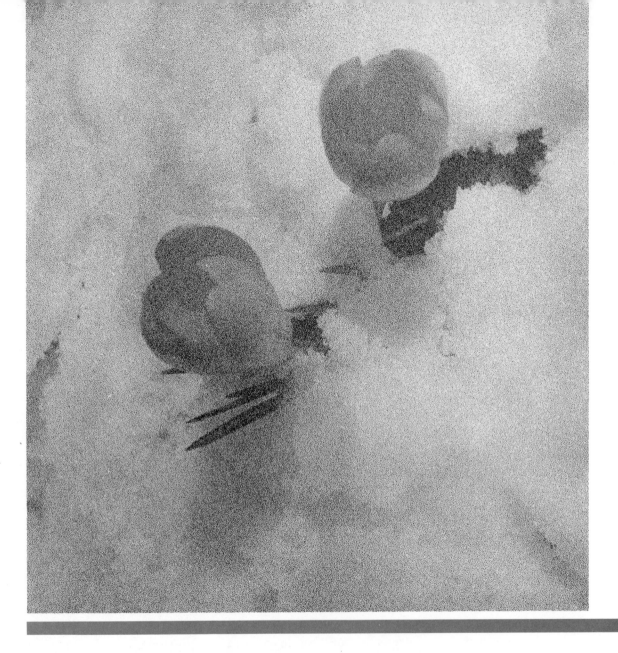

1 Your Dream: A Vision of Your Future

DREAMS have fascinated, inspired, driven, and energized people for thousands of years. In religious thought, the arts and literature, and civic speeches, references to dreams have a remarkably moving power. For instance, in the Jewish Scriptures, God said to the people of Judah:

"... I shall pour out my spirit on all humanity.
Your sons and daughters shall prophesy,
your old people shall dream dreams,
and your young people see visions.
Even on the slaves, men and women,
shall I pour out my spirit in those days.
I shall show portents in the sky and on earth,
blood and fire and columns of smoke."

(Joel 3:1–3)

In the classic musical *The Wizard of Oz,* Dorothy sings one of the most famous songs about dreams:

Somewhere over the rainbow
skies are blue,
And the dreams
that you dare to dream
really do come true.

Martin Luther King, Jr., portrayed the dream he wanted for all people.

Martin Luther King, Jr., the great civil-rights leader, portrayed the dream he wanted for all people in one of the most-quoted speeches of the twentieth century:

I have a dream that one day this nation will rise up and live out the true meaning of its creed: "We hold these truths to be self-evident; that all men are created equal."

I have a dream that one day on the red hills of Georgia the sons of former slaves and the sons of former slaveowners will be able to sit down together at the table of brotherhood.

Time to Dream

The Book of Ecclesiastes says that "there is a season for everything, a time for every occupation under heaven" (Ecclesiastes 3:1). Your senior year is a good time to dream—time to envision your **dream,** that is, to create an image of the future you wish to shape. But we are often scolded for daydreaming. To be called a dreamer is not usually a compliment. So why is it good to dream?

Destinations and Dreams

A life dream is like the destination for a trip.

Think for a minute about how a life dream is like the destination for a trip. If you are on a trip, you usually have a destination in mind. Maybe for a high school graduation trip you will drive to the Rocky Mountains or you will head to the beaches for a week of lounging in the sun. For the journey to come off without a hitch, you will have to spend time preparing: doing maintenance on your car, checking the route on a map, deciding who will go with you, and earning enough money to cover your expenses. Depending on your destination, you will have to bring specific items. If you are going to hike and camp in the Rockies, you will need the appropriate gear. If you are going to the beach, you will need at least a swimsuit, a towel or two, sunscreen, sunglasses, and a portable stereo. In short, your destination determines what sort of preparations you will need to make and the experiences you will have, just as a life dream helps you to focus on what you must do to attain that dream.

Of course, travelers can find that despite their best efforts at preparation, they may not always reach their destination—because of an accident, sickness, or a flight cancellation, for example. Or they even may find upon arriving at their longed-for destination that they are not so happy there. They might really prefer to be elsewhere, doing something other than camping in the Rockies or suntanning at the beach. In fact, travelers sometimes discover that a completely different destination than the one they originally had envisioned—a place they just stumble onto along the way—is what *really* satisfies them.

Dreams, too, can be altered. The dreams of our youth will be subjected to the mighty forces of personal crises, changing societal conditions, and changes in personal preferences. The point is that each of us needs a dream to give us focus, to mobilize our energies toward something outside of ourselves. In reality, this dream will be shaped, reshaped, tempered, refined, and in some cases tossed out in favor of an alternative dream as we move through years of experience. *But we have got to have a dream; we perish without a dream.*

Life is not terribly different from taking a trip. Our dream, or the goals we have for life, allows us to focus on what sort of education we will need, what kinds of friends we will have, and so on. A dream is important.

Dreams: Offering Truth, Idealism, and Courage

The dreams mentioned in the passage from Joel that opened this chapter were part of the prophecies that God was sending to the people of Judah. Joel knew that God speaks to us through the dreams of our sleep, which tell the truth in a way that many of our waking thoughts do not. Even contemporary psychologists say that if we bring the dreams of our sleep to consciousness and reflect on them honestly, these dreams will offer useful insights about ourselves and suggest areas in which we need to grow. A life dream, somewhat like a sleeping dream, comes from the core of us. It speaks the truth about who we are, what we yearn for, and how we need to grow.

In *The Wizard of Oz,* Dorothy's dream was the romantic vision of idealistic youth. Eventually it became tempered by experience, but it did lead her to adventure. Dr. Martin Luther King, Jr.'s, dream gave him the vision and courage to struggle for human rights. More important to King than winning the Nobel Peace Prize was the change in the whole U.S. social system that occurred in large part because he dreamed it could happen. If King had not been able to see a time when black people would have equal rights, he never would have been able to engage in the nonviolent protests that eventually brought equal rights under the law. Your dream, too, will help to create the lifestyle that you choose and the goals that you accomplish.

We have got to have a dream; we perish without a dream.

Dreaming the Good Life

After seventeen or eighteen years of life, you probably have images of what you want your life to be like in the future. You have some hopes, desires, and visions for yourself. Maybe you want

Our dream summarizes what we perceive to be the good life.

In writing, describe images or pictures that immediately come to mind when you think of the "good life."

to own an electronics firm, be married, have three children, be president of the local chamber of commerce, be a patient and caring person, and continue swimming competitively. Or perhaps you look forward ten years and see yourself as single, actively involved in church activities, and just getting settled into a dental practice.

Our Deepest Wishes

Our deepest wishes about who we will be as an adult make up our life dream. Our dream is more than a flight of fancy but less than a blueprint. We may have some specific images of what our life as an adult will be like, but some areas are still shrouded in a mist.

Our dream includes possibilities that excite and energize us. It may picture a future occupation: teaching, dentistry, plumbing, selling, engineering. However, our dream also ideally encompasses our vision of *who* we want to be, of what kind of person we will become. Sharon may want to be a biologist, but she also may want to be a kind, patient, assertive person. Vince's dream may project him as a counselor in a junior high school, but he also may want to be a speed skater and someone who is understanding of people.

Our dream summarizes what we perceive to be the "good life." The good life is what we plan for, ponder, and hold up as a goal for ourselves. Unless we have a concept, even if somewhat vague, of the good life, we can spend years wandering like a cross-country runner who has no idea of where the course or the finish line is.

A single, universal definition of the good life does not exist. For Christians, a description of the good life is contained in the dream that Jesus shared with us—the dream of a peaceable kingdom. Buddhists have a somewhat different concept of the good life: for Buddhists, it is liberation in the form of *nirvana*, or enlightenment. Materialists probably see the good life as one in which they own everything they want.

Our dream of the good life depends on three basic factors:

- what sort of person we are: our interests, abilities, past successes and failures, personality traits, and so on
- our relationships with parents, friends, teachers—anyone who has a substantial influence on us
- the larger set of circumstances that surrounds us: our church, the neighborhood and city we live in, distant relatives, and larger world events

Your dream is unique to you, and each of us must shape our own dream.

Giving Form to the Vision

We will turn our attention now to four steps that can help us to shape our dream so that we can move toward it.

Defining the Dream

First, try defining your dream as clearly as you can. Here are some questions that you can use:

- What will your personal life be like? For example, do you see yourself with several close friends? How involved do you want to be with your family—parents, cousins, aunts and uncles? How much private time do you need and want?
- Where will you live? Do you want to own property? Do you have a preference between living in a small town or in a large city? How important is having a large house to live in? Would you like to live very simply?
- Will you be married, single, a religious, or ordained? If married, what do you want your family life to be like? If single, what will that mean for you? If you were to join a religious order, which one might it be? Try to describe what the ordained ministry would be like for you.
- What sort of career do you want? Do you like technical work? Do you prefer working with people more than with objects? How much money and leisure time do you expect or want to have? Is enjoying your job more important to you than having a high salary and regular promotions?
- Where do religion and commitments to ideals like world peace and a clean environment fit into your dream?

In other words, you have to picture your dream in your mind in as much detail as possible. This requires some imagination; that is, you have to be able to make a mental image of your dream. Like an artist, you have to be able to picture the scene you wish to paint before you begin putting brush to canvas.

Finding Support

The second step in achieving your dream is realizing that you will need support from others. This support could be financial: you might need help to pay for your education or to begin a business. Or maybe you need someone to affirm that what you want to do is worthwhile. For example, if your dream is to be a veterinarian, your grades in college will have to be extremely

Starting with the question, "What will your personal life be like?" answer, as completely as possible, each of the questions listed on this page.

Your dream is unique to you, and each of us must shape our own dream.

high. Openings in veterinary schools are very limited, so these schools accept only the top students. During the four years of college before veterinary school, it will be difficult to maintain your morale without encouragement and support. Whether or not we like to admit it, all of us need help at one time or another. In the quest for your dream, ask yourself these questions:

- From whom can I expect support?
- Am I willing to seek help when I need it?

Essential sources of support or inspiration are our *models* and *guides,* the people whom we admire and wish to imitate. For instance, if you are a carpenter, working with a pro who is interested in you and who gives you well-timed advice can be a godsend. Most of us need this kind of guide to smooth the way or to exchange ideas and feelings with. In the same way, parents of small children frequently welcome the advice of older couples who have successfully raised their sons and daughters.

We need models—people we look up to who provide examples of what our fulfilled dream looks like. As children we might have tried to imitate star athletes or movie stars. Maybe we attempted to shoot baskets the way our favorite player did or to talk and look like our favorite actor or actress. The modeling appropriate for us as young adults is different, but we still need models. For instance, imagine that you tend to procrastinate. Your papers are always late. You delay changing the oil in your car until the warning light blinks on, and you regularly coast into gas stations with your engine running on fumes. You do not necessarily want to be this way. On the other hand, you do not want to be a fanatic about organization either. If you have a roommate in college who works efficiently and yet has a good time when she or he relaxes, this person can act as a model for your own change.

In the final analysis, much of our behavior is modeled on the behavior of other people. We learn good work habits, polite manners, the proper use of money, ways of being leisurely, and interpersonal skills from others. Unfortunately, it is also true that we learn negative behaviors from other people. For example, the majority of child abusers were abused when they were children. The treatment of children that was modeled for them was abusive treatment. So in shaping your dream, looking to positive role models is very helpful.

We need models—people we look up to who provide examples of what our fulfilled dream looks like.

Receiving Training

The third step in accomplishing your dream is receiving the training that you will need. Training for a career is only one type of skill development required. Learning to be a parent and deepening your understanding of your faith are essential if your dream includes having a family and growing spiritually.

Usually people have to be open to lifelong learning. Technology changes so rapidly that keeping up with new developments would be impossible without regular reading or skill development. Furthermore, the things that are important to us during the early stages of our life (such as the school years) usually change as we mature, yielding new interests, questions, and needs. These new directions in our life dream also require ongoing learning.

Acting on the Dream

Finally, you must begin acting on your dream. The training and support must be used to bring the dream to reality. You have to take action. However, a worthwhile dream does challenge us, and we may never seem to fulfill it perfectly. Moreover, our dream could develop in a different direction from what we had anticipated. Maybe the dream you have now will be too small for you when you are thirty. Worry about that bridge when you have to cross it. The important thing is what your dream is *now:* what sort of person you want to be, what you want to be doing, and what relationships you want to have.

A full life, the good life, will not happen unless we can imagine it. We cannot build a dream house unless we know what it is supposed to look like. It is virtually impossible to love unless we have an image of what love is. It is not only proper to dream in this course, it is essential.

Training and support must be used to bring your dream to reality.

Jesus' Dream

Building our dream is a call, or a vocation. After all, the word *vocation* comes from the Latin verb *vocare*, which means "to call." From a Christian point of view, our **vocation** is a calling from God. We were created to fulfill a dream that was best portrayed for us by Jesus:
• to build the peaceable kingdom
• to create a loving community
• to nurture and challenge people to grow fully alive
These were the three most important aspects of Jesus' dream for humankind.

It is necessary to remember that Jesus was no starry-eyed idealist. His dream was not the product of a child's overactive

imagination. When Jesus spoke of building the peaceable kingdom, creating a loving community, and nurturing people to be
fully alive, it was with a growing awareness that the price of his
leadership could be an agonizing death on the cross, at a time
when almost no one would call him friend.

The Peaceable Kingdom

As told in the Jewish Scriptures' story of Adam and Eve (Genesis, chapter 3), when the first two humans sinned, the earth
became a hostile place in which to live. Disharmony and violence
shattered the once peaceful Garden of Eden. To amplify this fact,
the authors of the Book of Genesis told the story of Cain killing
his brother, Abel (Genesis 4:3–8). The point of these stories is
that the peaceable reign present in Eden is gone because people
have sinned; they have harmed each other and creation.

Only when people truly love one another will the peaceable kingdom
come into existence.

The Jewish people believed that God would send a messiah
to reestablish the peaceable kingdom on earth. Christians, of
course, believe that Jesus is this messiah, who, if people really
believe in him, will lead humankind toward reconciliation of all
differences. One of the prophecies in the Jewish Scriptures clearly
illustrates Jesus' dream of the peaceable kingdom:

> The wolf will live with the lamb,
> the panther lie down with the kid,
> calf, lion and fat-stock beast together,
> with a little boy to lead them.
> The cow and the bear will graze,
> their young will lie down together.
> The lion will eat hay like the ox.
> The infant will play over the den of the adder;
> the baby will put his hand into the viper's lair.
> No hurt, no harm will be done
> on all my holy mountain,
> for the country will be full of knowledge of Yahweh
> as the waters cover the sea.
>
> (Isaiah 11:6–9)

This dream of a new Eden was clearly in Jesus' mind as he went
about his ministry. He preached love of neighbor because only
when people truly love one another will this peaceable kingdom
come into existence.

Further, Jesus pointed out to his followers that the kingdom
already existed among them—if they would only find it or admit it. The kingdom, or reign, of Jesus exists if we believe in

the presence of Jesus and act in accordance with his guidance: he said, ". . . 'For look, the kingdom of God is among you' " (Luke 17:21). Indeed, if people loved their neighbors as themselves, we would live in harmony and peace.

Jesus modeled love of neighbor by healing the sick, driving out devils, dying on the cross, and rising from the dead. But by reading about the Last Supper, we can have a clear image of what this love he talked about really looks like. At the Last Supper, Jesus presented the peaceable kingdom as a loving community.

A Loving Community

The story of the Last Supper is reenacted in the eucharistic celebration every day, and on Holy Thursday the story is read from the Christian Scriptures (John 13:1–15).

Jesus knew that he was going to die on the cross. This was the last time that he would be with his disciples before the Resurrection. As in all parting celebrations, much sadness surrounded the occasion. Jesus wanted to share his love for his friends and, at the same time, to remind them of how important—essential—it was for them to love one another. So he washed their feet. The disciples looked upon this act as servant work, not as something for the Master to do.

Jesus must have been frustrated when Peter resisted his efforts to wash his feet. All of his life Jesus had been telling and showing people that they must serve one another, that no one could be exempt from mutual service if a loving community was going to become a reality. So Jesus provided them all with one final example of service.

Then Jesus shared a meal with his disciples. It was simple, basic—bread and wine, the staples of the diet of the times. All of the participants were fed equally. Even Judas, who would betray Jesus, was welcome at the banquet. The sharing was a sign of their community, their love for one another. Jesus said that the bread and the wine were his body and blood. Christians should be known by this sharing of Jesus' body and blood and by the sharing of each person's own body and blood in service to one another.

This sharing was the very heart of Jesus' dream of community among all of humankind. The sharing of bread and wine at the Last Supper had been foreshadowed many times in Jesus' life. Indeed, eating together was often used as a sign of service and community. Jesus' public life began at a wedding banquet at Cana; there he turned water into wine (John 2:1–11). When

At the Last Supper, Jesus showed the Apostles that no one can be exempt from mutual service if a loving community is going to become a reality.

he was preaching later in his life, night was coming on and the crowds were hungry. He gave the people loaves of bread and fish to eat. Sitting together on the shoreline, he and his followers shared a meal (Matthew 14:14–21).

Jesus dreamed of creating a community based on shared faith and mutual service and motivated by love for all of humankind. He knew such a community would not come about in his lifetime, but this reality was acceptable to him. Jesus' followers would keep building this community.

Fully Alive Persons

Jesus knew that if people lived in peace with one another, served one another, and built a loving community, they would be fully alive. Jesus' dream was that all of us would be fully alive—people who fulfill our complete potential. This part of his dream is easily seen in the parable of the sower:

A sower went out to sow the seed. Some of it fell on a path; birds ate it. The seed that fell on rocky soil grew but could not take root, and it died. Some seed fell among thorns and was choked out. As Jesus explained the story, "And the seed sown in rich soil is someone who hears the word and understands it; this is the one who yields a harvest and produces now a hundredfold, now sixty, now thirty" (Matthew 13:23).

Jesus was not talking about the products of hard work in this parable. He meant that a person who really lives according to God's word will grow and fulfill his or her potential. This is why Jesus continuously challenged his disciples to grow, even though at times their understanding seemed dim and their commitment weak. Jesus believed in them, especially in Peter, who repeatedly failed and showed poor judgment. The harvest of the seeds planted in Peter and the other disciples began to be reaped in their own lifetimes, as the early church flourished. The seeds' potential is to become a huge crop of wheat—abundant, rich food for many people. Our potential is to be loving, lively people for our neighbors.

Through all of the seasons of Jesus' short life, his dream remained the same: to build the peaceable kingdom, to create a loving community, and to nurture people to become fully alive. Our dream is probably less clear. Thus, we are likely to adjust it throughout our life. Jesus certainly believed that his dream was worth giving his life to achieve. We also will spend our life

Jesus' dream may seem incredibly unreal sometimes. But what signs illustrate that Jesus' dream is in process? Bring into class an article from a newspaper or magazine that shows one of the following:
- the peaceable kingdom of harmony being created
- a loving community existing or being created
- people being fully alive by fulfilling their potential

Make some notes about why the article is a sign of hope.

fulfilling our dream. Our dream can be achieved if we are willing to pay the price. We must meet the conditions for our growth, or for the accomplishment of our dream.

Conditions for Growth

Some people pass through life with Teflon minds and emotions—nothing sticks. They learn little from their experiences and are insensitive to their own feelings and the feelings of others. Coming to completion as a person does not happen automatically by hanging around long enough. If fulfillment simply happened to everyone, then there would be no unpleasant, unhappy, and offensive adults.

So it seems that human growth happens only under certain conditions. Four important conditions are the following:

- willingness to take risks
- foresight
- support
- coming to terms with death

All areas of human growth require a willingness to take some risks.

Willingness to Take Risks

Every action involves some sort of risk. For example, if you invite acquaintances to go to a nice restaurant for dinner, you do not know if they will slurp their soup or eat with their mouths open. You risk being embarrassed if your dinner companions are rude. But if you do not invite your friends to dinner, you might be denying yourself and them a chance for a wonderful relationship. After all, what is more important—avoiding the possibility of a little embarrassment or taking the opportunity for a friendship?

You take some chances when your priorities are involved. What if your dinner partner does slurp the soup and eat spaghetti with an open mouth? A good sense of humor helps. Maybe you can still be friends. If we want certainty that everything will work out before every decision, then we will probably lead a very narrow life. The old saying, Nothing ventured, nothing gained, has more than a grain of truth to it.

Other risks are involved in growing:

- Telling people about our feelings is done at the risk of rejection.

Write down the following words, skipping eight lines between each word:
- *intellectual*
- *physical*
- *relational*

Under each category, describe two risks you have taken that have paid off. For example, under *relational* you might say, "Last year I took a chance and invited a transfer student to go out for pizza with me. I hardly knew him. We became good friends."

- Reading an important book might mean having to give up some fixed but secure ways of thinking.
- Traveling to Europe or Asia means adjusting to new cultures.
- Attending college away from home involves a new environment and unfamiliar faces.
- Marrying someone we love means the promise of lifelong commitment to that person, in good circumstances and in difficult ones.

Maybe the biggest risk, something that causes fear and trembling in many of us, is taking the time to look at ourselves.

Clearly, risk taking must not be equated solely with physical risks. It is hardly a growing or life-giving experience to drive recklessly or to see how many liters of Scotch one can consume. Rather, the risks involved in true growth have to do with new relationships, new revelations, and the use of one's talents more fully.

In a sentence or two, describe yourself as a risk taker according to the three types of risks:
- intellectual
- physical
- relational

How do you feel about your willingness to take risks for the sake of your growth?

Foresight

Simply put, foresight means thinking ahead, asking ourselves, What am I going to need (skills, knowledge, physical capacity, material resources, wisdom) five years from now to be who I want to be and to be doing what I want to be doing? Realistically, we will be who and what we want to be in five years only if we do some hard-nosed evaluation now.

Surprises are nice sometimes, but degrading or unfortunate surprises happen also. For example, many professional athletes never complete degrees or professional training in anything other than their sport. Then, between the ages of twenty-five and thirty-five, the pro athlete's career ends with an injury or because of the decreasing physical strength that comes with aging. Suddenly the person looks around and wonders what to do with the next forty years of life.

A more profound crisis can occur in personal or interpersonal matters. You probably know people who never seem to have much time for building friendships. They have acquaintances, and maybe they even date one or two people once in a while. But in general, projects, study, work, and extracurricular activities crowd friends from their lives. One day they will wake up alone in an apartment and wonder why no one calls and why they are so lonely. The patterns of life we choose now will dictate, in many ways, the conditions of our lives in five, ten, fifteen, or even fifty years.

List several events that will happen in your life between now and next September. Next to each event, write one or two ways in which planning will be needed.

Having foresight also means being able to take opportunities when they present themselves. Many times we overlook occasions for growth, potential friendships, or ways of serving simply because we do not look at events and people with fresh eyes. Sadly, we often do not know what we had until it is gone. If you have ever been to a funeral—especially the funeral of a younger person—you probably heard someone say something like, "I sure wish I had visited her more," or "I never had the opportunity to tell him that . . ." Coming to fullness means, in part, good timing—having the foresight to plan and taking opportunities as they arise.

Support

We need people who will listen to, care about, question, and challenge us, affirm our better instincts, and endorse our unique worth. Friends help us to feel good about who we are. They give us the strength to say, "I am a good person. I have worth, not so much for what I can do or produce as a valuable human being but because I am part of God's creation."

We need people who endorse our unique worth.

Perhaps this point needs little explanation, but it does require plenty of reflection. We may not always like to admit our need for the support of friends and kin, but we know deep down that we do need that support. We can learn about ourselves from just about anyone, but the unique gift of friends and family is that they know us and affirm us from a basis of knowledge. If people do not know us well, it is easy to undervalue what they say, but it is not so easy to ignore the affirmation of our friends.

Coming to Terms with Death

The last basic condition for human growth is one that we do not think about very often, yet it may be the most important requirement for human growth. We must come to terms with death because we are all going to die; we just do not know when, where, or how.

Avoiding the Inevitable

We cannot prevent death. Perhaps the most tragic aspect of death is that some people live their whole lives trying to avoid the inevitable. They live unreasonably narrow, stifled lives—never taking any risks, never making fresh plans, never reaching out to others, never trying anything new—thinking that they can somehow avoid death if they keep life under control, safe. But we cannot avoid death, and life is not controllable and not completely safe.

The meaningful question is not, How am I going to avoid death? The meaningful question is, How am I going to live so that when my dying comes, I can look back with a sense of completeness, with few regrets and much thanks? It is easy to fritter away the life we have been given, especially if we never commit ourselves to anyone or anything because such commitment might be painful, inconvenient, or risky.

Ivan's Emptiness

Much of the world's great literature treats the subject of how people experience dying. One of the most powerful stories is by the Russian author Leo Tolstoy. In "The Death of Ivan Ilych," Ivan dies a horrible death. Ivan had been a moderately successful government official. He owned a nice home, had a wife and two children, and seemed to have a comfortable and enviable life. However, when Ivan learned that he was dying of cancer, he began to struggle with the emptiness of his past. Early in the story, Tolstoy gives a hint as to why the death is so painful: "Ivan Ilych's life had been most simple and most ordinary and therefore most terrible." As his dying proceeds irrevocably, the nature of his torture becomes apparent:

> It was true, as the doctor said, that Ivan Ilych's physical sufferings were terrible, but worse than the physical sufferings were his mental sufferings which were his chief torture.
>
> His mental sufferings were due to the fact that that night, as he looked at [his servant's] sleepy, goodnatured face with its prominent cheek-bones, the question suddenly occurred to him: "What if my whole life has really been wrong?"

Have you ever asked yourself the same question that Ivan Ilych asks here? If so, why did you ask yourself this question? How did you answer it?

Tolstoy concludes that Ivan's life had, indeed, been all wrong: he had never really loved, he had been so busy avoiding conflict that he had never formed any convictions, and he had conformed even in the smallest customs so that he would be accepted by all the other boring men like himself. Ivan's death would have been easier if his life had possessed some meaning.

Jesus: No Clinging to Safety

Christians have a model of living and dying in Jesus, who—unlike Ivan Ilych—loved people, had a clear purpose for his life, and could leave this earth knowing that all of history had been changed because of his presence. Jesus dreaded dying. We have only to look at his agony in the garden. But this dread did not stop him from being fully alive and totally loving. Fear of death did not paralyze Jesus or prevent him from doing what he had to do on earth. He challenged the Pharisees, healed sick and possessed persons, forgave penitent sinners, and instructed his disciples. When it was time to go to Jerusalem and the death that he knew awaited him, a determined and compassionate Jesus entered the city. He proclaimed a profound truth:

"Anyone who wants to save his life will lose it; but anyone who loses his life for my sake will find it." (Matthew 16:25)

We should live so that when our dying comes, we can look back with a sense of completion.

A paraphrase of this statement by Jesus might be as follows:

Anyone who
    clings to the safety of self-interest,
    chooses to speak timid half-truths,
    and despairs of making a better world
will forfeit a meaningful and happy life.

But anyone who
    loves others,
    does good,
    has faith that Jesus spoke truly,
    and acts peaceably and justly
will find life, and therefore death,
    to be full of wonder and richness.

Jesus calls us to get on with life and love. Living tentatively, overly cautiously, and without commitments squeezes the love and joy that is God out of life. Jesus not only preached this message but lived it in his death and Resurrection.

The Stages of Life

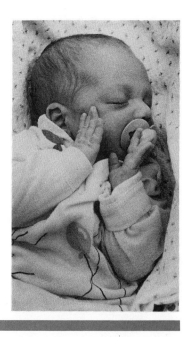

Human beings pass through eight stages of life, beginning with infancy.

As we move toward our dream, we pass through different stages. Psychologists who have studied human development have outlined the stages of growth in several different ways. However, most agree that at least eight stages, or seasons, in our growth can be identified:

- infancy
- early childhood
- play age
- school age
- adolescence
- young adulthood
- adulthood
- mature adulthood

The timing and experience of these stages is unique to each person, and it is important to remember that any description of life stages is very general. Some dilemmas that other people experience in a stage of growth may not be problems for you. Try not to compare or contrast yourself to your peers. Learning about yourself is accomplishment enough.

Each life stage begins and ends with a period of transition. These transitional periods are often difficult but always essential in the process of growth. Our dream, our vision, undergoes adjustments to our new skills and understandings and to changing circumstances. The period you are entering, the time between seventeen and twenty-two years of age, is an important transition into young adulthood. So that you do not go into young adulthood blindly and in order to make it a time of growth and progress toward your dream, you may find it helpful to understand the nature of transitional periods, particularly the period between the ages of seventeen and twenty-two.

Transitions

The word **transition** comes from the Latin word *transire*, meaning "to go across, to pass." Crossings and passages imply a certain degree of danger but also opportunity. Crossing the Golden Gate Bridge into San Francisco by car can be dangerous: the bridge could collapse, you could run into someone if the fog is thick, or your car could break down in the middle. But San Francisco, with all of its attractions, waits on the other side. Moving from grade school to high school was a passage: you faced some dangers but also some great new possibilities.

One of the most obvious examples of transition for you as a senior is the change in your relationship with your parents. You are more independent now than you were a few years ago. This independence has not been gained without pain on your part and on the part of your parents. You do not look up to them in the same way you did as a child, and they cannot treat you exactly as they did then. All transitional periods, when you are caught between an old way and a new way, are tough.

Reactions to Transitions

People react in all sorts of ways to transitions. After all, these periods entail ending old ways of doing things and modifying relationships. Some seniors try to deny that they are growing up. For instance, when deciding what to do after high school, they put off writing for college applications, visiting a technical school, or checking out other possibilities. Other seniors feel pressured in these situations and become angry. They feel that parents or friends are pushing them to do things. They become impatient. The source of the anger is often frustration because life seems to be too complex, but the person in transition might not know the cause of his or her anger.

Sometimes we want to be both free and safe all at once. We want to be more independent, but we expect financial aid from our parents. Another reaction to transition is that we may become depressed easily or experience tremendous emotional turmoil. In severe cases of depression, young people may even contemplate suicide. An individual who has serious difficulties in adjusting to transition may require the help of a counselor. Eventually, most people, including those who experience great stress in a period of transition, begin to accept the changes— the loss of familiar ways—and appreciate the new possibilities. They may not be very conscious of this process, but it does happen.

A Growing Time

These common problems with transition and the tensions and pressures they produce may lead us to ask more questions about life. Some people begin questioning the meaning of their religious beliefs. Others wonder whether they are too passive or insensitive. These questions can lead to an honest process of self-discovery that is growth-producing. A person may branch out. Someone who has been passive might try to be more assertive. College students who have hardly been out of their hometowns might become charged up to travel in Europe.

As a senior, some reactions to the transition you are in probably have begun already. Think of one change that you have already been through. List and describe the painful elements and the opportunities of this experience of transition. Overall, are you better off now, after the change?

Crossings and passages imply a certain degree of danger but also opportunity.

Our sense of who we are is shaped, in part, by how we relate to others.

Eventually people settle into some fairly stable pattern of doing things, and they make decisions that require commitments. For instance, a college student who studies liberal arts courses and is unsure of exactly what career she or he wants may finally say, "I'm going to law school." She or he takes the tests and settles down into the rigors of studying torts and contracts. This sort of settling down signals the end of a transitional period.

Adult life usually involves three transitional periods:

- ages seventeen to twenty-two
- ages forty to forty-five
- ages sixty to sixty-five

Because you are entering the first of these transitions, we will spend most of our time discussing this growth period.

Ages Seventeen to Twenty-two: The Passage to Adulthood

When developmental psychologists talk about any stage of development, they try to describe it in terms of **developmental tasks**. In other words, during the present transitional phase of your life, you will be challenged to grow in approximately eleven areas. Clearly, most people make this transition without being conscious of these eleven developmental tasks. The tasks are accomplished in varying orders by different people. They may occur simultaneously, and many of them overlap.

If you are aware of these tasks, you might be able to understand some of the feelings you are having. Understanding these tasks also will help you to plan for your dream. Actually, this whole course is designed to help you gain a perspective on these eleven tasks. What follows is a brief listing of each task.

1. Shaping an Identity

Who am I? What sense do I have of myself? These two central questions need to be answered by someone beginning the transition between adolescence and young adulthood. By growing in competence, becoming more autonomous, selecting a value system, and searching for a religious stance, we shape our sense of who we are—our uniqueness, our separateness, and our sense of how we relate to others.

By about the age of twenty-two, you will probably know what career you wish to pursue. If you are going to be a musician, you will have received appropriate training. If you are a leader, you will have had opportunities in school or on the job to demonstrate this quality. You will have a clearer sense of who you are and what you can do.

2. Becoming Autonomous

By the completion of this transitional phase, most young adults have become more independent physically, financially, intellectually, and emotionally. They are able to take care of the practical necessities of life effectively on their own. They are more emotionally secure; that is, they do not need as much approval from others. By age twenty-two, most young adults have the ability to initiate action on significant issues: they do not wait around for decisions to be made by other people. In other words, they become autonomous.

On the other hand, young adults can seek help when they need it without either feeling defensive or becoming too dependent. In other words, the truly autonomous person can be **interdependent** as well as independent. An interdependent person realizes that life is a two-way street. For example, if you expect help from your parents, you must be willing to interact with them and help them when you can. An interdependent person is able to give love and to be loved, and that person is not afraid of giving and receiving.

Two types of false autonomy should be mentioned:

Groupthink: Sometimes people in this transitional period make a sharp break from their parents and assume the practices and views of a different group of people. For example, persons who join cults often do so because they want to assert their independence from the values and lifestyles of their parents. Sometimes college sororities or fraternities function in the same way as cults do for dependent students who need a group to give them a sense of belonging and identity. In too many of these organizations, senseless initiations and substantial membership fees are the prices a person pays to assume the identity of the group. This is false autonomy because they have only traded one form of dependency for another.

The "jailbreak" marriage: Another false form of autonomy is the "jailbreak" marriage. Out of a desire to be free of their own family, some people contract into another family—a new one of their own. Instead of being free, they take on the tremendous task of being married without the necessary maturity and skills to make it work.

By the end of the transition to young adulthood, most people have become more independent physically, financially, intellectually, and emotionally.

Having a clear sense of your values will help you answer important questions.

3. Constructing and Living Out a Value System

In childhood and throughout high school, your value system—the code of conduct or group of moral principles by which a person makes decisions—has been more or less directed by your parents, your school, and your church. Perhaps you have accepted these values after careful consideration, or maybe you have gone along with them because it was convenient. In this transitional period, young people are more challenged to direct their own lives, using their own values. For instance, when a person goes to a university, class attendance may be supervised by some teachers but certainly not by all. No one calls mom and dad and asks why the student is not in class. To succeed in college, students themselves must value consistent attendance because they cannot depend on external forces to provide the motivation.

You soon will be faced with a career choice. Your values will influence that choice. Having a clear sense of your values will help you answer important questions like these:

- Do I want a job that is well-paying even more than one that is personally satisfying?
- Is there some ideal that I want to commit myself to through my career choice?

In sum, developing a clear value system is an important task of this transition.

4. Being Capable of a Loving Commitment

Most young adults grow in their ability to sustain and commit themselves to a stable, loving relationship with one person, but many people are choosing to delay marriage until their mid- or late-twenties. During this time of transition, people can gain the knowledge and skills required for marriage. Through friendship and dating, a person develops close relationships that might lead to a permanent commitment.

5. Reflecting on Religion

Many young adults sense that they need a place for religion in their life, but they have to make a personal search for a religious practice that expresses their own faith. Between the ages of seventeen and twenty-two, many people reject religious practices that have been part of their life until then. This turning away from religion often coincides with decreasing parental control, which shows that the young adults' former practice of religion was not really their own choice and rooted in their own faith. During this transition, one task is to begin developing one's own religious commitment.

6. Making Friends and Living with Intimacy

Generally, young adults deepen their relationships in this period. People in this age-group have a wider range of emotional and intellectual experiences to share, and they also realize the many dimensions and ways of being intimate with others.

7. Integrating Sexuality

During this transition, it is important to develop a set of values that guide sexual expression and to appreciate the role of sexuality in life. Sexuality needs to be integrated into the whole scope of personhood and how a person relates to others.

8. Gaining Competence

Competence refers to our ability to cope with our environment so that we can support ourselves and have the skills necessary to grow as persons and in careers. One sign of competence is the ability to cope with the developmental tasks of this transitional period. You are being challenged to develop the intellectual, physical, and relational skills needed to become the person you want to be.

9. Selecting a Career and Taking an Adult Job

Acquiring a broadly based competence in communication and other skills, at least in the first few years after high school, helps in preparing for any number of careers. However, in some areas (for instance, nursing), students follow a very structured program leading to more definite career slots. Either way, moving toward and preparing for a career is another developmental task.

Competence refers to our ability to cope with our environment, having the skills necessary to grow as persons and in careers.

10. Using Leisure Time for Renewal

With more and more leisure time available to North Americans in this century, the questions surrounding how best to use it have become more pressing:

• Will you use leisure time for expanding your abilities, for learning, and for building relationships?

• Or will leisure time mean passive relaxation?

You need to determine what you want leisure to be for you.

11. Taking Part in the Broader Community

Because eighteen-year-old people can vote, they have an opportunity to influence local, state, and national politics. On the global scale, young people have to decide what kind of world they wish to live in. For instance, the threat of nuclear war hovers over all of us.

• What is your attitude toward nuclear war?

• If you are opposed to it, what action can you take to make the world safer from nuclear war?

During this transitional phase of life, questions about your role in the world community must not be left unanswered.

You must not panic at how much "work" you have to do. Most seniors already are involved in accomplishing these developmental tasks. If you are committed to doing a good job in your studies, you already are gaining some of the skills of a competent adult. By building friendships, you are learning how to develop intimacy with other people. Maybe you are learning about the world of work by holding a job during summers or on weekends. By examining the eleven tasks of young adulthood, you have probably realized that fulfillment of these tasks will aid you in fulfilling your dream, which is a lifelong endeavor.

A Call to Fullness of Life

We are called to be fully alive—whole persons. Our growth to wholeness takes us through many stages—each with its own difficulties and opportunities. The dream that we form in our youth gives us a vision toward which to channel our energies. For Christians, Jesus offers a dream of the peaceable kingdom, a loving community, and full humanity.

The stage you are in now is a key transitional period in your life, with some important challenges and developmental tasks. The person you will be at eighty years old is, to a great extent, the person you are forming now. The fulfillment of your dream and the dream of Jesus for humankind is in process now. The following chapters will offer insights into and ask questions about important areas of the lifestyle that you are creating.

Choose five of the eleven developmental tasks for young adults. Write at least three concerns or obstacles you have in fulfilling each of the five tasks. For instance, under "becoming autonomous," you might list the following:
• I am easily swayed by my friends to do things even if I don't want to do them.
• I seldom bother to buy things I need.
• I let my parents choose my college major.

Refer to the list of fifteen concerns that you wrote in the previous activity. For each one, rate the intensity of your concern on a scale from little concern (1) to much concern (5). Then, circle the item from your list that bothers you the most and explain why in writing.

Write a prayer to help you talk with God about your dream and the developmental tasks ahead of you.

Review Questions

1. Why is having a dream important for each of us? What are the elements that make up a personal dream?

2. What are five questions that you can use to help yourself define your dream?

3. Why do we need models in the shaping of our dream?

4. What does the term *vocation* mean?

5. Describe the three aspects of Jesus' dream for humankind. Give examples from Jesus' life that show him modeling each facet of his dream.

6. Describe the first three conditions for growth described in this chapter.

7. Why is it more meaningful to ask yourself how you are going to lead a meaningful life than to ask yourself how to avoid death?

8. What did Jesus mean when he said, "Anyone who wants to save his life will lose it; but anyone who loses his life for my sake will find it" (Matthew 16:25)?

9. What does the word *transition* really imply?

10. What are some common reactions to periods of transition?

11. List and describe each of the eleven developmental tasks of the transitional period between the ages of seventeen and twenty-two.

2 Identity and Autonomy: Shaping Your Life

A dream is not only for the future; a dream is for now. It answers the questions, Who will I become? What will give my life zest, joy, and substance? What will I contribute with my life? This dream begins to take shape during a person's youth.

So your dream is already in process. The steps toward identity (who you are) and autonomy (your ability to direct your own life) that figured prominently in your adolescence are now assuming a central place as you move into young adulthood. These attempts to form an identity and a sense of autonomy are crucial to your dream.

Let's begin this chapter by taking a look at one young person's struggle to find his identity:

> Zack sat at the end of the cafeteria table, eating his ham and cheese on rye. Some mustard had just dripped off of the edge of the bread onto his blue pants. As he tried to scrub off the yellow glob with his handkerchief, the conversation about the coming weekend surged ahead without him. But, then, he was hardly ever included in the activities of the other seniors. Zack's position at the table defined his role with these guys; he was at the end, on the fringe.
>
> Jim brandished a letter announcing his acceptance to the state university. The others toasted him with milk cartons or pop cans held high.
>
> "You're just going there because Shelly is!" David announced.
>
> Everybody began ribbing Jim. Shelly and Jim had been going with each other for about two years.

A dream is not only for the future; a dream is for now.

When the bell rang at the end of the lunch period, the group split up and headed for different classes. Zack threw his garbage into a wastebasket and walked alone down the hall. "Why didn't I say something, anything? All I do is just sit like a lump. What a dummy!" he thought.

After Zack sat down in economics class, he flipped open his textbook to the page marked by a letter. He unfolded his letter of acceptance to the same state university that Jim and Shelly would be attending. "Maybe I can get involved more there." This was half question and half hope, spoken only in Zack's mind.

"Are you really going to ask him?" Jane asked. "You better be ready to talk for the two of you."

"He's quiet, but at least he has some brains."

Lisa walked quickly to economics class, wondering how Zack would react to her invitation to go to the chamber of commerce luncheon. She knew that he was shy but thought of him as intelligent and fairly handsome. Lisa had first noticed Zack when he nervously gave a speech in class about the need for equal opportunities for women. His hands had shaken and drawn aimless circles in the air; he had stared at the back wall. However, after a timid start, conviction had strengthened his voice. Lisa had wondered where Zack had been hiding for the past three years of high school.

After economics, Lisa walked beside Zack to their English class. She never felt nervous with anyone. Some people even found her to be too blunt.

"Zack, I have to go to a chamber of commerce luncheon to give a short talk about Catholic high schools. I was told that I could invite another student to go with me. I don't know how the food will be, but I'd like you to go with me. What do you say?"

Zack was stunned. He wondered if Lisa was kidding. "Well, sure. Great." He looked at her happily.

"I'll drive us. Friday. Meet me in the school office at 11:45." Lisa stopped walking and turned back to look at Zack. "Glad you're going, Zack. If you don't hurry, you'll miss the start of class."

Zack's situation is not unique; many of us exist on the fringes and wish we were somebody else at least part of the time. Fortunately, many people like Lisa exist, too. They are people who give us a richer sense of who we are because they recognize elements in our personality that we might not appreciate enough by ourselves. Developing a clear sense of your identity is important as you approach a career and greater responsibilities—a position in which you will have to depend more exclusively on yourself.

Depending on yourself is another way of saying that you have **autonomy.** An autonomous person is one who can make reasonable but often difficult choices on her or his own, sometimes in the face of disapproval or even contempt of others. A person who makes decisions by inner conviction rather than by social pressure or fear is truly free and autonomous.

The Christian View

As you consider different aspects of your identity and ways of establishing your autonomy, remember that in the Christian worldview, human beings are called to fullness of life. As Saint Paul said, ". . . you were called to be free" (Galatians 5:13). Valuing one's uniqueness and acting independently are central to Christian life.

Having a strong sense of identity, then, is part of being Christian. Consider one girl's situation:

- Michelle attends her first senior religion class and is told that she will be expected to do a service project for the course. She is at a loss. Michelle is not unwilling to serve, but she has no idea of her own talents or abilities. She can't imagine herself being of service to anyone.

Like Michelle, Zack did not appreciate his own intelligence or sensitivity. Perhaps Lisa will help him to recognize his strengths. To the extent that people like Michelle and Zack can discover their own unique gifts and their own identities, they will be able to live the full lives intended for all Christians.

Acting freely, autonomously, is also profoundly Christian in the sense that moral choices can be made only by *free* persons. Therefore, children are not considered responsible for their mistakes in the same way that adults are. A three-year-old girl who takes a handful of candy from a store might only be scolded gently, whereas a high school senior doing the same will probably be charged with shoplifting. The difference is that the little girl is not yet free—free of the ignorance and self-centeredness of childhood. She still depends on her parents to tell her what is right or wrong. However, as a young adult, the senior has to make moral choices with relative autonomy.

Identity and autonomy are at the heart of Christian life.

A person who makes decisions by inner conviction rather than by social pressure or fear is truly autonomous.

Identity: A Person in the Making

What Is Identity?

As a human being, you are called to be fully alive. Implicit in this statement is the need for you to be aware of and appreciate the person that you are. Your dog Rover, on the other hand, is not aware of himself as a Manchester terrier. Rover just eats, sleeps, looks at you eagerly for a friendly rub behind the ears, and behaves the way that instinct dictates to him. Essentially, he does not have any awareness of himself as a dog. Only humans are aware of themselves as separate, unique, conscious beings. We do not simply respond to circumstances through blind instinct—at least most of the time.

Your **identity,** then, is who you are—the marvelous combination of personality traits, abilities, strengths, weaknesses, interests, and values that is uniquely yours and that is still in the process of formation. This is distinct from your **sense of identity,** or your understanding of who you are.

Built on Past Experience

Your sense of identity is not developed in a vacuum. Your identity is composed of millions of bits of information that you gather about yourself from events, relationships with people, work, reading, and so on. Everything that happens builds your sense of identity. In turn, your future is built on the foundation of this sense of who you are.

The affirmation of other people, particularly of those who are significant to you, is important for achieving a strong sense of identity. If you have a notion that you are an intelligent person but other people treat you as dull-witted, you will live with a certain degree of insecurity about your intelligence. In this case, your *identity* may be that of an intelligent person, but your *sense of identity* is damaged or distorted by inaccurate messages given to you by other people.

Indeed, during much of your life, people have been affirming or challenging your identity, such as in the following instance:

> Joe plays the trumpet well, so his music teachers encourage him to apply for a university music scholarship. "Competence in music" becomes an affirmed part of his identity.
>
> On the other hand, every time Joe tries to fix his car, he either strips the threads off of bolts, puts wires back

To be fully alive is to be aware of and appreciate the person that you are.

Write fifteen sentences that begin with "I am . . ." Then pick the two sentences that best describe you. Put a check mark next to any statement that surprises you. Finally, write a summary of what you have learned about yourself from this exercise.

incorrectly, or in some way makes matters worse. After he botches a job, the mechanic that Joe takes his car to snickers and mumbles something about "some people have it and some people don't." Joe concludes that "mechanical ability" is not a part of his identity.

Like a Pearl

A clear and realistic sense of identity enables you to go forward with life choices about a career, hobbies, and so on. In addition, strong self-understanding is a center of strength that helps you to cope with conflicting demands, contradictory values, losses, and choices. Conversely, faulty perceptions about yourself may inhibit your development.

One caution: Before considering ways of gaining a stronger sense of who you are, realize that your identity is never final. Each accomplishment, every argument, and most events—the whole stream of life—continually shape you. Your identity is like a grain of sand that lodges in an oyster and over several years becomes a pearl as layer upon layer of pearly substance builds up around the grain. At each stage of development, the pearl has value, but it becomes more precious as it grows.

Knowing Yourself

Knowing yourself involves honestly addressing these questions:
- What am I feeling?
- What do I want?
- What are people telling me?
- What are my talents?
- What is out of my control? within my control?

What Are You Feeling?

Feelings are essential facets of who you are; they need to be acknowledged. Too frequently people are told to ignore how they feel: "Don't feel that way!" Think about how ridiculous that command is. You cannot help what you feel; you just feel. Emotions are reactions, not intentions.

Unfortunately, the message that some feelings, especially strong feelings, are unacceptable is often very powerful. So instead of facing emotions, people deny or suppress them. But strong feelings do not go away; they just bubble underneath the surface of our self-control, sometimes becoming a volcano that explodes.

Knowing yourself requires you to ask in a given situation,

Picture in your mind some of your past successes, recapturing the full scene:
- who was there
- what happened
- how you felt

Successes help us to form our sense of identity. Write about at least one success and why you felt good about it.

What feeling is hardest for you to express? Why? What feeling is easiest for you to express? Why? Write a personal goal about how you would like to handle your feelings.

Just how do I feel right now? Feelings can function as either friends or dictators. It is best to treat them as friends, or they will become dictators. This is illustrated in the following instance:

- *The dictator:* Troy has the habit of making Dan look stupid in class. Dan is furious but cannot find a way to express that anger. Maybe if he says something to retaliate, Troy's friends will come down hard on Dan or ridicule him. He is more than a little troubled, but he tries to tell himself that he is not angry anymore. Nevertheless, whenever Troy's name comes up in conversation, Dan says something rather nasty; he inserts innuendos that put Troy in a bad light. Dan finds himself tied in knots by his anger at Troy and is not himself. Clearly his anger is operating as a dictator here, although not consciously. A feeling is dictating Dan's behavior, making him less than free.

- *The friend:* Suppose that in the above situation, instead of denying his reactions, Dan treats his anger as an intimate friend who is letting him know just how hurt and humiliated he feels. Dan learns something about how sensitive he is and realizes for the first time how worried he is about looking intelligent to other people. Now he must decide what to do. Dan may opt to talk privately with Troy about how the cutting comments in class affect him. Or he may choose to say nothing to Troy. Then Dan might release his anger physically, by jogging. Either way, Dan decides not to let the embarrassing remarks affect his image of himself or the way that he treats Troy. In this situation, anger is Dan's friend, an affirming teacher who gives him insight into himself.

By treating our feelings as friends and refusing to let them be dictators, we can learn a great deal about ourselves.

What Do You Want?

Closely related to knowing your feelings is knowing your desires. You cannot decide what to do with your life unless you know what you want. You are barraged by other people telling you what they want you to want—in TV commercials, songs, billboards, fashion magazines, and even conversations with your family and your friends. As a consequence, knowing what you want is difficult. The tendency is to falsify your desires, to pretend that you want something in order to please someone important to you or to conform to some social norm.

Knowing what you want is not, in itself, selfish, although insisting that everyone else do what you want is. The point is this: that thinking realistically about your future requires serious

What you want forms your identity and shapes your life.

Write "I want to" fifteen times in a column, skipping a line after each phrase. Then quickly complete the statements. For example, "I want to learn how to cross-country ski."

consideration about what you want out of life and what you are willing to give to life. People who wake up at age forty realizing that they have never done anything that they wanted to do are sad indeed. In *That Hideous Strength* by British novelist C. S. Lewis, the character Mark comes to such a terrible realization:

> He looked back on his life not with shame, but with a kind of disgust at its dreariness. . . . When had he ever done what he wanted? Mixed with the people whom he liked? Or even eaten and drunk what took his fancy?
>
> . . . He was aware, without even having to think of it, that it was he himself—nothing else in the whole universe—that had chosen the dust and broken bottles, the heap of old tin cans, the dry and choking places. (Pages 287–288)

What you want forms your identity and shapes your life. Jesus recognized this fact when he said to his disciples, "For wherever your treasure is, that is where your heart will be too" (Luke 12:34).

The *Upanishads,* a collection of ancient Hindu sayings, make this same point: "And they say in truth that a man is made of desire. As his desire is, so is his faith. As his faith is, so are his works. As his works are, so he becomes."

Not all desires are good for human beings; not all desires lead to happiness. Christian desires can be identified in the dream of Jesus: to build the peaceable kingdom, to create a loving community, and to help persons grow fully alive. This dream is a broad framework within which thousands of decisions can be made about what we want—decisions regarding relationships, education, jobs, purchases, entertainment, or where to live. At each decision point, we can ask ourselves, Are my desires consistent with Jesus' dream for humankind?

Human beings cannot live in a condition of emptiness for very long. If we are not going toward something we really desire, we stagnate. Then our suppressed energy and potential turn to despair and sometimes destruction. But once we know what we want, life is motivated by an eagerness and a drive that would be impossible otherwise. Even though we make mistakes along the way, we are still headed for something we want.

You reflected on your life dream in chapter 1. That dream summarizes many of your desires. Review your dream now.
- Does it really represent *your* desires?
- Would you like to add any images to your dream?

What Are People Telling You?

Every conversation with another person—even the "Hello! How are you?" type—tells you something about yourself. "Hello! How are you?" is, at least, a recognition by the other person that you exist. If the other person says, "Hello, Terry!" you

List five comments that other people have made about your body. Next to each comment, describe how you felt about their remarks. Did you accept or reject their opinions?

know that you are acknowledged in an individual way. If the same person stops, looks attentively at you, and then says, "Hello, Terry! How are you?" you sense that you are significant in this person's eyes.

Your relationships provide millions of pieces of data about yourself, some of them affirmative and some of them negative. All of these pieces contribute to your sense of who you are. However, this information should not be accepted without examination.

In other words, we cannot become the unique persons that we want to be merely by living as others tell us to or as their perceptions define us. If Zack, from the first story in this chapter, had let his position on the fringe control him, he would not have had the freedom to accept Lisa's invitation. Freedom and uniqueness require that we listen to what others tell us about ourselves, whether in their words or in their deeds, and then decide within ourselves whether we accept those evaluations. Listening and deciding demand some time for pondering, time spent alone. People who are worried about finding themselves alone may never find *themselves* at all. A sense of identity is partially the fruit of silence.

What Are Your Talents?

Attentiveness to your feelings, your desires, and what others tell you about yourself builds a sense of identity. Added to these factors is awareness of your talents, or gifts.

The word *talent* comes from the Latin word *talentum,* meaning a unit of money used in ancient Rome. Today **talent** means an ability or an aptitude that has value. Talents are often called gifts because, in part, they seem to be inherited. A violinist does not choose to have perfect pitch; she or he is born with it. A great gymnast is born with an agile body. We say that these individuals are gifted. The discipline and practice needed to create a master violinist or a great gymnast have to be combined with the genetic gifts of musical aptitude and a certain body structure.

Talents are not just physical or intellectual. Aspects of personality can also be unique gifts. You have the potential to be a full person, but naturally you are more gifted in certain areas of your personality than you are in others. Some people are excellent listeners. Other people are witty or always seem to take the initiative. Unfortunately, people commonly forget about the gifts of personality because physical and intellectual gifts are easier to identify and recognize. School letters are given to athletes and band members. Few awards are given to recognize

Imagine that you are looking into the mirror before coming to school in the morning. Write a list of the mental comments you might make to yourself.
- Do you give yourself more positive or more negative feedback?
- Would you feel better if you glanced in the mirror every morning and said, "I am a terrific person, created in God's image"?

Write "I can" fifteen times in a column, skipping a line after each phrase. Then quickly complete the statements. For example, "I can relax with most people and become their friend."

the talent of being a good friend, listening with understanding, or acting with kindness.

Before talents can be developed, they first must be acknowledged. Saint Paul urged the Corinthians to recognize their individual talents as gifts from God:

> There are many different gifts, but it is always the same Spirit; there are many different ways of serving, but it is always the same Lord. . . . To one is given from the Spirit the gift of utterance expressing wisdom; to another the gift of utterance expressing knowledge, in accordance with the same Spirit; to another, faith. . . . But at work in all these is one and the same Spirit, distributing them at will to each individual. (1 Corinthians 12:4–11)

Aspects of personality can be unique gifts. For instance, some people are excellent listeners.

Each of us is gifted in some way; to be full persons we may have to take some time to reflect on exactly what our gifts are.

One disappointment some people feel sharply is that they do not have the talents they wish to have. Consider for a moment the feeling of defeat experienced by some students when rosters are posted after tryouts for sports, band, debate team, cheerleading, and so on. Students who are cut from sports or activities face disappointment in not being evaluated as talented enough. Even more disappointing may be the realization that they will not get a chance to be part of a group or team that they very much wanted to be part of.

Sometimes talents go unappreciated and, therefore, unused. Your talents may not be obvious ones; you may not have exactly the talents you wish for. Nevertheless, you are gifted in ways that will help you to fulfill your dream.

Compare the "I want to" statements you wrote in the activity on page 44 with the "I can" statements in the activity on page 46.
- Are there any patterns in the two lists? any differences?
- Are there any statements that most people would not know about you?

What Is Out of Your Control? Within Your Control?

To the extent that talents are inherited, they represent an area that is out of our control. However, what we do with our talents is very much within our control. In coming to a sense of identity, we would do well to sort out which of the factors that make us unique are out of our control and which are within our control. The factors that are out of our control include the following:

1. Cosmic: Your birth was a unique event over which you exercised no power. Likewise, someday you will die. These are givens. You are influenced by cosmic occurrences that insurance companies call "acts of God," such as earthquakes and hurricanes. Rainbows, gentle rain, and clean, new-fallen snow are "acts of God," too. All of these events have an impact on you.

Some factors that make us unique are out of our control, but we do have control over how we respond to them.

2. Genetic: Genes have a strong influence on who you are. From the moment of your birth, people may have been telling you how much you look like your mother or your father. As much as this may bother you, your looks are dependent on the chromosomes of your parents. Certainly, you are a unique combination of those genes, but a combination nonetheless. As discussed above, some of your talents may also be inherited. Not too many forwards on basketball teams are the offspring of short, stocky parents.

3. Cultural: You had no control over the culture into which you were born and raised—as a member of a particular family, living in a certain country and region, and as part of a particular religious, ethnic, and economic setting. These cultural factors have much to do with your identity. For example, if you live in Canada, you have educational opportunities that might not be available to you if you had been born in Mongolia. Canada has traditions that its citizens celebrate; these traditions are part of a Canadian's identity.

4. Circumstantial: Finally, you are shaped to a degree by circumstances: major historical events, accidents, chance meetings—occurrences that seem to be pure luck or pure misfortune. For instance, British young adults had no say in the outbreak of war with Nazi Germany, but it shaped their lives forever. You probably know or have heard about someone who became paralyzed by an accident; one event has given new shape to that person's identity. Many careers in music have been fostered because talented young performers have been fortunate enough to find equally talented teachers.

We can grow by using the talents we have in the circumstances in which we find ourselves.

In summary, your identity is influenced by cosmic, genetic, cultural, and circumstantial factors over which you have no control. However, you do have control over your response to these factors. You are a unique blend created by these four elements, and your reaction to them can be just as special. Your identity is in your hands to the degree that you understand where you have come from and can react consciously to that background.

The Apostle Peter, as portrayed in the Christian Scriptures, serves as a good example of someone shaping his identity. He was a fisherman, married, and probably illiterate. Peter lived in a land ruled by the Roman dictatorship. His work was hard. Some days his catch was good, and other days his nets were empty.

One day, along came a stranger, Jesus, who invited Peter to follow him. Jesus wanted to make him a fisher of people (Matthew 4:18–20). Peter was not a likely candidate to be the first apostle or the rock upon which Jesus would build his Church. Nevertheless, Peter accepted the responsibility. He overcame the parts of his background that would have kept him a fisherman and used the facets of his being that allowed him to be brave, impulsive, and resolute. Rather than letting genetics, culture, and circumstances largely determine the life we lead, we can grow, like Peter, by using the talents we have in the circumstances in which we find ourselves.

Autonomy: Directing Your Own Life

A strong sense of identity generally produces a healthy ability to direct our own life and actions—autonomy. The reverse is also true. Experience with being in charge of our own affairs and living with our own decisions brings about a more secure sense of identity. Therefore, identity and autonomy reinforce each other.

Living with Consequences

Independently making choices that have consequences—with the realization that you will have to live with those consequences—is the stuff of autonomy. Robert Frost expressed such choices symbolically in his poem "The Road Not Taken":

> Two roads diverged in a yellow wood,
> And sorry I could not travel both
> And be one traveler, long I stood
> And looked down one as far as I could
> To where it bent in the undergrowth;
>
> Then took the other, as just as fair,
> And having perhaps the better claim,
> Because it was grassy and wanted wear;
> Though as for that the passing there
> Had worn them really about the same,
>
> And both that morning equally lay
> In leaves no step had trodden black.
> Oh, I kept the first for another day!
> Yet knowing how way leads on to way,
> I doubted if I should ever come back.
>
> I shall be telling this with a sigh
> Somewhere ages and ages hence:
> Two roads diverged in a wood, and I—
> I took the one less traveled by,
> And that has made all the difference.

The consequences of our decisions sometimes include the disapproval of other people. Of course, affirmation is always welcome. Support is helpful; it gives us a lift. However, when we watch other people in order to imitate them or when we wait to see if everyone approves of an action before doing it, we are

A strong sense of identity generally produces a healthy ability to direct our own life and actions—autonomy.

Think about a recent situation in which you were too dependent on other people (for example, parents or friends). Write about that situation.

shackled by the need for approval. When independent decision-making is called for, an overly dependent person may be frozen, waiting for someone to give a clue as to what to do.

Not being dependent on the approval of other people does not mean that an autonomous person is insensitive to the needs, wishes, or opinions of other people; a mature person naturally takes others into account in decision-making. Autonomous decision-making does mean that the person is able to rely on his or her own judgment in weighing all of the factors in a decision.

Autonomy from Family

At this stage in your life, you are probably concerned about gaining increased independence from your family. The journey from dependence on your parents to an autonomous life lies just ahead of you. Perhaps you are already on that journey of learning to function capably on your own. Here are some examples of young adults who are struggling to develop this kind of autonomy, with varying degrees of success:

Write about recent situations in which you
- acted independently, resulting in personal growth
- acted independently, with negative results

- Linda, a high school student, commits herself to earning a significant part of her college tuition during the summer months. "It's important to me to rely on my own earning ability."
- After graduating from technical school, Rob could not get a job that paid well, so he went back home to live with his folks. Now Rob avoids his parents, staying in his room and rarely talking with them. "It feels like I'm in high school again."
- Mary, a college freshman who has led a fairly protected life until now, has joined a fundamentalist group on campus and lives in the members' house. "It is such a relief to find my real self apart from my family and to know that everyone in my house cares about me deeply and will keep me from going down the wrong path." Lately, though, a nagging thought has been recurring for Mary: "Why am I feeling sort of smothered?"
- Mike is in line to take over his parents' catering business when they retire. They have been grooming him for management, and he is good at it. But Mike has discovered that he wants to go to technical school to learn electronics. "It's not going to be easy to break the news to Mom and Dad."
- Cheryl is so delighted about having no curfew in her first year of college that she stays out every night until two or three in the morning. She is exhausted most of the day and skips

many morning classes. Finally, Cheryl admits, "This is crazy. My days and nights are reversed. I've got to get my schedule back to normal, or I won't be able to stay in school."

Becoming financially self-reliant (Linda), struggling with frustrations to our independence (Rob), spotting the tendency to substitute one form of dependency for another (Mary), asserting our own life plan in the face of our parents' contradictory plan (Mike), and having the freedom to learn from mistakes (Cheryl)—all are part of the journey to gain autonomy from family.

Whether we are striving for autonomy from parents, from the rules of peers, or from society's norms, it is important that our reasons for acting originate *within* ourselves rather than *outside* of ourselves in the approval or disapproval of others.

The Freedom to Be Responsible

Autonomy implies freedom from coercion or constraint. Such freedom is essential to directing our own life and development. However, we do not live alone; we live in a society of people who have rights and needs, who are all free. The freedom of all people requires that we respect and respond to the needs and rights of others. We are not responsibly free if we cannot see beyond our own noses to the needs of real situations and real people. If we are confined to the prisons of our own ignorance or if we view the world only through our own dream, we are not free. Freedom means that we direct our growth within the context of society. We must respond not solely to our own whims and wishes but also to people who need our nurturing and sharing.

For instance, a man racing his car down a city street at fifty miles per hour because he wants to see how fast his car can go is not acting freely. He is simply the prisoner of his compulsions and whims. He is not taking into account the real situation, which might include a child who wanders into the path of his speeding car. The man is acting without responsibility. However, if the man is speeding to the hospital because his grandfather has had a stroke while riding in the car, he might be choosing the most responsible free action. Considering the whole situation—life hanging in the balance, little traffic, and few pedestrians on the street—to drive slowly might be irresponsible. In other words, acting freely means that we consider the whole situation and respond accordingly for the good of all.

Consider the image of a river: Unlimited freedom, or license,

Write a goal for your growth in autonomy. For example, you might want to develop your judgment about study time so that you do not wait until the last minute or rely on how much time other students spend studying. Then list the concrete steps that will help you to reach your goal.

is like a river with no banks. The water is not directed, so it rushes through towns, flooding homes, overturning cars, and perhaps taking lives. On the other hand, responsible freedom is like a river flowing strongly in its channel. Towns use it for drinking water. Barges carry grain and coal up and down its length. Farmers irrigate their crops with its water. In short, the river fulfills its potential and helps everyone else at the same time.

For Christians, freedom is seen in the context of freedom from sin and freedom to love. In one of his letters, Saint Peter sharply rebuked people who lead others into error and perversity: "They may promise freedom but are themselves slaves to corruption; because if anyone lets himself be dominated by anything, then he is a slave to it" (2 Peter 2:19–20). Sin—selfishness, injustice, abuse of others, and so on—can dominate our life. The promise of Jesus' Resurrection is that sin can be overcome and that people can be free to love.

Freedom means that we direct our growth within the context of society.

Autonomy and Interdependence: Help Wanted

It is clear that genuinely autonomous people are neither lone warriors facing the world nor cold machines that operate unfeelingly. In summary, autonomous people can be described this way:

- They are strong enough to be sensitive to the needs of other people.
- They have firm identities that allow them to consider other points of view and to change.
- They are aware of their own resources—talents, skills, knowledge, and feelings—so that they can be confident, not threatened, in conflict.
- They realize that they sometimes need help and that they will not become overly dependent by occasionally accepting aid from others.

Autonomous people live interdependently.

To be interdependent means to function well on our own while realizing our need for others and their need for us. Most of the time, this give-and-take relationship feels comfortable. Interdependence also implies that others—teachers, friends, parents—help us to learn working knowledge and skills in a whole range of areas, from repairing flat tires and using computers to entertaining guests and listening well. We rely on others to teach us hundreds of practical life skills, and we teach others as well. This kind of interdependent lifestyle builds our sense of identity.

Write about a way in which you have been successfully interdependent, that is, involved in a give-and-take relationship.

Paul's Balance

The Apostle Paul is a useful example of the balance between autonomy and interdependence. Paul traveled all over the Mediterranean to spread the word about Jesus. He certainly coped capably with all of the problems that confronted him. In his second letter to the Christians at Corinth, Paul told them about some of his trials:

> Five times I have been given thirty-nine lashes by the Jews; three times I have been beaten with sticks; once I was stoned; three times I have been shipwrecked, and once I have been in the open sea for a night and a day; continually travelling, I have been in danger from rivers, in danger from [bandits], in danger from my own people and in danger from the gentiles, in danger in the towns and in danger in the open country, in danger at sea and in danger from people masquerading as brothers; . . . And, besides all the external things, there is, day in day out, the pressure on me of my anxiety for all the churches. If anyone weakens, I am weakened as well; and when anyone is made to fall, I burn in agony myself. (2 Corinthians 11:24–29)

No doubt, Paul was tough. He was autonomous yet in touch with the feelings of the Christians.

Paul's faith in God made him strong. His recognition of his own weaknesses made him sympathetic: ". . . It is, then, about my weaknesses that I am happiest of all to boast, so that the power of Christ may rest upon me" (2 Corinthians 12:9). Paul needed God's help and boasted about it. His letters to the Christian communities also are filled with requests for help.

Like Paul, we can be autonomous as well as interdependent. In fact, living in this way is part of growth.

Different Relationships Need Different Autonomy

One final note about autonomy: You will never be completely autonomous and interdependent with all people in all situations. No one is. You may feel a stronger need for the approval of your parents than for the approval of your teachers. You may feel more give-and-take with a close friend than with your younger brothers and sisters, who might take more than they give. Your relationships are important, and just as they differ from one another, so will your experiences of autonomy differ. At various times in your life, you will ask for the help of other people;

At various times in your life, you will ask for the help of other people; chances are that they will require your assistance at other times.

chances are that they will require your assistance at other times. What is important is that you grow in autonomy and in your ability to be interdependent.

Personal Power: Fruit of Identity and Autonomy

Growth in a sense of identity and in autonomy produces a welcome fruit—**personal power,** the ability to influence your own life and the people and events around you. You can be less of a victim to peer pressure, fancy advertising, and all other attempts to push you in one way or another. Naturally, this power has a positive effect on your sense of identity and autonomy; you begin to value yourself more and to take your own judgments more seriously. From a Christian point of view, people must be able to direct their own lives and influence events— that is, they must have power—if they are to build the peaceable kingdom, create a loving community, and become fully alive persons.

Power, of course, can be used in both good ways and bad ways.

Growth in a sense of identity produces personal power, the ability to influence your own life and the life around you.

Positive Power

Power is positive if it is used to influence your own life and the lives of others in growth-producing, healthy ways. Even planting a garden, studying the history of World War II, or asking a friend to a movie can be understood as power used well. Let's consider in more detail two positive types of power: nurturing power and shared power.

Nurturing Power

To nurture someone is to use power for that person. Parents exercise this **nurturing power** for their children by feeding them, changing their diapers, and later teaching them how to ride a bicycle. Jesus used this power to heal the sick, preach his message of love, and drive out demons. The power to nurture comes from a genuine concern for the welfare of other people, especially for those who have little power of their own— children, sick people, and poor people.

Shared Power

When our personal power is used to complement or increase other people's power, we have **shared power.** This kind of power can be very unfamiliar to us. We are accustomed to people in powerful positions who grasp their power tightly, hoarding it to exert maximum pressure whenever they desire to. But a different model of power can be seen in Jesus, who passed on his mission to the Apostles, sharing with them his power to build the kingdom. The early Christian communities, where the members held all property in common, give us a picture of shared power lived out. The Christians supported one another's efforts to preach the Good News. The power of each one enhanced the power of the whole group.

Being involved in a group in which power is shared rather than hoarded can be exhilarating. Consider the excitement conveyed by this young man in talking about a meeting that he participated in:

- It was a *different* kind of meeting. First of all, we were working on something we all believed in—raising money to help Katie's family with medical expenses when she got so sick. Somebody took the lead and got us started on coming up with tons of ideas to raise money. We all jumped in with suggestions. When it came to actually deciding which projects we should do, everyone spoke up and also listened; no one insisted on having it their way. By the end, we settled on two projects, and everyone took a piece of the responsibility. It was fun! These people are great to work with.

Shared power is evident in many friendships. For instance:

- Susan encourages David to try out for the school play and even listens to him practice because she knows that he would be excellent in it. Susan does this despite knowing that if David gets the part, he may be too busy to spend much time with her. She wants to see him use his potential because David has supported Susan on many important projects.

Sometimes shared power means speaking out or taking a stand so that others have a chance to better themselves—use their own power. The great Indian leader *Mohandas K. Gandhi* organized nonviolent marches to protest abuses by British colonial rulers. In one march, Gandhi led hundreds of poor people to the sea to make their own salt in defiance of a British ban on individuals making salt. Since the British had placed a tax on salt, a basic necessity for preserving food, salt had become too expensive for poor Indians to purchase. By leading the march, Gandhi empowered the Indian people to assert their rights. By marching with him, the people shared Gandhi's power.

Complete these two sentences with as many examples as you can think of for each:
- I used my power to nurture others when . . .
- I shared my power with others when . . .

Review your lists. How would you evaluate your sense of your own power?

Negative Power

Perhaps the word *power* has a bad reputation because power so often can be corrupt or inhumane. Power can be used in exploitative, manipulative, and competitive ways.

Exploitative Power

Using persons or nature for one's own purposes is **exploitative power.** Slavery is an extreme example, but exploitative power exists today in such forms as the following:

* Landowners in Third World countries devote increasing portions of the land to cash crops for export (sugar, coffee, pineapples) instead of crops that will feed the local, often hungry, population.
* Logging companies strip forests of trees, causing major erosion problems.
* Whalers hunt rare species of whales in order to make huge profits.

These cases are examples of exploitation.

Indian leader Mohandas K. Gandhi shared his power—used his personal power to increase other people's power.

Manipulative Power

Con artists, blackmailers, and many advertisers use **manipulative power.** This is power to maneuver people for one's own advantage. For instance, some years ago movie theater owners began inserting pictures of soft drinks or popcorn and signs saying "You are thirsty" into movies that were shown. Because these insertions consisted of only one or two frames of the film, they went by so fast that the moviegoers were not conscious of them. However, these pictures and signs seduced the viewers at an unconscious level. Soda and popcorn sales boomed. This form of manipulative power eventually was outlawed.

Competitive Power

Competitive power is something that most people are familiar with. In competition, power is exercised against another person or group; one wins and the other loses. Many people defend competition as useful and healthy, but it can harm a sense of community. After all, nobody wants to be a loser. When competition makes success or winning more important than relationships and compassion, it is power used badly.

The Need for Power

We need power in order to bring our dreams to fulfillment. Being powerful—that is, bringing about change in the world around

We know something of the joy of the Apostles at Pentecost when we realize our own power to reach out and make a difference in the world.

us—is not something that Christians should shy away from. We are meant to be powerful people. Consider some examples of what happens when people are powerless:

- Because they received no response to their repeated cries, many babies in a severely overcrowded orphanage in Peru stopped crying; they gave up on expressing their needs. Although the babies were being fed regularly, some of them died because they could no longer communicate physical distress. The inability to influence their environment in this most basic way became lethal.

- Many analysts of the causes of World War II cite the complete powerlessness experienced by the German people after World War I. The Versailles Treaty at the end of World War I so humiliated and punished the Germans that they turned to Adolf Hitler to exert their power in order to regain pride in their nation.

- People who are abused as children experience a terrifying form of powerlessness. They are more apt than other people to grow up and abuse their own children.

We need power. The deprivation of power, as demonstrated above, can lead to violence and tragedy. But we do not need the kind of power that exploits, manipulates, or competes with others. That is controlling power. What we do need are opportunities to nurture others and to share power. We need to be able to make a difference.

To go from hesitancy and a feeling of having no impact to a sense of being filled with strength can be a joyful experience. The Apostles felt this joy when they recognized that the power of the Holy Spirit had come into them at Pentecost. This power erased their fears about and barriers to communicating the Good News: "... There came from heaven a sound as of a violent wind. . . . They were all filled with the Holy Spirit and began to speak different languages as the Spirit gave them power to express themselves" (Acts 2:2–4).

A crowd gathered to listen to the Apostles, who, though mostly uneducated men, could now speak in a variety of languages: "Everyone was amazed and perplexed; they asked one another what it all meant. Some, however, laughed it off. 'They have been drinking too much new wine,' they said" (Acts 2:12–13).

The joy of the Apostles at Pentecost was not unlike the joy that we know when we realize our own power to reach out and make a difference in the world around us. This power, the fruit of a growing sense of identity and autonomy, can be called God-given because a person's journey to identity and autonomy is guided by the Spirit of Jesus, who dreams that each person will become all that he or she can be.

The Costs of Growth

Shaping our life is not accomplished without paying a price. Nothing worthwhile comes cheaply, so growth will involve pain and scars. For each friend that we find, we may lose another. Or we may discover that when we try a new skill, we fall flat on our face. Failure or rejection may haunt us. Sometimes, maybe many times, life is a muddle and a struggle.

But this pain of struggling to grow is not meaningless. In his journey to Resurrection, Jesus suffered the ultimate price for fulfilling his dream. He died on the cross. Even before this final agony, Jesus was rejected in his home province. He traveled and preached to demanding crowds, always being asked to perform miracles. Even after all of his efforts, the Apostles never seemed to truly understand what Jesus was doing and who he was. He was betrayed by Judas, a member of his inner circle of friends. Peter denied knowing Jesus, yet he was supposed to head the new community of Jesus' followers. The story of Jesus' life is hardly an average profile of success.

Nothing worthwhile comes cheaply, so growth will involve pain and scars.

"For the wonder of myself, for the wonder of your works—I thank you."

In the spirit of Psalm 139, write your own litany of personal aspects that you are thankful for, perhaps beginning with the phrase "I thank you, God, for . . ."

Our trials will not be exactly like those of Jesus. But at times, like him, we will be lonely, misunderstood, betrayed, and bothered by many demands. However, just as Jesus rose from the dead, all persons who love their neighbors, live in peace and justice, and help to build a loving community will share in Jesus' joy and glory.

Growing Day by Day

Do something every day to build your dream. Learn about one small aspect of yourself. Find out what others can teach you—either working skills or life skills. Affirm that you are a valuable person every day. To live fully is to change; to change is to grow to maturity. Maturity happens step-by-step, as you create it each day.

You are creating a lifestyle, a way of living in the world. Who you are, what you believe, what you do—all of these compose your lifestyle. If you are conscious of who you are and what you are creating, life becomes an adventure.

Shaping your life is an adventure full of risks, growth, pain, and joy. But the adventure is rooted in the mystery of your own identity, as you are known in your depths by God. Psalm 139 expresses this mystery:

> Yahweh . . .
> You created my inmost being
> and knit me together in my mother's womb.
> For all these mysteries—
> for the wonder of myself,
> for the wonder of your works—
> I thank you.
>
> (Psalm 139:1,13–14)

Review Questions

1. Why is freedom important to Christian life?

2. What is a sense of identity?

3. How does a person gain a sense of identity?

4. Why is it important to know what we are feeling? what we want?

5. Why are talents often called gifts?

6. List and describe in your own words the four uncontrollable factors that shape our identity.

7. In shaping our identity, to what degree do we have control?

8. Explain what the term *autonomy* means.

9. Describe the relationship between freedom and responsibility.

10. What does it mean to be interdependent? Explain how the Apostle Paul was interdependent.

11. What is personal power?

12. Describe the two positive types of power and give an example of each type from the chapter.

13. Explain the three types of negative power.

14. Why do we need power?

15. What are the costs of growth?

3 Love: A Focus for Life

LOVE. Most people desire it like marathon runners desire the finish line when they are halfway through the race. The runners' desire is sharp and painful, driving them out of fear of not finishing. They know that they will have a harder time living with themselves if they do not cross that line.

Love is the essence of much music, poetry, and literature—classical and contemporary—and the subject of endless speculation. People fight and die for it; blood has been spilled because of it since the start of humankind. Love of God has inspired missionaries all over the globe to die as martyrs. Without love, lives are empty and tragic.

Love appears in the human condition in so many forms that at first it might seem impossible to speak of love as one reality. The word *love* encompasses both the passionate love of a newly-wed couple and the familiar, almost unspoken love of two close friends.

Consider, on one hand, the kind of love expressed in this passionate poem from the Bible's Song of Songs, a collection of wedding feast songs:

Human love appears in many forms.

Beloved:
Set me like a seal on your heart,
like a seal on your arm.
For love is strong as Death,
passion as relentless as [death].
The flash of it is a flash of fire,
a flame of Yahweh . . .
Love no flood can quench,
no torrents drown.
Were a man to offer all his family wealth
to buy love,
contempt is all that he would gain.
(Song of Songs 8:6–7)

The fires of young love have dazzled and energized people throughout time. However, young people and passionate lovers are not the only ones who love. Consider, on the other hand, the mature love of a friendship that has endured for many years:

Ted and Iggy walked into the diner together at exactly 7:00 *a.m.,* just like they had for the last thirteen years since retirement. Every Friday morning, they met at church for Mass and then headed to the Chat 'n' Chew Diner for what they both called a "high-cholesterol, one-my-wife-will-never-fix-me" breakfast.

"Hi, Margaret!" they both chimed in.

"Must be Friday at 7:00 if you two are here!" she chided, friendly.

"You bet!"

"Margaret, I believe you get prettier each Friday morning."

Margaret beamed. "You old jokers just sit down. I know what you'll order, so don't even say it." She bustled around, readying their standard.

Ted and Iggy eased into "their" booth. If a stranger had come in and seen them, that person would have thought at one minute that they were planning a bank robbery—their heads bent close together as they talked furiously fast—and at another minute that they didn't know each other—their faces still, in calm repose.

The two men were seventy-eight years old. They had gone to high school together and had grown up in the same neighborhood. Ted had taken a job as a postal worker after high school, and Iggy had sold men's clothing at one of the big stores downtown. Each had been the other's best man and godfather to the other's first child.

During World War II, Iggy had been left behind at home because of a rheumatic heart. Every July 5 since the war, Iggy would tell his wife that that same day in 1942 had been the worst of his life. He had gone with Ted down to the train that would take him to San Francisco and then to the war with Japan. Iggy had grieved because Ted was going to war without him.

"Agnes," Iggy would tell his wife, "that's one of the few times I ever cried. I never thought I'd see Ted again."

When Ted had returned from the war, Iggy had been there at the station. The two old friends had shaken each other's hand, but becoming overwhelmed with emotion, they

Consider the mature love of a friendship that has endured for many years.

had hugged each other joyfully. "I didn't think you would make it without me!" Iggy had yelled happily.

Then, just for a moment, the smile had left Ted's face. He had looked at his friend seriously, "I wasn't so sure that I would make it either."

After Ted's return, they never talked about the war. With only a few short absences from each other, the two men had stayed close, watched their children grow up and move away, argued about sports, consoled each other when they felt hassled, fished together, and called each other regularly to see what was up.

At age seventy, Iggy had "got religion," as Ted said, and he had started going to Mass almost every morning. Now Ted would join him on Fridays, mumbling that once a week was "okay for Jesus, why not for us?" Then the pair would head for their breakfast at the Chat 'n' Chew Diner.

When you are seventy-eight years old, who might be your Ted or Iggy? Could you build such a lasting relationship with anyone you know right now? Write a brief paragraph about the possibilities.

Passionate love and the love of a friendship that has endured a lifetime—both are love, and both give life zest and meaning.

For a senior who is entering the transition period from age seventeen to twenty-two, a consideration of love, caring, and friendship is perhaps even more important than at other ages. Recall the developmental tasks of this transition period as listed in chapter 1. Among the tasks were these:
- constructing and living out a value system
- reflecting on religious beliefs
- being capable of loving commitments
- making friends and living with intimacy

These tasks center on an understanding of love and a growing ability to love, care, and make friends.

Growing in Love: How? Why?

Moments of Intimacy

Love of any kind doesn't just happen. It begins and is developed in moments of **intimacy**—that is, close association and contact. Intimacy can develop in just about any life activity or context that two persons can share. Intimacy in one area of a relationship may lead to closeness in another area, and then genuine love may grow between two persons. Consider the many types of intimacy:

Work intimacy: When people share tasks that bond them to one another in affirming ways, they experience work intimacy. Sharing responsibilities, decisions, and the satisfaction of a job well done brings people together because they can appreciate each other and feel mutual support. Think about how much time you spend talking about your work—being a student—with those around you. Schoolwork is a point of contact and a shared experience that can bring students together.

Emotional intimacy: Persons who share significant experiences and feelings that touch them in important ways have emotional intimacy. Most of us need—and perhaps have—someone with whom to communicate our sorrows, joys, angers, disappointments, and exhilarations, someone who will accept these feelings as important and maintain our confidences. Emotional intimacy can be the start of a deeper kind of mutual caring.

Intellectual intimacy: People who can talk about ideas and opinions and challenge one another to stretch their minds know the rewards of intellectual intimacy. They might exchange ideas about a movie, a book, or an exciting new computer program.

Crisis intimacy: Imagine that you are chairperson of the prom committee. The prom decorations are a disaster because the committee is disorganized. You turn to some people whom you trust, and they stay up with you until the wee hours to finish the preparations. While hanging decorations and setting up tables, everyone talks. You begin to see the true metal of these people. You have experienced crisis intimacy, which happens to people in disaster situations. For example, lifeboat survivors of a sinking ship, victims of war, and soldiers in the same outfit during battle frequently experience some of the most intimate moments of their lives. Veterans who come to the Vietnam Veterans Memorial in Washington, D.C., to see and touch the names of their dead comrades may weep openly, illustrating that crisis can bring a tremendous depth of intimacy.

Common-cause intimacy: The commitment of people who fervently share an ideal or cause often produces common-cause intimacy. For example, people in the antinuclear movement experience a genuine closeness with other members of the movement because of their strong, personal involvement in the common cause of disarmament.

Spiritual intimacy: The intimacy between people who share a similar sense of the meaning of life or a relationship with God

We should appreciate the opportunities for intimacy that exist in all areas of life.

is spiritual intimacy. It may be expressed in religious practices—worship and shared prayer—or in simple conversations about life and purpose.

Aesthetic intimacy: Watching a brilliant sunset, admiring an oil painting, or listening to a jazz quartet—when two persons appreciate beautiful scenes, music, art, literature, or cinema together, they experience aesthetic intimacy.

Recreational intimacy: Two women who jog together every morning might become close on the level of recreational intimacy. Doing something playful together can allow individuals to drop their masks and be themselves. This honest way of relating also fosters intimacy.

Creative intimacy: Avid gardeners can talk about miraculous varieties of cucumbers or roses with such enthusiasm that they find one another's company exhilarating. Likewise, parents, who are helping to nurture new persons while raising their children, find much to talk about—with each other and with other parents. The process of creating together brings about creative intimacy.

We can appreciate the opportunities for intimacy that exist in almost all areas of life: at work, in church, at school, in the library, in a restaurant, during a misty morning jog, or at an art gallery. Intimate relationships can be nurtured into loving ones if we use some initiative and a little imagination.

Write down the names of six of your friends in a column, skipping a line after each name. Next to each name, indicate the type or types of intimacy that you share with that person. Next to the names of your three closest friends, answer this question:
• What types of intimacy could I further develop with this friend?

Why Care?

We might be tempted to ask ourselves, Why bother to nurture relationships into loving ones? Isn't it easier not to become involved?

We are compelled by our very nature to love. The desire for intimacy with other people is deeply rooted in human beings. Every era has had its love poems, stories, and songs: The whole of the Jewish Scriptures is a record of God's love for Israel and Israel's on-again, off-again love for God. Each time the Israelites turned from God's love, they experienced regret. As the poet Emily Dickinson expressed the need for love,

> Parting is all we know of heaven,
> And all we need of hell.

By reminding us of how deeply we love someone, parting from that person gives us an idea of what the heaven of love is like, but the anguish of parting also suggests the pain of hell. Parting and other human experiences tell us that there are three reasons for our need to love and be loved:

Caring Overcomes Separateness

Overcoming the prison of our aloneness is a tremendous desire. We feel incomplete, limited, and threatened without love. We may try to substitute it with frantic activity, superficial socializing, group happenings, work, or the oblivion of drugs or alcohol, but finally we discover that caring relationships are the only ways to fill the emptiness inside of us and obliterate our loneliness.

Caring Gives Life

In one gospel story, Jesus raises Lazarus from the dead (John, chapter 11). Jesus' love for his friend brought Lazarus from the tomb and back to life. In our own time as well, love can literally snatch people from death—physical, social, or spiritual death.

One illustration of this life-giving quality of love is the commitment of Michael Geilenfeld, a lay Catholic who has opened a house for abandoned young boys in Port-au-Prince, the capital of the desperately poor country Haiti. There, parents sometimes leave their male children in the streets because they cannot feed them, and unlike the girls, who can become servants or prostitutes, the boys cannot produce an income. These abandoned boys do anything that they can—lie, cheat, steal—just to survive. They are considered to be the lowest rung of society. Even boys under ten years old end up in crowded jails for indefinite periods. Geilenfeld says this about his efforts:

> I want to get the younger ones out of prison—and ones still on the street—and bring them into a family atmosphere. To feed them and teach them. But primarily to show them that someone cares about them.
>
> This is what they need more than anything: The love God intends for all his children. . . .
>
> What we have is a family, and that's the most important thing. The kids have a lot of potential, but no one is interested in them.
>
> When they're on the streets, they can find food [scrounged from garbage], a place to sleep, and rags to wear. They can't find love. I show them I care for them, that I think they're good. By example, they show each other the same thing.

Describe in writing your most recent experience of loneliness. Include the following factors:
• what led up to the lonely time
• what may have caused it
• how you felt during the loneliness
• what you did about it
• any beneficial effects of the loneliness

The commitment of Michael Geilenfeld, who has opened a house for abandoned boys in Haiti, illustrates the life-giving quality of love.

Geilenfeld's love is literally life-giving. He feeds, shelters, and educates the boys, giving them a motive for living. Through the giving of life, Geilenfeld himself also receives life.

Caring Brings Security and Self-esteem

When people care about us, their love affirms the best aspects of us. This affirmation brings a degree of security, and it heightens self-esteem. In addition, those people who love us may challenge our ideas, listen to us, and probe our motivations, enabling us to become clearer about what we think and who we are: we grow even more secure.

The affirmation of people who care about us brings a degree of security, and it heightens self-esteem.

We develop security and self-esteem not only by receiving love but also by giving it. Life becomes centered and purposeful as we use our talents, skills, intellect, and emotions for the ones we love.

The Apostle Paul summarized why we need to love: ". . . If I am without love, I am nothing" (1 Corinthians 13:2). We need to love in order to overcome our aloneness, give life, and bring security and self-esteem to other people.

What Is Love?

An Inclusive Definition

The reasons for loving and being loved can be found deep within the human spirit. But we still do not have a definition of love that will encompass all types of love—from the passionate love expressed in the Song of Songs to the familiar love of friends like Ted and Iggy.

Love means to seek and then foster the good of others in the context of their concrete situations.

Find a printed advertisement that uses the word *love* in connection with a product. Write a paragraph that summarizes how the word *love* is used in the ad. Does the ad distort the meaning of love as it has been defined in this chapter?

One of the most inclusive definitions may be this one: **love** means to seek and then foster the good of others in the context of their concrete situations. This definition may not sound very romantic, but it will serve us well after some explanation. Let's consider the definition in three parts:

To Seek and Foster

First, love means *to seek and then foster*. *Seek* and *foster* are active terms; love demands activity. That is, love entails finding out what another person needs and then doing something about that need. To love means to be active, to exert our power for another.

The Good of Others

Second, love means to seek and then foster *the good of others*. The good of others is the same good that we would do for ourselves. Jesus made this very clear when he said, " '. . . You must love your neighbour as yourself' " (Mark 12:31). If we like to hear affirmative remarks about our accomplishments, we must compliment other people about what they do. If we wish that someone would listen to our problems, we should gladly listen to the persons we love. The good of others is what we would wish for ourselves.

In the Concrete Situation

Third, love means to seek and then foster the good of others *in the context of their concrete situations*. Love respects a person as he or she is—not as we might wish him or her to be. Each of us is unique, and we wish to be seen that way. So love must take the uniqueness of the other into account. For example, if the person you love does not like bowling but you insist that bowling would be good for her or him, you may be overlooking the concrete situation.

Loving within the concrete situation may require that we take painful or difficult steps for the good of another person, as in the following instance:

Rosemary had been afraid of her father for years; he ruled the family with an iron hand. However, now that she was in her twenties, Rosemary could see that it wasn't just the force of his personality that made her fearful; it was the fact that her father was drunk on almost every occasion that she visited home. He was wildly unpredictable when he had been drinking. This was a man who was in terrible trouble.

In spite of her fear, Rosemary loved her father. She had always been the one he could joke with and show his best side to, in between the fearful times. Her brothers and sisters also loved their father, each in his or her own way. Unfortunately, their mother was too afraid to intervene in order to help her husband with his alcoholism. Because of her own need to escape, their mother was also becoming dependent on alcohol.

After building up her courage for weeks, Rosemary finally came to this conclusion: Love required that she and the other children, if they were willing, confront their father and mother about his alcoholism and her growing dependency. Regardless of the conflict and upset feelings that no doubt would be kicked up, she had to try to help her father get the treatment that he needed so desperately and could not ask for on his own.

When we love another person, as Rosemary loved her father, we affirm that the other has value and that his or her development and needs are as important as our own. But we do not surrender our uniqueness, our identity. The situation is quite the opposite: In love, the identity of each person is strengthened. Love affirms the beloved. It is power shared. Love creates new possibilities for a relationship. It starts with respect for another person as uniquely valuable and filled with potential. Rosemary could not have made the difficult decision to help her father without believing deeply in the possibilities within him.

Have you ever known someone who confronted another person out of love? If so, describe in writing what happened.

Saint Paul: Love Never Ends

Saint Paul summarized many of the characteristics of love in his advice to the Christian community in Corinth:

Love is always patient and kind; love is never jealous; love is not boastful or conceited, it is never rude and never seeks its own advantage, it does not take offence or store up grievances. Love does not rejoice at wrongdoing, but finds its joy in the truth. It is always ready to make allowances, to trust, to hope and to endure whatever comes.

Love never comes to an end. (1 Corinthians 13:4–8)

Love persists patiently—in times of convenience and inconvenience. Love never ends. But the world we inhabit has become accustomed to looking for quick solutions, immediately fulfilling experiences, and continually gratifying relationships. How thirsty the world is for the witness of people who love deeply.

The Types of Love

Love is concerned with the good of the other, affirms the other, is patient and enduring with the other. But who is "the other"? Specifying that "other" gives us a good way to categorize the types of love.

Self-love

Self-love may be the least understood of the types of love. It is neither selfishness nor conceit; rather, self-love is essential to loving anyone else: " '. . . You must love your neighbour as yourself' " (Mark 12:31). This commandment implies that we *do* love ourselves.

Self-love begins with self-acceptance, that is, the discovery and valuing of the qualities we possess and of who we are. Self-love fosters our best qualities in the context in which we find ourselves. We must try to see ourselves from God's vantage point. God loves us unconditionally—even (perhaps especially) when we make a mess of things.

Most people have a hard time loving themselves. A variety of social and psychological factors accounts for this lack of self-love. One significant cause is the false messages given by others and by our culture about what constitutes worthiness. People are told that their worth is measured by ungodly standards, such as how much money they make, how well they do in school, where they live, how beautiful or handsome they are, how much attention they receive, and so on. These things have nothing to do with God's view of human value. God created us and loves each of us just as we are.

These signs of having difficulty with loving oneself may sound somewhat familiar:

- She would never go out with me. She probably thinks I'm the lowest form of life.
- I'm too tall! I hate looking down at guys.
- This speech is going to be terrible. The *B* on my last one was probably just a gift to encourage me.
- I would rather go along with what he wants than let him know what I really think. I just cannot let him get mad at me. That would be awful.
- What a bunch of creeps. I wouldn't want to be seen with them.

In each of the above statements, the individual is worrying about how she or he will come across to others—in other words, how she or he is "packaged"—rather than simply accepting the

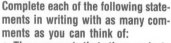

Complete each of the following statements in writing with as many comments as you can think of:
- The comments that others make to me that increase my feelings of self-love are . . .
- The comments that others make to me that decrease my feelings of self-love are . . .

Then think about this question, and answer in writing:
- Do I love myself as much as God loves me?

gift of who she or he is, including flaws. The last example illustrates that a wound in the ability to love ourselves can be evidenced in a conceited or superior outlook, which is another form of worrying about how we look to others. The person who puts others down is usually having a problem with self-love.

Volumes have been written on self-love and self-hatred; psychologists stay busy treating people who do not seem able to love themselves. The realization of God's unconditional love enables many believers to break through the barrier of worrying about packaging to care genuinely for themselves as God cares.

Friendship

Friendship is universal. Saints and criminals have friends. **Friendship** is characterized by mutual caring between two people, usually involving loyalty, support, and a shared view of the world. Friends are capable of helping each other to achieve what is good.

The following passage from the novel *Ironweed* by William Kennedy illustrates how friendship can exist anywhere, even under the most strained circumstances. Imagine a mission for down-and-out people on skid row. The time is the winter of 1938, in the midst of the Great Depression. Francis, Helen, and Rudy—all hobos—listen to the preacher's sermon inside the mission. Sandra is outside, passed out in the alley:

The preacher then took the beatitudes for his theme. Blessed are the poor in spirit, for theirs is the kingdom of heaven. Blessed are the meek, for they shall inherit the earth. Blessed are they that mourn, for they shall be comforted.

"Oh yes, you men of skid row, brethren on the poor streets of the one eternal city we all dwell in, do not grieve that your spirit is low. Do not fear the world because you are of a meek and gentle nature. Do not feel that your mournful tears are in vain, for these things are the keys to the kingdom of God."

The men went swiftly back to sleep and Francis resolved he would . . . hit Chester [the preacher] up for a new pair of socks. Chester was happiest when he was passing out socks to dried-out drunks. Feed the hungry, clothe the sober.

"Are you ready for peace of mind and heart?" the preacher asked. "Is there a man here tonight who wants a different life? . . . Will you stand up now? Come to the front,

Many times small acts of love and concern are overlooked. Love often comes to us in small gifts. List ten specific expressions of concern that were extended to you in the last twenty-four hours.

Friendship is characterized by mutual caring between two people, usually involving loyalty, support, and a shared worldview.

kneel, and we will talk. Do this now and be saved. Now. Now. Now!"

No one moved.

"Then amen, brothers," said the preacher testily, and he left the lectern. . . .

Then began the rush of men to table, the pouring of coffee, ladling of soup, cutting of bread by the mission's zealous volunteers. Francis sought out Pee Wee, a good old soul who managed the mission for Chester, and he asked him for a cup of soup for Sandra.

"She oughta be let in," Francis said. "She's gonna freeze out there."

"She was in before," Pee Wee said. "He wouldn't let her stay. She was really shot, and you know him on that. He won't mind on the soup, but . . . don't say where it's going."

"Secret soup," Francis said.

He took the soup out the back door, pulling Rudy along with him, and crossed the vacant lot to where Sandra lay as before. Rudy pulled her onto her back and sat her up, and Francis put the soup under her nose.

"Soup," he said.

"Gazoop," Sandra said.

"Have it." Francis put the cup to her lips and tipped the soup at her mouth. It dribbled down her chin. She swallowed none.

"She don't want it," Rudy said.

"She wants it," Francis said. "She's just [angry because] . . . it ain't wine." . . .

Francis put the cup down and slipped her ratty shoe onto her left foot. He lifted her, a feather, carried her to the wall of the mission, and propped her into a sitting position, her back against the building, somewhat out of the wind. With his bare hand he wiped the masking dust from her face. He raised the soup and gave her another swallow. (Pages 35–36)

On another night, the person in need might be Francis or Rudy. Even though Francis is down-and-out himself, he takes care of his friend Sandra. He is, in his own way, loyal, generous, and respectful. Francis clearly understands Sandra's view of the world.

Most of us are down-and-out at one time or another. Maybe we flunked a big test, parted from the person we have dated for a long time, were refused admission to the college of our choice, or were injured and could not play in a crucial game. The story

Our friends are incredibly important to us when we are down-and-out.

of Francis, Rudy, and Sandra is a story about hitting bottom. Our circumstances may be different, less drastic, but we can know what it feels like to be out in the cold, isolated, and hurting. This is when our friends are so incredibly important to us.

The story illustrates another aspect of friendship, too—that its origins are often circumstantial or even mysterious. We may find ourselves tossed together with someone in a situation. If we are open, hopeful, and willing to initiate, friendship often grows.

The friendship between Francis, Rudy, and Sandra is not marked by a high degree of intimacy. Deep intimacy is experienced with only a few friends in life. In addition to being loyal and supportive and sharing a similar view of the world, our self-disclosure is deeper with our dearest friends, and we are far more vulnerable. Other friends may know a lot about us, but our closest friends know almost as much about us as we know about ourselves—the good and the not so good, the interesting and the boring. A friend lets us pull off our mask and be ourselves.

When two people can enjoy being together without having to do anything in particular and when they stay close through disagreements and separation, they have real friendship—the kind that lasts, holding on stubbornly through adversity and always hoping that new life and growth will burst forth.

A relationship in which one person conforms to every wish of the other person simply to hold on to him or her can masquerade as a friendship, but it is actually a form of *destructive dependency*. Devotion to another person may look like love. However, in an overly dependent relationship, the uniqueness and individuality of each person is not respected. One person twists his or her personality and interests to coincide with the other's. The dependent person may fear that if he or she does not conform to the ways of the other person, the beloved will reject him or her. The trouble is that this is not love. It does not foster the good of both people. There is no mutual respect or care.

Can you think of some overly dependent relationships that have not been helpful or healthy? Describe one of these relationships in writing.

Erotic Love

Erotic love is the desire two people have for union of their bodies and souls, hearts and minds. This is the love described in many passages from the Song of Songs. Erotic love, like all types of love, fosters the good of each person. The specific element that distinguishes erotic love from other types is the yearning for sexual expression of that love. In erotic love, lovers place their own relationship in the center of their lives.

From a Christian point of view, the nature of erotic love is such that expressing the love in sexual union implies total commitment of the partners. Unlike simple friendships (of which we may have many), erotic love is meant to be exclusive to the two persons. Saint Paul, echoing the creation account in Genesis, described erotic love in this picture of what marriage means: "This is why a man leaves his father and mother and becomes attached to his wife, and the two become one flesh" (Ephesians 5:31).

Not all married couples reach the depth of commitment, passion, and intimacy that ideally is involved in the union of erotic love. This kind of love will be treated more completely in later chapters on courting and marriage.

Romantic Love

Romantic love may come most readily to mind when we think of the word *love.* After all, most of the poetry and songs about love throughout history have described this kind of love.

The wonderful feeling of falling in love is probably one of life's peak moments. You may have experienced it already, and you may likely experience it again. Here is one young woman's description of falling in love:

- All I can do is think of him. I cannot wait to be with him all the time, and what's so fantastic is that he feels that way about me, too. Just thinking of him makes my heart race. We find all these special ways to say I love you—little gifts and surprises. All that matters is that we love each other. This feels so right, so *meant to be,* so *forever.*

Eventually, this "falling" phase passes into a less intense form of romantic love (no one could stand the intensity of falling in love for very long), and this carries people into periods of dating steadily and even into engagement. Romantic love can be beautiful and energizing.

However, romantic love is not the whole story—or even most of the story—about what brings and keeps people together for a lifetime. Romantic love, precious as it is, cannot by itself sustain a relationship forever. This is why you may fall in and out of love several times with several different people. Though romantic love *feels* incredibly eternal and destined, it is not necessarily or even probably so. Most romances do fade in time. In a marriage, romance will certainly reappear as time goes on— but not as the sustaining force in the marriage. A deeper and more solid kind of mature love, based on knowledge of and care

Respond in writing to these questions:
- Do you agree that romantic love alone will not sustain a marriage?
- Can you think of any examples to support your response?
- Why is romantic love so powerful?

for one another over the years, has to sustain a lifelong relationship through good times and bad. When people convince themselves that the only real love is romantic love and they set out on a perpetual quest for romance, they are apt to be disappointed—perhaps even divorced—many times..

Infatuation: A pitfall of romantic love is that it tends to set us into an emotional whirlwind that hinders clear perception and good judgment. In addition, infatuation and love at first sight are varieties of romantic love that may provide roots too shallow for love to grow from. The two persons may be so enamored with the thrill of infatuation that they fail to really discover each other. Infatuation is like a roller coaster. It zooms along with everything passing in a blur, and when the cars go plunging downhill, people get dizzy. Infatuation can be a thrill a minute, but like most rides, it ends, leaving us a bit shaky on our feet.

Idolizing: Another problem related to romantic love is the phenomenon of idolizing another person—seeing her or him as perfect, wonderful, the answer to all prayers and dreams. The failure to acknowledge faults in the other person is as unfair and hurtful as the failure to acknowledge her or his good qualities. For in treating someone as an idol, we do not really love *the person,* we love *our image of the person.* Someday that image, that idol, will probably crumble in the face of evident flaws, and both persons will be hurt badly, particularly if they are married.

Romantic love, rich and joy-filled as it can be, needs to be seen with a certain objectivity.

Romantic love, precious as it is, cannot by itself sustain a relationship forever.

Nutritive and Parental Love

Nutritive love: Fostering the good of needy, poor, homeless, or helpless persons is **nutritive love.** It starts with the belief that all people are our sisters and brothers, so we treat them as we would wish ourselves to be treated if we were in their situation.

The Christian Scriptures are filled with stories of Jesus healing the blind and the lepers, feeding the hungry, and raising the dead. Jesus stated that nutritive love will be the chief criterion for separating the "sheep" from the "goats" at the Last Judgment, when he will speak these words:

". . . 'Come, you whom my Father has blessed, take as your heritage the kingdom prepared for you since the foundation of the world. For I was hungry and you gave me food, I was thirsty and you gave me drink, I was a stranger and you made me welcome, lacking clothes and you clothed me, sick and you visited me, in prison and you came to see me. . . . In truth I tell you, in so far as you did this to one of the least of these brothers of mine, you did it to me.' '' (Matthew 25:34–40)

Nutritive love is not an option for Christians; it is a requirement. As Latin American theologian Segundo Galilea wrote, "Christianity comes to be the only religion where we find God in human beings, especially in the weakest of them. There is no Christianity . . . without a sense of the poor" (*Following Jesus,* page 31).

Parental love: Closely related to nutritive love is parental love. **Parental love** is the affirmation of, care, and responsibility for one's children. As in nutritive love, parents exercise their power for the good of children who cannot feed, clothe, and shelter themselves. Additionally, parental love fosters the intellectual, spiritual, and emotional growth of children.

In his memoirs about his large family, Eugene S. Geissler conveyed sensitively some of the qualities of parental love.

- *On treasuring each child:* "I am convinced that every family should have a Sheila [one of Geissler's sixteen children]. . . . A Sheila is worth waiting for. . . . A family does not know what it is missing until it has a Sheila.

    "And that is true of every child."

- *On waiting, not pushing:* "It takes a long time to get across a big yard with a little boy on a September evening. But it is better to go a hundred feet with him at his pace than a thousand other [feet at your own pace]."

- *On learning:* "I like to think that I have taught my children many things, and now I discover that the greatest teachers in my own life have been my children."

In nutritive and parental love, persons give because the ones they love have such an aching, sometimes urgent, need for what they can provide. But it is not entirely a one-way street. As Geissler expressed so well, and as the quote on the Last Judgment speaks so powerfully, *those who need us show us the face of God.* The persons whom we love are gifts to us as much as we are gifts to them.

Love of Nature

In shaping our lives around love, we should not assume that love is confined to people. God has created the earth as a home for humankind. Just as a married couple wants to provide a fitting home for their children, so we are called to **love of nature,**

The persons who need us are gifts to us as much as we are gifts to them.

Parental love is a wonderful gift to parents and to their children, but it demands self-sacrifice from parents. List and describe five sacrifices that your parents have recently made for your benefit.

caring for the earth as the fitting home of all God's children. In loving the earth, we love all human beings as well.

When God created the world, God declared that "it was good" (Genesis 1:18). The earth is worth loving, not only as a home for human beings but also as a good in itself. Saint Francis of Assisi, known for his appreciation of and reverence for the natural world, prayed in "The Canticle to the Sun" about the elements of creation as his family members, with whom he had a deep, personal connection:

Praised be thou, my Lord, with all thy creatures,
Especially the honored Brother Sun,
Who makes the day and illumines through thee. . . .

Praised be thou, my Lord, for Sister Moon and the stars,
Thou hast formed them in heaven clear and precious and
    beautiful.

Praised be thou, my Lord, for Brother Wind,
And for the air and cloudy and clear and every weather,
by which thou givest sustenance to thy creatures.

Praised be thou, my Lord, for Sister Water,
Who is very useful and humble and precious and chaste.

Praised be thou, my Lord, for Brother Fire,
By whom thou lightest the night,
And he is beautiful and [merry] and robust and strong.

Praised be thou, my Lord, for our sister Mother Earth,
Who sustains and directs us,
And produces various fruits with colored flowers and
    herbage.

Praise and bless my Lord and give him thanks
And serve him with great humility.

As is the case with all forms of love, loving the earth means that we give it respect, understanding, and protection. Loving the earth means that we love it as we love ourselves.

Love of God

Love of God is almost unimaginable unless we first love ourselves, our neighbors, and creation. As Saint John said, ". . . Whoever does not love the brother who he can see cannot love God whom he has not seen" (1 John 4:20). Love of other people and of creation is the school in which we learn to love God—the creator of all that is.

Love of God is almost unimaginable unless we love ourselves, our neighbors, and creation.

Describe the following situations in writing:
- two ways in which you have cared for the earth over the last two days
- two ways in which you could show more respect for the earth

We love our parents, who have given us birth and have brought us this far in life. If we believe in the creator, then we believe that God gives us everything: the parents who nurture us, the food we eat, the air we breathe, and the friends who are our companions. If we love our parents, friends, and nature, we are loving God, who is the source of all of these gifts.

Religious practices are the formal way of recognizing God's love for humankind and a way for human beings to express their love of God.

Love: The Core of a Christian Lifestyle

Caring, or love, is the center of meaning in a Christian lifestyle. Love is not a given; we do not automatically love. Rather, we must decide to love; we must choose it as the focus of our lives. This is the essential, most important choice in a Christian's life.

The Law of Love

Jesus gave this blunt answer when asked which was the most important commandment:

> ". . . This is the first: . . . you must love the Lord your God with all your heart, with all your soul, with all your mind and with all your strength. The second is this: You must love your neighbour as yourself. There is no commandment greater than these." (Mark 12:29–31)

Jesus' answer was direct: love is what the Christian life is all about. Jesus lived out this love by giving up his own life for us. No greater love exists.

Christianity is a religion of love, even though Christians are not always the best models of caring. The religion of Christians—that is, its ultimate concern or focus—*is* love. The first letter of John makes this point very directly, equating God with love itself:

> . . . God is love,
> and whoever remains in love remains in God
> and God in him. . . .
> Anyone who says "I love God"
> and hates his brother,
> is a liar,

"God is love, and whoever remains in love remains in God."

since whoever does not love the brother whom he can see cannot love God whom he has not seen.

(1 John 4:16–20)

The whole of Christian tradition has made it clear that love of God and love of human beings are inseparable.

Throughout the centuries, Christians have been recognized as holy people who not only care for poor, needy, and sick people but also maintain mutual friendships. The great friendships between Saints Paul and Timothy, Francis and Clare, Teresa of Ávila and John of the Cross, Ambrose and Monica are legendary in church history. The saints were not dried up, loveless, stifled people. They were passionate and loving people who knew the suffering and joy that love implies.

Remember that Jesus' dream had three aspects: building the peaceable kingdom, creating a loving community, and becoming persons fully alive. Love is at the heart of this dream and is the only real measure of following Jesus. Saint Paul stressed the importance of love in one letter to the Corinthians:

> Though I command languages both human and angelic—if I speak without love, I am no more than a gong booming or a cymbal clashing. And though I have the power of prophecy, to penetrate all mysteries and knowledge, and though I have all the faith necessary to move mountains—if I am without love, I am nothing. Though I should give away to the poor all that I possess, and even give up my body to be burned—if I am without love, it will do me no good whatever. (1 Corinthians 13:1–3)

Paul—and Jesus—helps us get down to the basics: the most important life decision we will ever make is the choice to love.

Sin: The Choice Not to Love

Despite the fact that Christian lives are meant to center on love, we do violence in big and small ways; we lie, we gossip, we overlook serious wrongs in society. In short, we sin.

To sin is to turn our back on God, who is love. Sin is the opposite of love. If love is fostering the good of others, then sin is harming others. But the decision to sin may not be truly conscious or deliberate. Sin may happen through passion, blindness, insensitivity, or sheer inertia. Nonetheless, it is a decision not to love.

Some acts are obviously sinful: physical abuse to another

Keeping in mind the different types of love discussed in this chapter, list all the times that you have loved in the last three days, focusing in particular on the following:
- how you have loved yourself
- how you have loved other people in a nutritive way
- how you have loved nature
- how you have loved God

person, stealing, cheating, slander. These are acts of *commission*. But sin can take the form of *omission*, too—in other words, the failure to act. In the description of the Last Judgment (Matthew 25:31–46), those who have neglected to feed and clothe unfortunate persons, and so on, are guilty of sins of omission, for they have failed to love when given the opportunity.

Sins of omission can be collective, or social, as well as individual. For instance, if, as a society, we neglect to clean up our lakes and rivers now, we are allowing the next generation to drink polluted, carcinogenic water, and we are condemning species of wildlife to extinction.

Formulating a value system is one of the developmental tasks of this period in your life. A value system is formed not in one conscious choice but in thousands of daily choices that together make up a person's response to life.

The Christian life asks us to set out on a journey toward loving others as God loves us—to choose a path toward love.

What Love Asks of Us

Love certainly challenges us, calling us to use all of our human potential and all of the help and inspiration that God gives us.

Even with our best efforts, we can reach toward loving relationships but never attain them perfectly. The Christian life, however, does not demand perfection; it asks us to set out on a journey toward loving others as God loves us—to choose a path toward love. Along the way, we need to develop some life skills of loving.

1. **Knowledge of the other person:** We attempt to understand the other person in depth so that we can respond to his or her real needs.
- Beth thinks about her friend Jim at lunch before the pep assembly: "I can tell he's nervous about speaking in front of the group, but I know he can do it well if he just believes he can. I'll encourage him by letting him know all the good things I saw him do last time he had to speak."

2. **Practical knowledge:** We develop the skills and know-how that are useful in the ways we want to serve—whether in car repair, listening, or organizing a fund-raiser for hunger.
- Gary says to himself before he goes to the hardware store, "I better get things straight. If I make a mess of this plumbing job, Grandma will be worse off than she was before she asked me for help."

3. Flexibility: We are able to respond to change in the person we love and to shifts in the relationship.

- Len explains to a friend how things are going since his wife began college: "With Barbara in college now, I have to spend a lot more time on housework and taking care of the kids. And she's not as available to me as she used to be. But I want to help. I know how important a college education is to Barbara."

4. Handling conflict: We bring out in the open what bothers us in a relationship and try to resolve problems in a way that respects the value of both persons.

- Jane says to her friend Maria, "When you say you'll be here to pick me up at a certain time, it's up to a half hour later when you get here. It's been irritating me because I could be doing other stuff while I'm waiting if I know you won't be here for thirty minutes."

A value system is formed in thousands of daily choices that together make up a person's response to life.

If we are patient, we respect the other person's timetable for growing.

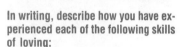

In writing, describe how you have experienced each of the following skills of loving:
- practical knowledge
- patience
- honesty
- trust

5. Patience: We hang in there with the other person through difficult times, and we respect the other person's timetable for growing.

- A mother describes to a friend the behavior of her two-year-old daughter: "Lately, Jenny has been throwing tantrums when we're in stores. It used to drive me crazy when little Gary did that; I would holler and threaten to spank him to make him calm down. But now I know that this tantrum thing is just a phase for Jenny. So when it happens, I say firmly, 'No, Jenny,' and take her out of the store."

6. Honesty: We are genuine in our caring and do not put on masks to pretend we are something we are not.

- Diane tells her friend about a discussion she had with her boyfriend's mother: "I was afraid that Kurt's mother would think I was a terrible person if she knew about my family and all the trouble we've had. But one night we talked about it, and it felt good to tell her where I've come from. Now we're really close friends."

7. Trust: We let go of our concern about constantly protecting our own interests in a relationship so that the other person can grow.

- Dan confides to a friend about what hard experience has taught him: "I learned my lesson about trust when Melissa broke up with me. I was trying to hold on to her. I wouldn't let her be with other people because I was so afraid of losing her. Now I see that she just felt mistrusted and smothered."

8. Trustworthiness: We can live up to the other person's trust in us.

- Linda talks with a friend about her relationship with her parents: "After I got caught shoplifting, I thought my parents would never trust me again. They knew I had lied to them several times, too. But instead they told me that they forgave me, that they believed in me, and that I could turn around from this. Now I'm totally honest with them. I wouldn't dream of breaking their trust."

9. Humility: We acknowledge our real situation—our accomplishments as well as our limits and flaws—and recognize that we are like all human beings, no better and no worse. We treat others as dignified and deserving of respect.

- Jeremy describes his work at a local shelter for the homeless: "The people who come to the shelter teach me more about life than I ever learned in school. They're remarkable; they know about enduring, suffering, and trying to cope. I feel fortunate that I've had the chance to know them."

10. Hope: We are ready at each moment to foster new growth in a relationship and are open to new relationships without putting heavy expectations on another person.

* Julie thinks to herself about getting to know Jeff: "I have a feeling that something really special may eventually come out of this friendship—what it will be, I'm not sure. Meanwhile, it's so much fun just getting to know Jeff."

11. Courage: We have courage to face the unknown—possible rejection, conflicts, separations, the death of another person, abandonment, and the day-to-day demands of working out a relationship.

* Wayne hasn't heard from Mark in over a week. Wayne is a bit sensitive about the possibility of being left out: "Maybe Mark's tired of getting together with me. On the other hand, maybe I should take the initiative and call him for a change. That's what I'll do."

Write a paragraph describing from your own experience why courage is needed in any caring relationship.

12. Forgiveness: We do not hold the other person's hurtful behavior or wrongdoing over his or her head. We talk about it with the person; then we go forward in the relationship with a generous spirit of forgiveness.

* Sally says to her sister Megan, "I understand what you did and why you did it. I know you didn't mean to hurt me, even though it did hurt. I forgive you, and I don't hold anything against you."

We have the resources within us to love, and God's grace is always present within us. After all, God created us to love! However, the skills of genuine loving described above do not come instantly; they develop over a lifetime. When we make the choice to love, we do not automatically possess these skills, but we choose to try to develop them, being patient with ourselves in our attempts just as God is patient with us.

List two or three skills that you would like to develop in your ability to love and care for others. Specifically describe what you would like to work on for each skill.

A Vocation to Care

We are compelled by our very nature to love and to seek love. The Christian vocation, or call, is to love. For most of us, it is the focus of our dream. Love is not simple. It challenges us in ways that call upon all of our resources, but it also energizes us and brings us to life.

All of us have much to learn about love. None of us are perfect. Even so, God has claimed us as lovable just as we are. If a person believes in God's love, perhaps that person will believe in his or her own ability to love. That is the experience described in the poem "A Gift" by Mary Eleanore Rice:

you have touched me
you have cradled me in your security
until i found my own
given me words
when they were unknown to me
tenderly you have held my heart in your hands
your firmness has given me strength
life itself wrapped in love
was your first gift to me
to love you is to love myself
to love myself is to love you

To love you is to love myself; to love myself is to love you.

This kind of love is possible for us. Loving depends on the daily choices we make—saying yes to the call of love.

Review Questions

1. Describe each of the nine types of intimacy.

2. Explain the three forces that motivate us to love and be loved.

3. Define the word *love*.

4. Why is it imperative that we have self-love?

5. What is one reason that we find it hard to love ourselves?

6. What is meant by destructive dependency?

7. From a Christian point of view, what is meant by erotic love?

8. Why is romantic love not a solid foundation for marriage?

9. Describe nutritive love. How is it a requirement of the Christian life?

10. Why is love of nature part of the Christian call to love?

11. How can we tell whether we love God?

12. What did Saint Paul say about the importance of love?

13. What is the relationship between sin and love? Explain the difference between sins of omission and sins of commission.

14. List and describe in your own words each of the twelve skills of loving.

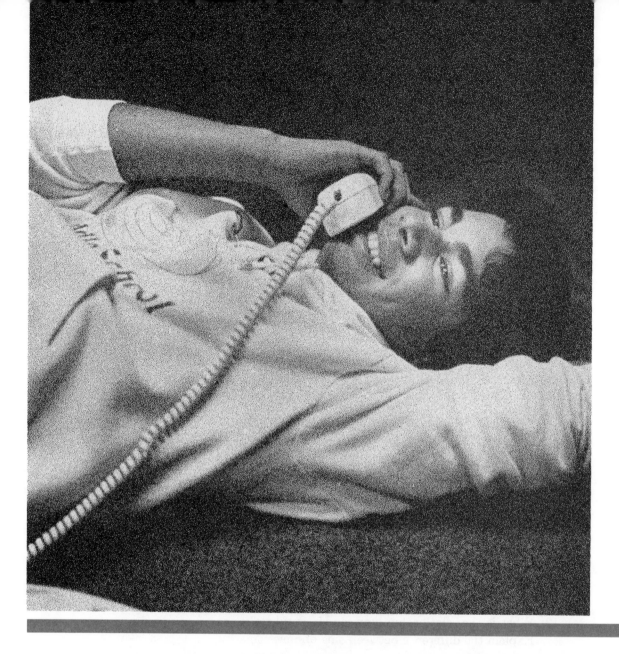

4 Communication: A Skill for Lifelong Caring

YOU probably remember *Through the Looking-Glass* and *Alice in Wonderland* by Lewis Carroll as zany tales of a girl who alternately shrinks and grows huge, making her way in a world of weird characters and bizarre, dreamlike situations. The stories, however, are more than that; they are classic accounts of miscommunication. Consider, for example, this frustrating dialog between Alice and Humpty Dumpty:

"There's glory for you!"

"I don't know what you mean by 'glory,' " Alice said.

Humpty Dumpty smiled contemptuously. "Of course you don't—till I tell you. I meant 'there's a nice knock-down argument for you!' "

"But 'glory' doesn't mean 'a nice knock-down argument,' " Alice objected.

"When *I* use a word," Humpty Dumpty said, in rather a scornful tone, "it means just what I choose it to mean—neither more nor less."

"The question is," said Alice, "whether you *can* make words mean so many different things."

"The question is," said Humpty Dumpty, "which is to be master—that's all."

"The question is," said Alice, "whether you *can* make words mean so many different things."

Humpty Dumpty very obviously was not operating in good faith. He was making communication impossible by distorting the meaning of words. By his own admission, he was using the conversation to set up himself as master. Manipulation, not communication, was what Mr. Dumpty was after.

This bizarre conversation can begin to sound terribly familiar. It is not uncommon for language to be distorted and words to be used for manipulation rather than for communication. Words like *love* have been so corrupted by advertisements that we are not sure of exactly what they mean anymore. Governments manipulate language to distort reality and shape public opinion: nuclear missiles are called "peacekeepers," and bombing raids are dubbed "protective reaction strikes."

At the level of our everyday life, how often do we see people—like Humpty Dumpty—using a conversation to get the upper hand? Miscommunication, of course, is the result.

Communication is an exchange of ideas, feelings, or meaning between two or more persons. It implies that two persons give and receive information. Each person must pay attention to the other. A person who is communicating well knows and feels, even if only partially, what the other person knows and feels.

Communication takes place in many ways. We are accustomed to thinking of communication as words, but words are only part of the picture. The exchange of ideas, feelings, and meaning happens in three ways:

- body language
- listening
- verbal language

Though people tend to emphasize the last method, which involves words, the other two methods are just as significant, if not more so. We will focus on these three methods later in this chapter.

Clearly, communication is integral to love, the subject of the preceding chapter. In addition, communication is involved in every other topic that will be covered in this course: sexuality, learning, work, the use of money, leisure, courting, marriage, and so on. Every developmental task of your age-group depends on communication for its accomplishment. So the topic of communication is pivotal to this entire course.

Our Need to Communicate

We have a deep need to communicate—stemming partly from the drive to love and be loved and partly from the simple desire to express ourselves and to gain from the expressions of others. In the exchange of feelings and ideas with other human beings, we learn what being human is all about. This situation illustrates the universal need to communicate:

Jeff was a transfer student who had quickly gained the reputation of being a snob. He made straight *A*'s, always

In the exchange of feelings and ideas with other human beings, we learn what being human is all about.

raised his hand to answer in class, and even took a first-place prize in the state speech competition. Added to that, Jeff defeated the junior class president for the position of starting shortstop on the baseball team. His classmates thought that he was snobbish, not because of what he said (he never bragged about his accomplishments, never even talked about them) but because he walked around with his head tilted up in the air. When students talked to Jeff, he had the appearance of looking down on them.

One day at lunch Jeff overheard two guys talking. One of them said that Jeff was "such a snob, always walking around with his nose in the air." Jeff was hurt and angry. Even though he was very shy, he walked over to the student and confronted him.

"I heard what you said," Jeff snapped. The boy who had made the remark began to turn flaming red. "I can't help walking around with my nose in the air. I have an eye problem, and to see okay I have to hold my head the way I do. I don't like this problem, but I have to live with it and with people like you who make no attempt to understand." Jeff turned on his heel and stormed off to his next class.

The two students were deeply embarrassed. Soon word got around that Jeff had been seen unfairly. Jeff's classmates began to view him in a new way. Before long, he had the reputation of being a very generous guy who knew how to have a good time, too.

The students in this story learned a few things about the need to communicate:

- Having accurate knowledge about an individual is the key to opening up a relationship with that person.
- It is easy to misinterpret body language—in this case, the way Jeff tilted his head—so it is important to be sure of interpretations.
- Communicating directly with an individual is better than speaking behind the person's back.
- Confrontation can lead to a welcome shake-up in stale patterns of thought and behavior. In this case, Jeff's confrontation with the gossiper was risky for him. It took courage because it made him vulnerable to further ridicule. But Jeff's act gave the students a chance to throw off an old and destructive pattern of thinking and behaving—slanderous gossip.

By trying to understand what Jeff had felt because of his

List the names of your five closest friends. For each of them, recall the first conversation you had together. In a sentence or two next to each name, describe what you talked about and what your first impressions were. Did you have to overcome any negative preconceptions about any of your friends?

Recall an incident when you did not check to see if your perceptions of another person were correct and you acted on an incorrect assumption. Write a brief description of what happened.

eye problem, the students developed *empathy*, the ability to walk around in another person's shoes, to see and experience the world as that person sees and experiences it. Empathy comes through communication.

Communication and the Christian Life

Communication gives us empathetic knowledge of other people, the kind of knowledge that we must have in order to love them. So communication is at the core of love. Since love of God and neighbor is the heart of the Christian vision, communication is essential to Christian life. We must communicate in order to be the fully alive persons of Jesus' dream.

Jesus and the Apostles as Communicators

The mission of Jesus on earth was to communicate God's love for all of humankind. His words and stories are called the Gospels—the Good News. His actions communicated love, too: he healed the sick, gave sight to the blind, confronted injustice, and drove out devils. Jesus' message was communicated through his whole way of being in the world—his lifestyle.

After he had risen from the dead, Jesus directed the Apostles to continue communicating with the whole world to spread the message and way of life that he had shown them: "And he said to them, 'Go out to the whole world; proclaim the gospel to all creation' " (Mark 16:15). Jesus did not come into this world so that only a few people could experience God's love. He came so that all people might know that God loves us— weak, silly, sinful, strong, serious, and good as we are. Jesus spoke of this love, but he also communicated it by his actions.

In the discussion of power in chapter 2, you read about the Apostles being filled with the Spirit at Pentecost and speaking in many languages. Jesus knew that to communicate effectively the Apostles had to speak in words that their listeners would understand. So he gave them the ability to do this through his Spirit. To communicate in a way that our hearers can understand us, with a sensitivity to *their* perspectives and experience (which was what the gift of tongues was really about), is to communicate with empathy.

The mission of Jesus on earth was to communicate God's love for all of humankind.

Avoiding Vicious Talk

The Apostle James spoke most strongly about the destructive use of speech and about the relationship between bad deeds or vicious talk and the true condition of one's heart. Here are some words of caution from the letter of James about practices to avoid:

> Nobody who fails to keep a tight rein on the tongue can claim to be religious; this is mere self-deception; that person's religion is worthless. (James 1:26)

> Anyone who is wise or understanding among you should from a good life give evidence of deeds done in the gentleness of wisdom. But if at heart you have the bitterness of jealousy, or selfish ambition, do not be boastful or hide the truth with lies; this is not the wisdom that comes from above, but earthly, human and devilish. (James 3:13–15)

> Brothers, do not slander one another. . . .
> There is only one lawgiver and he is the only judge and has the power to save or to destroy. Who are you to give a verdict on your neighbour? (James 4:11–12)

Lying, slander, and an uncontrolled tongue are the opposite of communication. Christ called his followers to communicate with care so that loving relationships could be born and nurtured. As we build relationships, we build the peaceable kingdom.

Attitudes: Avenues and Roadblocks to Communication

Nurturing relationships through communication requires a receptive and open frame of mind. Picture communication as a car that carries information, feelings, and opinions back and forth from one person to another. The ideal situation is that the car moves freely on wide avenues, with no kinks and twists in the road. To move easily, the car must not encounter any roadblocks.

The attitudes that make up our frame of mind when relating to other people can be either *avenues* or *roadblocks* to communication. Attitudes that are avenues can ease the passage of information, feelings, and opinions. Attitudes that are road-blocks can throw up all kinds of barriers that make communication nearly impossible. The following paragraphs describe some of the most significant avenues and roadblocks.

Trust Versus Self-Protection

The avenue of trust: With an attitude of trust, we act on the assumption that the other person will not disappoint us or hurt us; we do not demand evidence that the other person is trustworthy and will not let us down. Trust involves risk, and communication requires this willingness to take risks.

When we protect ourselves because we think people are not interested in us, those people stop trying to communicate with us.

The story of "doubting Thomas" in the Gospel of John is a good example of what a lack of trust does to communication. Thomas refused to trust the other disciples when they told him that Jesus had risen from the dead: ". . . 'Unless I can see the holes that the nails made in his hands and can put my finger into the holes they made, and unless I can put my hand into his side, I refuse to believe' " (John 20:25). Eight days later, Jesus came to Thomas and the other disciples and presented Thomas with the physical evidence of his wounds. Thomas finally believed that Jesus had risen. Jesus' words to this skeptical disciple speak to all of us about our need to trust in communicating with our friends: ". . . 'You believe because you can see me. Blessed are those who have not seen and yet believe' " (John 20:29).

The roadblock of self-protection: The opposite of trusting others is overprotecting ourselves. We insist on seeing evidence that communication will involve no risk before we attempt to relate to another person. So we might not talk to certain people because we think that they are too intelligent for us. Or we may share very little of our thoughts and feelings because we think that people would not like us if they truly knew us. This risk-free, self-protecting approach tends to create a self-fulfilling prophecy. That is, when we protect ourselves because we think people are not interested in us or do not like us, those people stop trying to communicate with us.

Hope Versus a Win-Lose Attitude

The avenue of hope: We enter into dialog with someone because we hope that our conversation will have a desirable outcome. Hope is a readiness to respond to a person without necessarily knowing exactly what the outcome of communicating will be. With a spirit of hope, we treat communication as an adventure. In other words, we take a trip through another person's experience and ideas—taking a chance that positive results will happen between us but not insisting that the results happen *our* way.

The roadblock of a win-lose attitude: Conversely, carrying a win-lose attitude into a relationship is bound to bog down communication. With this approach, being right is more important than understanding or relating. Instead of listening and getting to know the other person's ideas in a hopeful spirit of adventure, we use the conversation to establish that we are on top or better. This need to win can push us to distort the ideas of others, become sarcastic, or preoccupy our minds with impressing others. A person with this attitude quickly shuts down communication.

Acceptance Versus Stereotyping and Judging

The avenue of acceptance: We need to accept people as they are, in their uniqueness and specialness, in order to have an interchange of experience and understanding with those people. We do not have to like all of their attitudes, ideas, and mannerisms, but we do need to respect their right to be different and to try to see the world through their eyes. When people feel accepted, they usually react by being more open, by revealing more of who they are. They communicate more freely because they feel that the other person is not about to make swift judgments about them or evaluate their every word. People grow—they become their best selves—in a genuinely accepting relationship.

The roadblock of stereotyping and judging: He's a dumb jock! She's stuck up. He's just a class clown; don't take him seriously. Such statements are evidence of stereotyping, the tendency to put people into a neat role that does not take into account their individuality and to judge them on the basis of that role. Once we have stereotyped someone, we do not have to treat that person as the complicated and interesting individual that he or she is. We also may develop a judgmental attitude toward a person based on some behavior of his or hers that is a pet peeve of ours. As surely as the acceptance of an individual helps her or him to communicate openly, stereotyping and judging will cut off communication with that person.

List ten of your pet peeves about people. Rank them from 1 (most bothersome) to 10 (least bothersome). Ponder your list for a few minutes and check those items of which you are guilty yourself. Finally, answer this question in writing:

- When I am bothered by someone because of a pet peeve, how does that influence my ability to communicate with him or her?

Body Language

Earlier in the chapter, these three ways of communicating were identified:
- body language
- listening
- verbal language

Most of the remainder of this chapter will focus on listening and on several aspects of verbal language that can present problems for people. First, however, we will turn our attention to the area of **body language**.

Through body language, we give messages even when we are not speaking words.

We often give messages even when we are not speaking words. Usually we are not conscious that our bodies as well as our words are speaking to other people. These *nonverbal* cues—consisting of such things as bodily gestures, facial expressions, posture, tone and pitch of voice, rate of speech, clothing, and the use of physical space—form a language of their own. Here are some examples:
- *A wink:* Depending on the context, a wink could mean "This is a joke" or "Let's get together after the party."
- *A hug:* A hug usually communicates affection, but its spe-

cific meaning may vary from "I'll protect you" to "I sure do need you."

- *A scowl:* A scowl can indicate "I'm disgusted with you" or "This situation is making me furious."
- *Crossing arms:* Crossing one's arms can often signal "I need to protect myself."
- *Looking away from the speaker:* Depending on the situation, looking away from the speaker may mean "You are boring me," "I'm anxious about what you're saying," or "I'm preoccupied with other concerns."

Directing What We "Say"

Most of the time we do not need to consider our body language. We act naturally, and that is fine. However, just as with our use of verbal language, the situation sometimes calls for us to direct what we "say" with our bodies.

For example, if you are giving a speech, waving your note papers around anxiously or swaying from side to side can make your audience uncomfortable because these movements give them the feeling that you are nervous. In more intimate communication—for instance, in trying to help someone open up and talk—sitting behind a desk will put a physical and psychological barrier between you and the other person. Sitting behind the desk tells the other person, "I am protected from you; there is a distance between us." If you want the other person to talk freely, sit across from him or her at eye level—on equal terms—with no physical barrier.

Body language is very important because people tend to believe these nonverbal messages more readily than verbal messages. Nonverbal behavior is less conscious, less subject to control. So when there is a discrepancy between words and nonverbal messages, the nonverbal behavior has more credibility and therefore is seen as the "real" message. For instance:

- Kelly had planned to go to a movie with Jan on Friday night. But when another girl whom Kelly had been trying to be friends with offered her a chance to get together, Kelly suddenly changed her plans and told Jan that she was busy. Jan now feels hurt and tells Kelly so. Kelly's response is to cross her arms, tap her foot, purse her lips, and say in a somewhat heated tone of voice, "Listen, I'm *sorry!* I didn't think this would hurt you!"

If you were in Jan's place, would you believe Kelly's words or her body language?

Although people tend to believe body language more readily than verbal language, body language can be easily misinterpreted. For instance, looking away can mean either boredom or anxiety. How does the person watching the nonverbal behavior know what the action actually signifies? Many other cues have to be taken into account, and these, too, may be misread. The earlier story of Jeff and the students' interpretation of snobbishness gives witness to the intricacies of reading body language accurately.

Touch and Communication

The area of physical touch deserves special mention in our consideration of body language.

Most children love to crawl into a parent's lap to be held, cuddled, and kissed. Children thrive on this physical expression of affirmation and affection. As mentioned in the discussion of power in chapter 2, infants whose cries go unanswered and who are therefore deprived of regular, caring touch have been known to withdraw and even die. Touch as a means of communicating love can be intensely meaningful, especially in circumstances where words cannot be found. For instance, at funerals close friends often console each other simply by embracing; in the face of death, words seem hollow.

As people grow into their teens, they become more wary of touching. For instance, sons and fathers may cease to hug each other. The need for signs of affection remains, but the fear of being thought of as weird or the desire to appear independent may make affectionate touch taboo.

Interestingly, cultures vary widely in their norms about who may touch whom. In North American culture, a man and a woman walking hand in hand are considered acceptable, but two men or two women walking this way might be suspect. However, in many places in Asia and the Middle East, just the opposite is true.

In any case, most human beings of all ages relish simple, affectionate touch. Relationships suffer without any physical sign of caring. Touching without love or care, though, is meaningless and may be exploitative. Perhaps the best guideline is this: touch only to give, not to get. The person who touches benefits, but his or her motives for touching should be to offer sympathy, encouragement, or friendship.

Human beings of all ages relish simple, affectionate touch, and relationships suffer without physical signs of caring.

Because communication tends to be equated with speech, the highly significant area of body language is often overlooked when people are considering how they communicate. We must remember that our bodies send off a constant stream of quiet but powerful messages.

Listening

Listening may be as overlooked as body language when we consider all the ways in which we communicate. We are not accustomed to fine-tuning our listening skills, perhaps because we think of listening as simply the absence of speech. But listening is much more than that.

An Overlooked Essential

If you are like most people, you have often wanted to say, "You're not listening! No one ever listens to me." It is not a nice way to feel. We want to be taken seriously. We prefer to think that what we have to say is important and that how we feel is worth attention. Indeed, one characteristic of friends is that they listen to each other.

- Susan looked around at her classmates at graduation. She thought about all of the people with whom she had trudged through four years of high school. So many characters, so many laughs, so many crazy memories. Now everyone would be going their separate ways. Who would she miss and what would she miss the most? Susan realized with a pang how much she treasured her friendship with John—John, who listened to her heartaches, her plans, her worries, and her exciting news in a way that made her feel wonderfully understood. Susan knew deep down that she and John would always be friends.

Listening is important not only in friendships but in other relationships as well. Top-caliber students tend to listen in class better than moderately performing students do. Successful salespersons usually listen carefully to customers' wants and needs. The most effective managers usually listen well to their employees. Listening is crucial to success. What is more important from a Christian perspective, though, is that listening is essential to caring and loving.

Out of all the people you know, who is the best listener? Describe in writing what makes him or her a good listener.

Guidelines for Listening

You are probably listening well if the other person keeps talking and tells you about what is important to her or him. Good listening is *not* advice giving, problem solving, or a time for you to tell your story. These three things may happen later, after you have listened. But for the time being, the listener's job is simply to let the other person talk and to speak only to encourage her or him to continue talking. Listening well involves both body language and spoken language.

Here are some helpful guidelines for good listening:

Hold your tongue and be attentive. Being quiet does not necessarily mean that you are listening, but it is almost impossible to listen and talk at the same time. So do not interrupt the speaker out loud, and also hold the tongue that may be running in your own mind. That is, do not formulate your response mentally while the other person is still talking. In effect, that is the same thing as interrupting the speaker, and it conveys disrespect. Besides, if you plan your response halfway through the conversation, that response may be appropriate only to the half of the conversation that you were listening to.

Convey an open spirit with your body language. Sit up attentively and face the other person, being aware that your facial expressions, posture, and positioning can convey either openness or a closed feeling. If you sit too far away, frown, or tap your fingers impatiently on the arm of the chair, the other person will probably clam up rather quickly.

Stay in eye contact. This tip is closely related to the last one. Look at the other person. This shows that you are focusing your attention on him or her, not on the sun peeking through the clouds or the ugly painting hanging on the wall. However, do not stare; just be sure that your eyes meet the other person's eyes regularly and attentively.

Avoid assuming anything about what the other person will say. When someone starts speaking and you assume that you know what the person is about to say, your mind may race in a direction different from that of the actual conversation.

Give signals that you are listening. When it feels natural to do so, nod and say "yes" or "okay" or "uh-huh." These little signals let the speaker know that you are following carefully.

You are probably listening well if the other person keeps talking and tells you about what is important to her or him.

Briefly describe in writing five things that make listening hard for you. Then describe five features of listening that you enjoy.

Help by summarizing occasionally. Sometimes a speaker becomes stuck or confused, especially if she or he has been talking for a long time or is very upset. If it seems appropriate, you might say something like, "Let me see if I have it straight. What you just said is . . ." Your summary may or may not be accurate, but your attempt to let the person know what you understood will encourage her or him to clarify thoughts, perhaps overcome confusion, and keep talking. However, avoid the temptation to use the speaker's concerns as a takeoff point to talk about yourself. Stories that begin "That reminds me of when I . . ." or "You think *you've* got it bad . . ." derail the conversation and do not help the speaker.

Ask clarifying questions. Help the other person to say more by asking questions that clarify what the problem or feeling is: "So how did you react when he did that?" Or you may simply want to ask a question to clear up your own confusion: "I'm not sure I understand what happened, Jake. Could you go over the last part of what you said?" Such clarifying questions are especially important in disagreements, where differing uses of words sometimes lead to misunderstanding.

Check your perceptions of the speaker's body language. If a speaker is red-faced and clenching his or her teeth but is talking in a hushed tone, he or she might be looking for an opening to express some stronger feelings—or he or she might just be warm. So perhaps say something like, "You sound pretty calm to me, but when you clench your teeth and because your face is red, I wonder how you are feeling about this issue."

Let the person know if you cannot listen at the time. It is better to let a person know that you have something else you need to do and that you do not have time to listen than to agree to listen and then spend the listening time thinking about what you have to do. Honesty conveys respect for the other person.

Being listened to well is a priceless gift, one that should not be taken for granted. If you are on the receiving end of some good listening, be sure to express your appreciation to the listener.

It is safe to say that the world's best communicators are also the world's best listeners. Listening skills are indispensable to communication. But some of us are more skilled at listening than others. We need to accept that we are not perfect listeners

Being listened to well is a priceless gift, one that should not be taken for granted.

Using the guidelines for good listening, what grade would you give yourself as a listener: *A, B, C, D,* or *F?* Write down your grade and your reasons for giving yourself this grade. Then write one specific goal you might work toward to improve your listening skills.

while we make an honest attempt to develop our abilities in that area. Listening is a very concrete way of following the commandment of Jesus to love your neighbor as you love yourself.

Verbal Language

At this point, we will turn to several aspects of verbal language that can be particularly challenging in communication, especially the kind of communication that aims at nurturing intimate relationships. We will cover these aspects of **verbal communication:**

- self-disclosure
- "I" messages versus "you" messages
- giving feedback
- asking for and receiving feedback
- handling conflict

Although these topics certainly involve body language and listening, we will concentrate on the verbal dimensions of these areas of communication.

Self-disclosure

Friends share something of themselves with each other. They share facts about themselves and, perhaps a bit later, their ideas and opinions about what matters to them. But for the friendship to move to a deeper level of intimacy, the friends must begin to communicate about what is most personal to each of them—their own feelings. This gradual, mutual process of **self-disclosure,** all the way from sharing facts to sharing feelings, is what builds lasting, intimate relationships.

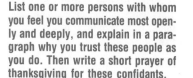

List one or more persons with whom you feel you communicate most openly and deeply, and explain in a paragraph why you trust these people as you do. Then write a short prayer of thanksgiving for these confidants.

Communicating Feelings

When we open up to a friend and talk about our emotions, we are offering a special gift to the other person. We are saying, in effect, "I trust you with this very personal information about myself. I'm telling you how I feel because I want you to understand me, to appreciate me—all of me, including my deepest feelings."

Communicating or disclosing our feelings, however, can be threatening. We might be afraid that others will take advantage of us if they know that we are sensitive about a particular issue. Or perhaps we are afraid that if we share our emotions, others will think of us as weak. So maybe we keep a stiff upper lip: we push all of our feelings inside and hope that they will go away. In Judith Guest's novel *Ordinary People* (also an Oscar-winning movie), Conrad is a young man who is troubled and haunted by his brother's accidental death. Dr. Berger, the psychiatrist whom Conrad has been seeing, tells him this:

> "People who keep stiff upper lips find that it's damn hard to smile.
>
> "... Feeling is not selective, I keep telling you that. You can't feel pain, you aren't gonna feel anything else, either. And the world is full of pain. Also joy. Evil. Goodness. Horror and love. You name it, it's there. Sealing yourself off is just going through the motions, get it?" (Pages 225, 227)

Those who cannot acknowledge and express their painful feelings can find themselves denying almost all of their feelings—even the joyful ones. Sharing feelings with a friend not only builds the friendship but also enables us to experience the richness of life.

The wonder of self-disclosure is that it leads to more self-disclosure—most of the time. However, we cannot and should not open up to *everyone*. Some people will use our self-revelations against us. We have to carefully choose those with whom to share our inmost selves. But to share our feelings and deepest experiences with no one condemns us to a lonely life, a life in which we never feel solidarity with other people. The trust necessary for love or friendship is built on mutual self-disclosure.

Confidentiality

A key principle about communicating personal and important matters is this: maintain the privacy and the confidentiality of your conversations with other people unless they give you permission to discuss what they have revealed to you. Physicians, psychologists, lawyers, and priests are expected to keep confidences because people need to feel secure that whatever is said to helping professionals will be held private. In this way, people can confide sufficiently to solve their problems or to free their souls of the burdens of sin.

Confidentiality in a friendship is just as important as it is in the professions cited. Without a mutual deep respect for and protection of self-disclosures, each person begins to distrust the other and to hide significant areas of life from the other. Unease grows between the two people. Since few people like to be

Reflect on the last month, remembering a time when you needed to and did talk to another person about something important to you. Maybe you were angry, happy, worried, full of plans, or confused. Describe the situation in a paragraph:
- what you needed to talk about
- who you talked to first
- how the talk was or was not helpful

"People who keep stiff upper lips find that it's damn hard to smile."

around those with whom they feel uncomfortable, the relationship usually comes to an end.

Self-disclosure and the mutual confidentiality that enables risk taking form the soul of a deep friendship.

"I" Messages Versus "You" Messages

Alice in Wonderland again can provide us with a fine example of a tendency that we see too often in communication. Consider this bit of dialog between the Mad Hatter and Alice:

> "Your hair wants cutting," said the Hatter. He had been looking at Alice for some time with great curiosity, and this was his first speech.
>
> "You should learn not to make personal remarks," Alice said with some severity: "It's very rude."

First, the Hatter made a subjective judgment about Alice's hair, which he pronounced as a fact. For her part, Alice defended herself by scolding the Hatter and making the subjective judgment of her own that the Hatter was rude.

The problem in the dialog above is "you" messages. A **"you" message** is a comment that we make to another person that implies a negative judgment of that person. "You" messages seem to be designed to annoy and anger. Here are some typical "you" messages:

Self-disclosure and the mutual confidentiality that enables risk taking form the soul of a deep friendship.

- You ought to listen more carefully.
- You don't care.
- You should ask for others' opinions.
- You must be nuts.
- Your clothes are weird.

The above remarks usually evoke responses like the following:

- I'm a better listener than you are.
- I do so care.
- I'm always asking others to tell me their ideas.
- You're the one that's nuts.
- I wouldn't be caught dead in those rags you're wearing!

"You" messages typically force people to defend themselves. Instead of fostering the exchange of communication, these messages make others close their gates and guard their fortress.

In contrast to "you" messages, which label others with our own judgments about them, **"I" messages** tell another person, "Here I am; this is the way I feel, think, and see things. These are my reactions, and I hope that you will listen and understand them.''

For example, Alice might have responded to the Hatter's remark with an "I" message: "I feel quite insulted when you say things like that." That would be an "I" message because Alice would not be blaming the Hatter or accusing him. She would be expressing her reaction as just that—her *own* reaction.

Consider the way each "you" message from above has been changed to an "I" message:

"You" message	"I" message.
• You ought to listen more carefully.	• When you stop me while I'm speaking, I don't feel listened to.
• You don't care.	• I feel left out.
• You should ask for others' opinions.	• I wish that I had the chance to give my opinion.
• You must be nuts.	• I am very upset.
• Your clothes are weird.	• I have different tastes.

Notice that the "I" messages state observations, feelings, thoughts, and wishes. They do not blame, judge, or belittle the other person. "I" messages express the speaker's concerns, but they leave the other person free to respond or not to respond.

Two Dialogs

Observe what happens to communication in this dialog between Amy and Mike:

"You" messages typically force people to defend themselves.

Last night Amy waited for Mike to pick her up to go to a movie. Mike never showed up, despite having called Amy yesterday afternoon to decide on a time. Mike did not even phone afterward to explain why he had not picked her up.

Amy meets Mike ten minutes before their first class.

"You didn't show up last night, and I waited around for you. The least you could have done was call."

"If you were a real friend, you would trust me. You obviously don't want to know what happened."

"Of course I want to know, but why were you so inconsiderate?"

"What do you mean, 'inconsiderate'? I had to take my father to the hospital. He had a heart attack." At this point Mike storms off.

Obviously, "you" messages are flying everywhere in that interaction. Compare that dialog with the following one:

"Mike, we were supposed to go out last night. I waited. What happened?"

"Oh, no! I forgot to tell you."

"I was pretty upset when you didn't come."

"Really, I'm sorry. I had to take Dad to the hospital. He had a heart attack."

The second dialog begins with statements of fact and a question; Mike does not have to defend himself because Amy simply asks him to explain. Amy expresses how she feels, but she does not blame her feelings on Mike. Consequently, when Mike explains that he had to take his father to the hospital, Amy does not need to feel embarrassed at having made an accusation, and Mike does not have to feel angry at Amy for being insensitive.

A certain humility underlies an "I" message. It is not arrogant. Instead it implies that what the speaker says is simply his or her reaction, opinion, or version of a story—not the whole or absolute truth. "I" messages imply a willingness to *take responsibility for owning one's communication.* In other words, with an "I" message, a person says, "This is how *I* am reacting," not *"You* shouldn't be that way." Recall the earlier discussion of avenues and roadblocks to communication. "I" messages travel on those wide, spacious avenues of trust, hope, and acceptance.

Assertiveness and "I" Messages

An "I" message is an accurate description of the speaker's own feelings about what happened, yet it permits the other person to explain. Allowing the other to explain and withholding judgment take a good deal of courage, for in doing so an individual gives up the illusion that he or she can control the other. "I" messages do not imply weakness in the speaker. To say, "I am very angry because I had to wait" instead of "You are always late" is not feeble behavior. Far from being a sign of weakness, "I" messages are a crucial part of being assertive.

Assertiveness shows a healthy respect of self and other people. To be assertive means to respect the rights and dignity of others but also to communicate our own views, feelings, and needs. Assertiveness should not be confused with **aggressiveness,** the attempt to dominate others by making them do what we want them to do. Assertiveness demonstrates strength of character; aggressiveness illustrates the character of a childish

Imagine that you have to talk with a friend about something he or she did that really bothered you. Write what you would say, using "you" messages. Then change your complaints or criticisms into "I" messages.

bully who has to have her or his own way and who cannot permit other people to be themselves. It probably has become obvious to you that aggressive people pepper their speech with heavy doses of "you" messages.

Besides aggressiveness, the other extreme to avoid in communication is **nonassertiveness.** Nonassertive persons devalue themselves; they find life frustrating because they assume that their own feelings, ideas, and wants are not as worthwhile or as valid as those of other people.

Of course, all of us behave with some combination of assertive, nonassertive, and aggressive behaviors, depending on the circumstances and on the particular relationships we are in. But we can aim to nurture a healthy, assertive style of communicating. These general guidelines are helpful:

State in specific terms what you want to say. Avoid generalizations. Say, "I feel taken advantage of when the only time I hear from you is if you need a ride someplace," not "I just don't feel right about things."

Do not apologize for what you say and do. (This presupposes that what you say and do is legal, moral, and reasonable.) Say, "This feeling of being taken advantage of is beginning to make me resentful when we get together," not "I know I probably shouldn't feel this way, but I do."

Make specific requests. Indicate what you want from the other person. Do not leave the situation unclear. Say, "Can we talk about this? I'd like to figure out a way to stay friends without my feeling resentful," not "I don't suppose there's anything that can be done about it because you don't have a car."

Listen. Hear what the other person has to say, recognizing that his or her feelings and ideas may be different from yours but that they are valid, too. Say, "Do you have any reactions to what I just said?" not "Well, I've said what I wanted to say. You can take it or leave it."

People need to behave assertively in order to be healthy. Sitting on feelings and wants and stuffing them inside ourselves (nonassertiveness) or operating as if our own feelings and wants are the only ones that count (aggressiveness) can only bring havoc to our well-being. The skill of using "I" messages wisely is a key to a healthy, assertive lifestyle as well as a loving one.

"I" messages imply a willingness to take responsibility for owning one's communication.

The Gift of Feedback

All types of verbal communication require that we be in touch with our feelings and reactions and that we *express* these to another person. In this sense, verbal communication can be a gift of self. Closely related to the forms of spoken communication that we have been discussing—self-disclosure and "I" messages—is feedback, which is a gift in a particular way.

Feedback is useful information given to a person about his or her behavior and how it affects others. Whether the information given is positive or negative, feedback conveyed sensitively is a gift because it can both affirm the person and help the person to grow.

Feedback does not imply a judgment about the worth of the person receiving it. Rather, it is the sharing of perceptions or observations about that person's behavior. "I" messages, not "you" messages, form the core of feedback. So all that has been said about "I" messages applies to feedback.

Giving Feedback

Here are some tips on giving feedback:

1. **Make feedback specific and descriptive, not general and judgmental.** For instance, compare these examples of negative feedback:

- *General and judgmental:* "You never listen to anything I say." This comment is unhelpful because it gives the receiver no specific behavior to think about. In addition, it is a "you" message.
- *Specific and descriptive:* "When you look away from me when I'm talking, I feel like you're not listening to me." This comment identifies a specific behavior—looking away—that the speaker perceives as a sign of not listening. The receiver can consider whether he or she wants to change the behavior. Note, too, that this is an "I" message.

Positive feedback also needs to be specific and descriptive to be helpful:

- *General and judgmental:* "You are a super person! How can I thank you enough?" Even though the judgment is positive, this comment does not offer the receiver much information.
- *Specific and descriptive:* "I felt better after talking with you. That story you told me about your uncle really encouraged me." Here, a particular behavior is identified and affirmed.

Feedback is useful information given to a person about his or her behavior and how it affects others.

2. Give feedback for the good of the other person and your relationship with him or her. Even if worded correctly, feedback that is given for the wrong motive—for example, to put someone down or to manipulate the person—is not beneficial. Offer feedback out of a desire to help, not out of a need to feel powerful.

3. Be sensitive to the timing of your feedback. If you know that the receiver is under a lot of strain, you might want to delay sharing negative feedback. Generally, however, feedback is most helpful when it is given at the earliest opportunity after the related behavior. With negative feedback, bad feelings will not have the opportunity to fester and harm the relationship. With positive feedback, the affirmation of the good behavior will be strengthened.

Did you receive any positive feedback in the last week? Write down what you heard and how the comments made you feel. Was the feedback specific or general? Do the same with any negative feedback you have received in the last week.

4. Share something of yourself in the feedback. If the feedback you are giving is negative, the receiver may begin to feel inferior to you—or think that you are stressing your own superiority. But if you share something—for instance, a story or some of your own feelings that identify you with the receiver—he or she might feel a sense of mutuality with you:

- "I've had the tendency, too, not to really look at people when they talk. Then my mind wanders and I'm not following the other person. I remember the time I got in big trouble with a friend for that. I didn't even realize I was doing it until she pointed it out to me."

Write five items of positive feedback that you could give to specific persons this week. Is there anything stopping you from sharing these comments?

5. Make sure that the feedback was clear. Find out if what the receiver heard is what you intended to say:

- "Am I being clear? Let me know what you understood me to say."

Asking for and Receiving Feedback

Feedback given well is a treasure that marks the depth of maturity in a friendship. Yet people generally dread receiving feedback, at least the negative kind. They fear that anything negative will hurt. (Some people have trouble accepting positive feedback, too.) The following tips can make receiving feedback easier.

1. Ask for feedback. The best way to receive feedback is to ask for it. Of course, this does not mean that you should refuse to hear others' comments unless you have asked for them. But asking does let other people know that you are receptive, and it encourages them to be honest. Asking for feedback is not a sign of weakness. However, before asking, decide if you truly want an honest answer from the person or if you are simply fishing for compliments or support. Also decide whether you trust his or her ability to hold a confidence and to be sensitive to your needs.

2. Be specific in your request for feedback. As with giving feedback, being specific when seeking feedback yields better results.

- *General:* "What do people think of me?" This question is too broad to invite a helpful, descriptive answer.
- *Specific:* "Do you think I should have said those things to Mary and Phil? How do you think they took what I said?" These questions increase the chances of receiving useful answers.

3. Listen carefully. Do not interrupt the person giving feedback to you. Think about what is being said. Ask questions if you need to clarify the comments. Avoid becoming defensive.

4. Try summarizing the feedback. Let the giver of the feedback know that you have heard and comprehended what was said, even if you disagree with the comments. You may need more time to think about the feedback.

5. Point out what you agree and disagree with. After thinking about the feedback, decide what you agree and disagree with. Perhaps comment on why the statements you agree with seem true for you. Try to delay comment about areas with which you disagree. After all, people usually need time to digest feedback that is not to their immediate liking.

- "What you said about my comments sounding sarcastic seems true. I can get pretty sarcastic when I'm mad, and I was fuming! But the part about sounding like I didn't want Phil and Mary to go with us—I'm not sure about that. I wasn't aware of that. I'll have to think about it."

Handling Conflicts

Inevitably, value disagreements, misunderstandings, competing interests, complaints, or criticism will cause conflicts in a relationship. Pain and frustration often result. However, conflicts

What is one aspect of yourself about which you would like some feedback? Write it down with the name of a person you would trust to give you helpful feedback. List two questions that you could use to solicit feedback.

can be handled so as to minimize anger and hurt. Furthermore, they can become growth points for the relationship, particularly if certain principles are kept in mind by both persons in the conflict.

The first principle in a conflict situation is to treat other people as we ourselves would want to be treated.

Do unto Others . . .

The first and most important principle in a conflict situation is to treat other people as we ourselves would want to be treated. If we do not like being spoken to in a condescending manner, then we must not use a condescending tone with others. If we like being reasoned with, then we should reason with other people. If we expect some compromises from others, we must be willing to compromise.

Go to the Source

The second principle in handling conflict is to go directly to the source, the person with whom you are in conflict, and talk about the matter. Going to a third person or talking about the problem to everyone but the individual involved usually accomplishes little and makes the situation worse. Eventually, if the direct approach breaks down, you may need a third person or a higher authority to intervene. But starting with the other individual involved in the conflict is important. Consider what happens to communication when the third-person approach is taken too quickly:

> Nicole needs the family car on Saturday night to pick up her friends, but her younger brother Jay already has permission from their parents to use it. Instead of talking with Jay to see if he and she can make some arrangement, Nicole pleads with her parents. She tells them that because she is older than Jay and has more important things to do, she deserves to use the car. Her parents tell her to settle it with her brother.
>
> Meanwhile, Jay finds out that Nicole has pleaded with their parents; he feels insulted that she thought so little of him that she would not even talk to him first. Consequently, when Nicole finally does ask him about giving up his use of the car, Jay simply says, "No."
>
> Now Nicole must enter into lengthy negotiations with Jay to soothe his hurt feelings and then to get him to budge on this issue. The energy that could have been spent on thinking of alternative arrangements for use of the car is instead being used on repairing a wound in the brother-sister relationship.

Get the facts straight before rushing into battle.

Get the Facts Straight

A third principle in handling conflict is to have the facts straight before rushing into battle. For example, if we think that someone is spreading rumors about us, we should do some careful verification before making accusations. Many of us have had the embarrassing experience of charging into combat only to find out that we have accused someone of doing something that she or he did not do.

This principle is also important in less personalized conflicts. For instance, if you are making a proposal to a committee or club, make sure that you have all of the information you need to discuss the proposal and debate it with those who might disagree. The club will benefit if its decision is based on solid information.

Take a Problem-Solving Approach

The fourth principle in handling conflict is to treat the conflict as a problem to be solved by both persons, not as a win-lose situation. These suggested steps to problem solving will help to solve a conflict:

1. **State the problem clearly.** Use "I" messages, not judgments or accusations, and allow the other person to state his or her perceptions about the problem, too. Sometimes no conflict exists once both parties have tried to define exactly what they think the problem is. Limit the conflict under discussion to a particular issue; try not to bring a whole history of conflicts into the discussion.

2. **Brainstorm for solutions.** It takes two people to create a conflict and therefore two people to create a solution. Brainstorming together means coming up with as many ways to solve the problem as possible—from the lofty to the ridiculous. You will be surprised at how often a creative solution emerges.

3. **Evaluate each proposed solution and choose one.** Reflect on the solutions together, and talk about which will work best for the two of you. Then choose the one most acceptable to both of you. Sometimes the only solution seems to be for one of the parties to give in—a win-lose outcome. This is a sad situation because a win-lose outcome ultimately harms the relationship. A solution that both persons can at least live with—a win-win outcome—is always preferred.

Sometimes resolving a conflict requires a *mediator*—someone who can step in and help the two people to agree. This mediator must be trusted by both persons and must be a good listener. Although a mediator helps two people to work out their conflict, she or he does not impose a solution. Often the best result is a compromise.

Conflicts are not always bad; they are normal. If two people are committed to finding a solution to a conflict, their relationship can be stronger in the end. After all, wrestling through a problem together, with all of the listening and talking involved, can lead to greater mutual knowledge and self-understanding. This knowledge can support and build friendship. Conflicts also push us to clarify our thinking, sharpen our principles, and test our skills of communication.

Recall a recent conflict that you had with someone. Write a brief paragraph that answers these questions:
- Did you use any of the principles for handling conflict?
- Which principles were used and which were not used?
- Which principle is hardest for you to follow?

Describe the most significant realization you have had in this study of communication. In what ways do you think that you will be a better communicator?

A Rich Harvest

Communication requires patient effort as we try out different approaches, stumbling at times and feeling accomplishment at other times. But a conscious attempt to become more aware of body language, to develop skills in listening, and to use language carefully yields a rich harvest of friendship, intimacy, and self-respect. In our own small part of the world, we may then experience something of Jesus' dream for us: the peaceable kingdom, a loving community, and becoming fully alive.

A conscious attempt to communicate well yields a rich harvest of friendship, intimacy, and self-respect.

Review Questions

1. What is communication, and why is it so important for us?

2. What is the relationship between communication and the Christian life?

3. List and explain the avenues and roadblocks to communication.

4. What is body language? Why is body language more readily believed but more easily misinterpreted than spoken language?

5. What does this course recommend as the best guideline for communicating through touch?

6. Why are good listening skills important? How can you tell when you are doing a good job of listening?

7. List and explain the nine guidelines for good listening.

8. How is self-disclosure sometimes threatening?

9. Why is confidentiality important in relationships that involve self-disclosure?

10. What are "you" messages and "I" messages? Give three examples from the text of each type of message.

11. List and explain the four guidelines to healthy, assertive communication.

12. What is feedback? What are the five tips on giving feedback?

13. What five tips make receiving feedback easier?

14. List and explain the four principles of conflict resolution.

5 Sexuality: A Great Gift

WE were created as sexual creatures—male and female. Sexuality is integral to who we are. Yet, despite the tradition that "God saw all he had made, and indeed it was very good" (Genesis 1:31), sexuality has been a source of apprehension for human beings throughout the centuries. We experience the power and urgency of the sexual drive, but we wonder how to channel it. For young adults, integrating sexuality into the larger framework of life, identity, and dream is a challenging developmental task.

The Meaning of Sexuality

The Mythical Origins of Male and Female

One way to understand sexuality is to examine myths or stories about the creation of men and women. Although these myths, which date from the earliest years of recorded history, are not intended to record scientific facts about creation, they do tap into deep levels of human wisdom about what it means to be sexual creatures.

According to a Greek myth, each human being was originally both female and male. Zeus, the king of the Greek gods, punished humans by splitting them into female and male. (Interestingly, the word *sex* comes from the Latin word *secare*, which means "to cut" or "to sever.") We might say that ever since Zeus split human beings into female and male, women and men have sought to reunite themselves in order to be whole once again. This would explain the powerful drive that compels women and men to bond.

The Greek myth strikes a familiar chord when we consider the creation story in the Jewish Scriptures. In that account, God separates the first human being into a man and a woman:

> Then, Yahweh God made the man ["earth creature"] fall into a deep sleep. And, while he was asleep, he took one of his ribs and closed the flesh up again forthwith. Yahweh God fashioned the rib he had taken from the man ["earth creature"] into a woman, and brought her to the man. And the man said:
>
> This one at last is bone of my bones
>   and flesh of my flesh!
> She is to be called Woman,
>   because she was taken from Man.
>
> This is why a man leaves his father and mother and becomes attached to his wife, and they become one flesh. (Genesis 2:21–24)

A bit of explanation about terminology will help in our understanding of this passage. In the ancient Hebrew language, the word translated into English as "man" actually means "earth creature," which is neither male nor female. The Hebrew terms for the human male and the human female are not introduced in the creation account until after the rib episode. What the writers of the account intended to convey was that both man and woman were created from the same earth creature.

In both the Greek and the Jewish stories about the creation of man and woman, sexuality can be seen as a force that draws two people together into oneness. However, in the Jewish Scriptures, the original split of the human being into man and woman was not done as punishment by God; rather, it was done so that the earth creature would not have to be alone. From this account, we can learn that men and women spring from one source—God's love and life.

Another important aspect common to the Greek and the Jewish creation stories is the implication that both femaleness and maleness were originally inside of each human being. Today, psychologists who take a *Jungian perspective*—that is, follow the theory of noted psychologist Carl G. Jung—assert that within each female lies a masculine dimension and within each male lies a feminine dimension. To become whole, a person must bring this dimension to awareness and allow it to be integrated into her or his personality. Sexuality not only drives us to be unified with another person but also propels us to be whole persons, using the full range of our intellectual and emotional capacities. This is what God created us for.

Sexuality: Seeking Fulfillment Outside of Ourselves

Given the insights into the meaning of sexuality provided by the Greek and the Jewish stories, we can see the wisdom of a definition of **sexuality** given by two authorities on sexuality, Mary Perkins Ryan and John Julian Ryan:

> Sexuality . . . is the force in human nature meant to provide psychophysical impetus [motivation] and urgency to the drive of our whole being to find fulfillment . . . with others; it urges us, physically and psychophysically, to seek completion in an "opposite" to ourselves. Our sexuality at once makes it evident that we are not self-sufficient and impels us to seek fulfillment outside ourselves. (*Love and Sexuality,* page 43)

Sexuality urges us to overcome our sense of loneliness and selfishness. This strong, basic drive is part of our humanity.

Write your responses to these questions:
- Do you agree with the definition of sexuality given in this course?
- Would you add, subtract, or alter anything in the definition? If so, what?

Sexuality is a force that draws two people together into oneness.

Naturally, people tend to associate sexuality most closely with erotic love and the power to conceive new human life. In one of the creation accounts, "God blessed [the male and female], saying to them, 'Be fruitful, multiply, fill the earth and subdue it' '' (Genesis 1:28). Even this purpose of sexual union—the conception of new life—points us toward the broader meaning of sexuality. As the Ryans added in their discussion of sexuality,

> The biological purpose of sexual union, one aspect of human sexuality, suggests its total purpose: to impel us toward life-giving union with other persons and with God. (Page 44)

Notice the Ryans' comment that sexual union is only one aspect of human sexuality. Sexuality, and sex, is more than sexual intercourse. It is the emotional, physical, and psychological drive to be bonded to another person in a life-giving way.

A Tradition of Affirming Sexuality

In the Scriptures

The Jewish Scriptures and the Christian Testament continually affirm the goodness and life-giving nature of sexuality. In the Jewish Scriptures in particular, the sexual attraction of lovers is described in beautiful and moving terms. For instance, the Book of Proverbs declares the following:

> Find joy with the wife you married in your youth,
>   fair as a [doe], graceful as a fawn;
>   hers the breasts that ever fill you with delight,
>   hers the love that ever holds you captive.
>
> (Proverbs 5:18–19)

The most famous hymns of love in the Jewish Scriptures are found in the Song of Songs, a collection of wedding feast songs. Supposedly dedicated to Solomon, the greatest lover of the Jewish Scriptures, these songs were written for a husband and a wife to sing to each other. For example, the wife sings these words:

> I hear my love.
> See how he comes
> leaping on the mountains,
> bounding over the hills.
> My love is like a gazelle,
> like a young stag.

Sexuality helps to make us who we are and is part of our desire to love other people and God.

. . . .
My love lifts up his voice,
he says to me,
"Come then, my beloved,
 my lovely one, come.
For see, winter is past,
the rains are over and gone."

. . . .
My love is mine and I am his.

(Song of Songs 2:8–16)

In his letters, Saint Paul continued the tradition of recognizing the dignity of sexuality. Paul believed that the body is to be used for love, not for short-term pleasure or, worse, for selfish enjoyment that implies no commitment to the other person:

Do you not realise that your body is the temple of the Holy Spirit, who is in you and whom you received from God? . . . So use your body for the glory of God. (1 Corinthians 6:19–20)

In the Church Tradition

Throughout the centuries since the time of Jesus, the church has consistently maintained the dignity and worth of sexuality in human life. A recent statement from the Vatican's office on education, *Educational Guidance in Human Love,* sums up the church's affirmation of sexuality:

Sexuality is a fundamental component of personality, one of its modes of being, of manifestation, of communicating with others, of feeling, of expressing and of living human love. Therefore it is an integral part of the development of the personality and of its educative process: "It is, in fact, from sex that the human person receives the characteristics which, on the biological, psychological and spiritual levels, make that person a man or a woman, and thereby largely condition his or her progress towards maturity and insertion into society." (No. 4)

Simply put, the church believes that sexuality helps to make us who we are and that sexuality is part of our desire to love other people and God.

Both in the Bible and in the church tradition, the Christian

Write a paragraph that describes how the affirmation of sexuality in the Jewish Scriptures and the Christian Testament and in the church document matches—or does not match—what you have learned in the past about the Catholic view of sexuality.

worldview calls us to appreciate our own sexuality as an integral part of our humanity.

The Power of Sexuality

We can acknowledge the humanness and goodness of sexuality, but it is also important to recognize its power. We are not addressing faint emotions or weak energies when we talk about sexuality. For the adolescent whose sexuality is being awakened by immense biological and hormonal changes, this deep creative drive transforms, enlivens, and expands the person's whole being. Curiosity and imagination are stirred, thinking is colored, and the body is transformed. The power of sexuality to make us feel different—new and charged with energy—is part of its potential to help us realize our humanity.

Intense and Conflicting Reactions to Sexuality

Sexuality frequently leads us to be physically attracted to another person. Romantic love (see pages 76–77) and eventually erotic love (see pages 75–76) may follow. These experiences can create many intense and conflicting reactions to sexuality—such as those described in this poem by the Spanish poet Jorge Manrique:

Love "sometimes shows sadness, at other times, joy."

> Love is a force so strong
> it rules all reason.
> A force of such power
> it turns all minds
> by its power and desire.
>
> . . . .
> 'Tis pleasure with sorrow
> and sorrow with joy.
> Pain with sweetness
> and might with fear.
> Fear with daring
> and pleasure with rage.
> Glory with passion
> and faith with desire.
>
> . . . .
> A kind of madness
> in the changes it makes.

Sometimes shows sadness,
at other times, joy,
as it wishes and pleases.

Manrique described well the power and the effects of the strong attraction that is part of our sexuality: It urges us, physically and psychologically, to seek completion in an opposite to ourselves. We may become drawn toward another person, but he or she may not be interested in us. Or we initially may become close, but then the other person might back away or fall in love with someone else. We may find someone who is attracted to us and love may grow, but then we must wait to consummate that love in marriage. Such intense and not always comfortable experiences can result from the powerful life energy that sexuality gives us.

Because it is so powerful, particularly in adolescence, sexuality normally assumes enormous importance in a young person's awareness and growth in identity. Eventually, healthy, mature people are able to put sexuality into perspective and learn to integrate it into the whole of life.

Sexual Intercourse and Commitment

The role of sexual intercourse in a loving, committed relationship fulfills the need to experience sexuality as a part of the whole of life, not as something that dominates life. Marriage is intended to be such a relationship.

Sexual intercourse is undeniably the most obvious expression of sexuality, though not the only one. Intercourse can bond two people into "one flesh" (Genesis 2:24), but this expression signifies much more than physical unification. To say that two people are "one flesh" implies that they also reach a depth of knowledge of one another. In fact, in the Bible, another term used for sexual intercourse is *knowledge*. For example, Mary questioned the angel who told her that she would bear a son: " '. . . But how can this come about, since I have no knowledge of man?' " (Luke 1:34).

Intercourse in the context of a total, committed relationship can lead to profound mutual understanding because the commitment allows a couple to become intimate on many levels, not only on the physical level. Recall the many types of intimacy discussed on pages 66–67 in chapter 3. Those who commit themselves to one another permanently pledge to share deeply the whole of their lives—emotions, struggles and joys of parenthood, appreciation of beauty, vision of life, attempts to make

Have you ever experienced some of the confusion and madness of romantic love? If so, how did you order or cope with those feelings? Write your reflections.

The sharing of life brings people closer to fulfillment.

In writing, compare the need to have a permanent commitment as the context for sexual intercourse with the attitudes toward sex that prevail in our culture.

a welcoming home, a sense of fun, efforts at work, or sorrow from loss or tragedy.

When living a total life together, the bonding of sexual intercourse brings two persons closer to fulfillment. Intercourse does not magically make people whole and fully alive. What does bring people closer to fulfillment is the sharing of life. As an act of trust, joy, and emotional and physical renewal, sexual union celebrates that sharing in the most intimate way. Without a commitment to the long-range existence of a relationship, sexual intercourse becomes hollow, even if somewhat pleasurable.

Most loving and committed couples do not instantly have

"perfect" sexual relationships. However, their long-range commitment to each other can take away much of the pressure and anxiety to perform perfectly. The Ryans described the relationship between intercourse and commitment in this way:

> If sexual intercourse is to become the human experience and act of love it should be, it needs freedom from worry, freedom to take time, freedom not to succeed perfectly and [freedom] to try again, in the context of a lovingly shared life. . . . These freedoms cannot ordinarily exist outside of marriage. (*Love and Sexuality,* page 77)

Sexual intercourse needs to be experienced as part of the whole of a shared, committed life.

Ordering Our Sexuality

Like other kinds of power, sexuality needs to be **ordered**—that is, directed and channeled through responsible, loving choices.

We have already seen that the permanent commitment of marriage provides the best atmosphere for the most obvious expression of sexuality, sexual intercourse. Intercourse is ordered within marriage. Perhaps the explanation above about why intercourse belongs in marriage made sense to you—or perhaps it raised questions for you instead.

Sometimes it is difficult to understand why limits need to be placed on sexuality by society or religion. We might ask these questions:

- Why should sexuality be ordered?
- Wouldn't life be ideal with no restrictions?
- Why can't people do whatever they please sexually?

We might, at times, imagine a world without restrictions on sexuality.

Society, however, could not survive without some customs or principles that limit sexual activity. Even the most primitive societies developed codes of sexual conduct. They realized that the uncontrolled expression of sexual power is destructive of social order. It is also destructive to the person whose sexuality is uncontrolled.

If we examine what happens in our own society when sex is not ordered by responsible choices, the fantasy of a world without sexual limits begins to look less attractive and more

Bring to class one newspaper article that illustrates the harm that results from disordered sexuality. Write a brief reflection on how the disorder caused harm.

genuinely disturbing. Here are a few examples of *disordered* sexuality that we find in our own society:

Rape

The most extreme example of disordered sexuality is rape. This act is condemned by society not because it is sexual but because it is essentially violent, brutal, and dehumanizing. Rape robs the victim of her or his rights and dignity as a human being. The rapist is also a victim—a victim of uncontrolled, violent emotions.

Teenage Pregnancies

The drastic increase in pregnancies among unmarried teenagers, and the alarming increase in abortions to "handle" them, is evidence of disordered sexuality. Whether a baby is aborted or comes to term and is born, the implications of such a pregnancy for the persons involved and for society as a whole are extremely serious. Too often the teenage mother and father are too young and immature to assume the enormous task of bringing up the child.

These pregnancies are not the result of responsible, loving choices about sexuality. Instead, the unexpected pregnancies often result from ill-considered, shortsighted decisions and sometimes even from coercion or selfish manipulation.

Lust

Lust is the desire to use another person as an object for one's own sexual pleasure. Treating another person as an object is always disordered. Lust is sexuality gone sour; it may sound like love, but it is not. Frequently a person preoccupied with lust focuses so exclusively on self-gratification that he or she cannot direct energies into the development of friendships, creative projects, service to others, and so on.

Pornography

Pornography reduces sexuality to a depersonalized, second-hand experience of genital sex. It tries to substitute mental pictures, photographs, or movies for human love. It is a form of deception, ultimately degrading and misleading. Pornography cannot deliver what it promises. It may seem nonthreatening to readers or viewers because it demands nothing in terms of a human relationship, but it does not prepare them to relate to real persons.

Write responses to the following questions:
- Why do you think teenage women are becoming pregnant in record numbers today?
- What are the effects of teenage pregnancy, or the pregnancy of any unmarried woman, on herself, the father, the baby, their families, and society as a whole?

Pornography frequently involves acts of violence, especially against women, which humiliate and brutalize persons. Some people feel powerless or inadequate with real human beings, so they gravitate toward pornography for sexual stimulation and as a substitute for direct human relationships.

Selling Through Sex

Another example of disorder is the abuse of sexuality by the electronic and print media as a means of selling products. When these media tell us that a product will make us alluring to the other sex, they are telling us that a certain look, piece of clothing, smell, or possession is what composes our sexuality.

Equating commercial products with sexuality degrades us because this equation says, "You as a person are not essentially attractive; this product is what attracts someone to you." Those who abuse sexuality by using it to sell products are simply trying to manipulate us by taking advantage of the powerful and common desire to feel attractive.

Valuing Ourselves as Sexual Persons

As we discussed earlier, sexuality is much more than sexual intercourse; it is the force that drives us to find fulfillment with others. A healthy expression of that sexuality depends on many factors. One factor is that we value ourselves as sexual persons. We will consider two aspects of that valuing:
* having a positive body image
* appreciating our maleness or femaleness

Having a Positive Body Image

Having a positive body image means that we feel comfortable with our bodies and that we love our bodies enough to take care of them.

Feeling Comfortable in Our Own Skin

To be comfortable and feel at home in our own bodies is not as easy as it might sound. We have discussed how readily the media take advantage of our need to feel attractive by equating our attractiveness with their products. Discomfort with ourselves as bodily persons seems to be on the increase

Describe in writing what you think is the North American culture's attitude toward pornography. Does it fit the view presented here about pornography?

List and describe aspects of your body that you like and aspects that you would change if you could. Next to each aspect, write down one or more experiences that have caused you to like or dislike that aspect (such as hearing the comments of other people).

Advertising uses tactics to make us dissatisfied with our own bodies.

List the attributes of the perfect male body and of the perfect female body as they are depicted in magazines and on television. Then write your answer to this question:
• How has my perception of the perfect body for my sex influenced my acceptance of my own body?

in this society. Here are some examples of the tactics used in advertising to make us dissatisfied with our own bodies:

• TV, magazine, and radio ads scream at us for being too fat, too thin, too short, too tall, pimply, yellow-toothed, dull-haired, or just plain homely.

• Health clubs and tanning spas make big profits as they promise to give us gorgeous bodies.

• Fashion magazines do a thriving business by convincing us that what we are currently wearing will not make us suitably attractive to the other sex. There is even a fashion magazine for big (meaning "fat") and tall men; of course, its purpose is to sell clothes that hide bigness.

A lot of businesses would close if people were comfortable with their bodies, if they valued themselves more as persons and less as appearances. Tragic evidence of the obsession with bodily perfectionism in our society is the dramatic increase in cases of the eating disorders *anorexia nervosa* and *bulimia,* particularly among young women. Both of these disorders are characterized by a pathological fear of gaining weight. With anorexia nervosa, this fear leads to faulty eating patterns, malnutrition, and excessive weight loss. Persons who have bulimia tend to go on food binges and then induce vomiting to avoid weight gain.

So it is not easy to feel at home in our own skin, even though our bodies—plump, thin, weak, or strong—are marvelous creations given to us by God. Too many messages tell us to be ashamed. Shame, however, makes us more unattractive than any deviation from the norms of beauty. Shame makes us shy, awkward with others, and hesitant to try new relationships. We can probably think of people who refused to feel shame about their far-from-perfect bodies and whose lives were therefore filled with friendship and significant accomplishments.

At some point in life, we must look at ourselves in the mirror and say something like, "I'm five-four, a short guy, but I am lovable and I can love others," or "I'm six-three, tall for a woman, but I am lovable and I can love others." In Christian terms, we need to love ourselves in order to love others.

Caring for Our Bodies

Accepting and loving ourselves implies that we care for our bodies—by eating wisely, exercising, and taking precautions to prevent illness and exhaustion.

In recent years, researchers have identified seven habits that are effective in promoting health and increasing life expectancy:

- Three meals a day, avoiding snacks
- Breakfast every day
- Moderate exercise two or three times a week
- Seven or eight hours of sleep at night
- No smoking
- Moderate weight
- No alcohol, or only in moderation

(Doris Janzen Longacre, *Living More with Less,* page 41)

By keeping our bodies healthy and fit, we have the energy and stamina to enter life-giving relationships. Suppose, for instance, that a young woman wants to nurture a relationship with someone who loves to bike. If she is out of shape and smokes heavily, she is unlikely to experience recreational intimacy with that person through biking together. Fitness and health also enhance mental alertness, so even the capacity for intellectual intimacy can be affected by the physical well-being of a person.

Appreciating Our Maleness or Femaleness

- Women are sensitive but unreasonable.
- Men are insensitive but logical.

- Women should take primary responsibility for child rearing.
- Men should be the breadwinners.

- Women should stick to the liberal arts.
- Men should be engineers, doctors, or accountants.

Until the last two decades, these statements stood in public opinion as mostly unquestioned truths about what it means to be male or female. Although fewer people would make these comments today than in earlier years, many people still act out of these prejudices. Valuing ourselves as sexual persons by appreciating our maleness or femaleness does *not* mean that we lock into such stereotyped notions of masculinity and femininity. That would be a distortion of sexuality. Yet such distortions are still common in our society.

By keeping our bodies healthy and fit, we have the energy and stamina to enter life-giving relationships.

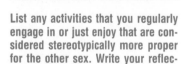

List any activities that you regularly engage in or just enjoy that are considered stereotypically more proper for the other sex. Write your reflections on how you feel about doing these activities.

Stereotypes confine us and eventually warp our personalities.

Refuting Stereotyped Notions

A stereotyped notion of what manhood is all about is represented well in this man's childhood memory:

> I had a wonderful feeling inside me, a feeling you can't know about unless you've had it—but if you're a man you'll have had it some time. . . . It's a wonderful thing to be a boy, to go roaming where grown-ups can't catch you, and to chase rats and kill birds . . . and shout dirty words. It's a kind of strong, rank feeling, a feeling of knowing everything and fearing nothing, and it's all bound up with breaking rules and killing things. The white dusty roads, . . . the dirty words, . . . the stamping on the young birds, the feel of the fish straining on the line—it was all part of it. Thank God I'm a man, because no woman ever has that feeling. (George Orwell, *Coming Up for Air,* page 75)

The adult version of this boyhood stereotype of masculinity can be seen in the common expectation that men should strive for control, competitive power, and domination. They should be tough, not tender and emotional. Above all, men should not be needy. The female counterpart of this stereotype is that women should be soft, dizzy, and helpless.

Sojourner Truth refuted this notion of being female with passionate conviction. Truth (1797–1883) was a brilliant orator who toured the United States, preaching for the abolition of slavery. She had been born a slave but escaped. She never learned to read or write, but her words were so inspiring that others recorded them. After the Civil War, Truth supported the issue of women's rights. This passage from one of her speeches seems directed at the man quoted above and at any others who stereotype women:

> That man over there says that women need to be helped into carriages, and lifted over ditches, and to have the best place everywhere. Nobody ever helps me into carriages, or over mud-puddles, or gives me any best place! And ain't I a woman? Look at me! Look at my arm! I have ploughed and planted, and gathered into barns, and no man could head me! And ain't I a woman? I could work as much and eat as much as a man—when I could get it—and bear the lash as well! And ain't I a woman? I have borne thirteen children, and seen them most all sold off to slavery, and when I cried out with my mother's grief, none but Jesus heard me! And ain't I a woman? . . .

Then that little man in black there, he says women can't have as much rights as men, 'cause Christ wasn't a woman! Where did your Christ come from? Where did your Christ come from? From God and a woman! Man had nothing to do with Him.

If the first woman God ever made was strong enough to turn the world upside down all alone, these women together ought to be able to turn it back, and get it right side up again! And now they is asking to do it, the men better let them.

Obliged to you for hearing me, and now old Sojourner ain't got nothing more to say.

Sojourner Truth's point was this: we are more than the stereotypes about womanhood and manhood allow us to be.

Stereotypes confine us and eventually warp our personalities. For instance, if a woman cannot be assertive and independent, she might deny herself the training or education she needs to establish herself in a career suited to her gifts. If a man needs help in a situation but is so afraid to show his vulnerability and to be dependent that he will not ask for assistance, he contributes to his own suffering. In both cases, stereotyping harms their capacity to be fully alive persons.

A Season for Everything

To paraphrase a part of the Jewish Scriptures, "There is a season for everything. . . . A time to be logical, a time to use intuition; a time to be gentle, a time to be firm; a time to be vulnerable, a time to be strong" (Ecclesiastes 3:1–8). These times occur for men and women alike. To be men and women who are whole people, we must break through the stereotypes that confine the expression of all that we are.

Appreciating our femaleness or maleness does not mean that we endorse and fulfill the stereotypes of femininity and masculinity that are pushed on us by many elements of our culture. It does mean that we cherish ourselves as *physically* male or physically female. We must resist the pressure from our culture to identify femaleness or maleness with stereotypical notions. To appreciate our true femaleness or maleness is to transcend those artificial distinctions.

The Greek and Jewish stories about the creation of man and woman hint at the idea that whole human beings bring together what are traditionally considered masculine and feminine traits. After all (according to these myths), in the

In your own words, summarize in writing Sojourner Truth's argument against stereotyping women.

Do any stereotypes about your sex feel particularly stifling to you? List these, and give an example of a situation in which you felt the impact of each stereotype.

Sojourner Truth was a former slave who crusaded for women's rights.

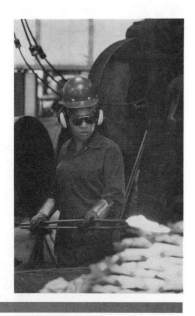

Most men and women long to express their feminine and masculine sides: they long to be whole human beings.

Choose a line from the poem "For Every Woman" that most speaks about your experience of yourself. Write an explanation of why this line has meaning for you.

original human condition, male and female were united in one human being. The longing that both men and women have to express their feminine and masculine sides—the longing to be whole—comes through in this poem by Nancy R. Smith entitled "For Every Woman":

> For every woman who is tired of acting weak when she knows she is strong, there is a man who is tired of appearing strong when he feels vulnerable.
>
> For every woman who is tired of acting dumb, there is a man who is burdened with the constant expectation of "knowing everything."
>
> For every woman who is tired of being called "an emotional female," there is a man who is denied the right to weep and to be gentle.
>
> For every woman who is called unfeminine when she competes, there is a man for whom competition is the only way to prove his masculinity.
>
> For every woman who is tired of being a sex object, there is a man who must worry about his potency.
>
> For every woman who feels "tied down" by her children, there is a man who is denied the full pleasures of shared parenthood.
>
> For every woman who is denied meaningful employment or equal pay, there is a man who must bear full financial responsibility for another human being.
>
> For every woman who was not taught the intricacies of an automobile, there is a man who was not taught the satisfactions of cooking.
>
> For every woman who takes a step toward her own liberation, there is a man who finds the way to freedom has been made a little easier.

Jesus: The Complete Person

The best model that we have of someone who transcended sexual stereotypes and used the full range of his intellect and emotions in loving others is Jesus. He was sensitive when that was required and assertive when that was the proper response to a situation.

A Tender and Nurturing Healer

Crying is not stereotypically masculine, but Jesus wept. He cried over the death of his friend Lazarus (John 11:32–36), and when he came in sight of Jerusalem and realized that he would be rejected by the people there, "he shed tears over it" (Luke 19:41).

Nurturing weak persons or children is associated with stereotypes of femininity. But Jesus made the care of sick, lame, and poor people and children a necessary part of his command to love others. He held up to his followers the model of the good Samaritan, who "was moved with compassion" and "bandaged [the beaten man's] wounds, pouring oil and wine on them" (Luke 10:33–34). Jesus told his followers about the tender mercy of the prodigal son's father, who, when he saw the young man return to him, "ran to the boy, clasped him in his arms and kissed him" (Luke 15:21). Jesus was not concerned that anyone would think him feminine. He knew that love calls for nurturing in the form of physical care and gestures of affection.

Jesus knew that love calls for nurturing in the form of physical care and gestures of affection.

- Most directly, Jesus showed his sensitivity by healing lepers, blind people, and those filled with demons. For example, when two blind men came to him, "Jesus felt pity for them and touched their eyes, and at once their sight returned and they followed him" (Matthew 20:34).

- At one point Jesus compared himself to a mother hen. When he pondered the stubborn people in Jerusalem who had killed the prophets and would now try to destroy him, he said, ". . . How often have I longed to gather your children together, as a hen gathers her brood under her wings, and you refused!" (Luke 13:34).

- The Middle Eastern custom of washing the feet of guests was considered the job of slaves or women. So at the Last Supper, the Apostles were shocked when Jesus, whom they considered their Master, washed their feet. The point that Jesus made was that we should serve one another by doing whatever is needed, whether the necessary action is considered feminine or masculine by society.

A Strong and Confronting Leader

When leadership and strength were required, Jesus could fulfill these stereotypically masculine roles, not because he needed to prove his masculinity but because love demanded leadership and strength.

- It must have required tremendous personal courage and a

sense of his own leadership ability for Jesus to walk up to a group of tough fishermen and say, ". . . 'Come after me and I will make you into fishers of people' " (Mark 1:17). Peter and Andrew followed him at once.

- Jesus had to put up with a life of wandering: "Jesus said, 'Foxes have holes and the birds of the air have nests, but the Son of man has nowhere to lay his head' " (Matthew 8:20). He was weathered and toughened by a hard life.

- Jesus was also strong in his convictions. He knew that he was on earth to do the will of God. Consequently, he confronted head-on the religious powers of his day, the scribes and the Pharisees: " 'Alas for you, scribes and Pharisees, you hypocrites! You shut up the kingdom of Heaven in people's faces, neither going in yourselves nor allowing others to go in who want to. . . . Alas for you, blind guides! . . . Fools and blind! . . .' " (Matthew 23:13–17).

- The sensitive and caring Jesus was also the Jesus who drove the merchants out of the Temple: ". . . He went into the Temple and began driving out the men selling and buying there; he upset the tables of the money changers and the seats of the dove sellers" (Mark 11:15).

In short, Jesus could be feminine or masculine, as the situation demanded; he was free of the stereotypes that confine most people. As a perfectly whole person, Jesus gives us a model of what it means to live a full life as a male or a female. He was chaste and never married, but Jesus expressed his sexuality by directing its energy and power into his ministry.

Write a description of a time when you were a "nurturing healer" and a description of a time when you were a "strong and confronting person."

Identify two areas of sexuality that most people your age have questions about. Do some library research and also interview teachers, parents, or helping professionals to gain information and insight about these topics. Prepare a written report on each topic to summarize your findings.

Created to Be United

The powerful nature of sexuality is both a gift and a challenge. If sexuality were not so powerful, we would not be so wonderfully transformed and enlivened by it. On the other hand, the intensity of sexuality can be difficult to order through responsible, loving choices. Furthermore, the misunderstandings of sexuality promoted by the media do not help us to integrate sexuality into a whole and healthy way of life.

In spite of the dilemmas that sexuality can present to us, we know that we were created as sexual persons, whose destiny is to be united with others. Whether we eventually marry, remain single, enter religious life, or become ordained, our sexuality will be with us, moving us to break out of our separateness and to seek loving relationships as whole persons.

Review Questions

1. How does the Greek myth explain the origins of male and female? What story from the Jewish Scriptures parallels the Greek myth?

2. What are some implications about sexuality that can be drawn from the Greek and the Jewish creation stories?

3. How did the Ryans define sexuality?

4. Cite one instance from the Jewish Scriptures in which sexuality is affirmed.

5. What does the church teach about the place of sexuality in human life?

6. What are some examples of the intense and conflicting reactions people can have as a result of sexuality's power?

7. Why is commitment necessary in order for sexual intercourse to be fulfilling?

8. Why does society always seek to order sexuality?

9. Why are rape, teenage pregnancies, lust, pornography, and selling through sex considered disordered uses of sexuality?

10. Give some examples of why discomfort with one's body is increasing in our society.

11. Why should a Christian value his or her body?

12. How does sex-role stereotyping distort sexuality?

13. What human longing is expressed in the poem "For Every Woman"?

14. How was Jesus a complete person who fully expressed his sexuality?

6 Lifelong Learning: Growth Beyond High School

MOST seniors will be completing their formal education either this year or in a few more years at the end of college or technical school. You may be anticipating the end of your school days with some enthusiasm, looking forward to the day when you no longer will be preparing for real life but instead will be living it. After twelve or so years of school, you may feel that learning is something to be finished as quickly as possible in order to get to the real business of living. So why discuss the topic of *lifelong* learning? Learning is important because it is a lifetime effort, not simply a school effort.

You already have learned a tremendous amount in school, and college or technical school offers more to learn. However, the great bulk of **learning**—or growth in knowledge, insight, and skills—is done outside of formal education, in the school of life. You have been a pupil in *that* school since the day you were born, and you will remain enrolled until the day you die.

This is not to downplay the importance of the formal education you have received or the further education you may be about to undertake. Those forms of learning are crucial to your development as a person and as a competent, contributing member of the community. But the notion that learning is lifelong, not temporary, casts a new light on how to approach the rich world of experiences you are about to enter: you can view new situations as opportunities to learn.

The rich world of experience is the school of life; you have been a pupil in that school since the day you were born.

The School of Life

The following examples illustrate people who are growing in knowledge, insight, and skills in the school of life—at times with pain or with joy, through mistakes and through small victories:

- Now that he is away from home, Ted has his own checking account, but he has never bothered to balance his checkbook.

One day four checks bounce, costing him sixty dollars in penalties and plenty of embarrassment. Ted learns very quickly how to balance his checkbook.

- Carmen was laid off when the factory she worked for closed down. She has two children to support. After a period of shock and then restlessness, she decides to open a small carpentry business, doing interior remodeling, garages, and room additions. Carmen has always had a knack for carpentry, but she has no business experience. So she soaks up every bit of information she can about how to operate this kind of business—advertising, obtaining loans for equipment, buying supplies, billing and accounting, and eventually managing workers. Carmen becomes very successful at her business.

- Since their baby was born three years ago, Laura and Rob have become experts in childbirth, breast-feeding, nutrition, childhood illnesses, stress management, infant and child development, discipline for young children, safe and enriching toys, day-care options, and fun ways to pass rainy days.

- Jenna's father has lung cancer, with no hope of recovery. In the last four months, Jenna has learned a tremendous amount—about cancer and its many forms and treatments, about controlling pain and other symptoms, about the emotional stages of a person who is dying, about how a family can cope in a crisis, about how difficult but necessary it is to grieve and talk with her father, about ways to provide home care, and about what it means to faithfully support someone who is suffering.

- Len's first college roommate is from Japan. At first he wondered if they would have anything in common, but now he is learning some Japanese words and is beginning to appreciate his roommate's culture. Len thinks that he would like to travel to Japan someday to study Japanese business.

- Meg's parents have discovered that she has a severe drug addiction. The treatment program that they find for her involves the whole family in counseling, which enables Meg, her parents, and her brother to see what kinds of family situations have been affecting Meg negatively. Now they are trying to relate to one another in new ways.

- Tom became frustrated during his first semester at the huge state university when he couldn't get into most of the classes that he wanted. At second-semester registration, he follows the example of an experienced sophomore, picking up her

Persons who can draw meaning and growth out of all of life's events are the deepest learners.

techniques for maneuvering through the bureaucratic maze to get specific classes.

- Nancy studied the U.S. Constitution in a government class, but it had seemed like an abstract, dry document. Now she is watching TV coverage about a major scandal in the federal government that involves constitutional issues. Suddenly Nancy understands what the concepts of "separation of powers" and "checks and balances" mean in the real world.

- Jerry's mother lives in a nursing home. He visits her regularly and occasionally volunteers to play the piano and lead a sing-along at the weekly social hour. Soon Jerry develops a sensitive grasp of how music can speak to the hearts of older people, especially to the most impaired, and how it helps them to communicate feelings that would otherwise go unexpressed.

All of the people in these examples are letting life be their teacher. Because they are open to their experience—whether it be a minor crisis (bounced checks), a marvelous joy (the birth and growth of a baby), or a major sorrow (a parent's dying process)—they are growing in knowledge, insight, and skills.

Those who can draw meaning and growth even out of seemingly devastating events rather than retreat from life in fear are the deepest learners. Author Molly Dee Rundle expressed this quality of openness to experience that leads to fullness in living:

> Sometimes we are prisoners in prisons of our own design. We've carefully built our walls; we've made our prison safe and comfortable and then we have chosen to lock ourselves inside. And we do not call it a prison at all, we call it our home or work or responsibility. We are very careful to post guards so that nothing threatens the security of our prison. Some of us live and die there and suppose that we have been happy and that living was good.
>
> But sometimes, something or someone happens to us and the walls are shattered, and we lie helpless and exposed . . . in view are new horizons, new ideas, new experiences. When this happens many of us quickly gather the stones and rebuild our prison and retreat inside, but some few look around and crawl out of the rubble and gaze into the distance and wonder what "stuff" the world is made of. They venture out to taste and smell and feel. These people never build prisons again. They are willing to risk the

Describe three lessons you have learned in the school of life during the past six months.

Ignorance is a prison. All of us have experienced our own ignorance. Write about one time when your lack of knowledge about something has confined and hurt you.

hurt and possible failure of living and loving and dying with no guarantee of safety. They live with only the promise that there is fullness in living. They take the risk and choose life.

To be a lifelong learner in the school of life is to choose freedom over the prison of security and sameness.

In addition to the chances for informal learning from experience, opportunities abound for adults to learn formally as well. After the years of high school, college or technical school, or graduate school are over, many people take advantage of continuing education courses, community classes, certificate programs, parish sessions, and training programs sponsored by employers.

Whatever means we use to learn, formal or informal, the growth of learning frees us for a fuller life.

Learning and Our Dream

What Learning Does for Us

The moment we gave our first cry at birth, we learned our first lesson. We felt hands touching us, a body warming us. As we experienced hunger, we cried. Instinctively we nursed. That satisfied our hunger. We struggled to focus our eyes on our parents. Although we did not have any words for the people and things that we saw, tasted, touched, heard, and smelled, we were learning.

By our nature, we are learners. From birth on, learning is life-giving; it enables us not only to survive but also to have a full life. Here are some of the things that learning does for us:

Offers choices: Acting out of ignorance is like walking into a pitch-black room expecting to put together a thousand-piece jigsaw puzzle. Learning is the light that allows us to see the pieces. We may still have a hard time doing the puzzle, and perhaps we will decide not to complete it. But without light, we cannot see to make the choice. Learning helps us to see clearly and thus gives us the chance to choose among options in life.

Overcomes fear: Walking in the dark can be fearsome. If we walk blindly, we might crack our shin on the sharp corner of an end table or stub our toe on a chair leg. Living in the darkness of ignorance can be threatening, too. For example, ignorance of other cultures can lead to fear of people from those cultures, especially if they do not look, dress, speak, or act like

Describe an incident in which you experienced the freedom to choose that comes from knowledge.

us. By dispelling ignorance about what causes us to be fearful, learning opens the way for enriching experiences.

Gives competence: Competence (the eighth developmental task for young adults) is the ability to engage effectively in specific behaviors that lead to our important goals, our dream. Competence includes a working knowledge and the skills needed to accomplish our goals—from being a great softball player to being a good friend, from being a concert pianist to sewing patches on jeans, from leading a meeting to toilet training a child. Our dream will require some combination of intellectual, physical or manual, and social competencies. These competencies are the products of learning—whether in formal educational programs or in the school of life.

Helps us to cope with change: People change. Governments change. Technology changes. In fact, change seems to be one of life's few constants. If we are to cope with the challenges of such changes, lifelong learning is essential. At various points in life, we probably will need to know how to do the following:

- refocus relationships
- gain new job skills
- become accustomed to different work environments
- respond to new requirements of family members
- adapt to a changed standard of living

Learning enables us to cope with these types of adjustments.

Write an inventory of forty of your intellectual, physical, and social competencies: for example, using a computer graphics program, driving a car, helping people feel at ease. Then write your reflections on these questions:

- Could you add even more capabilities to this list?
- What do these competencies tell you about your own ability to learn?
- Which of these competencies will be most important for you throughout life?

Getting Ready: As Important as Getting There

A few years ago, a group of adventurers trekked by dogsled to the North Pole. For years they had dreamed of attempting this feat. Their desire to fulfill this quest was overwhelming. Rather than being swept up in delusions of easy success, the group worked through every aspect of the trip before daring to head across the vast wasteland of ice, deep crevices, bone-freezing winds, and whiteness that could cause snow blindness.

In preparation for the trek, each piece of equipment was checked, tested, and double-checked. The sled dogs were carefully tried and selected. The team of explorers made practice runs, got to know each member's strengths and weaknesses, and worked their bodies into peak condition. They also charted their journey as meticulously as possible—given the fact that ice packs shift constantly. Only when these extensive preparations were complete did the team embark on its great adventure.

In much the same way, we all need to prepare as completely as possible if we want to reach our dream. Great dreams require great preparation, extensive competencies, and continual learning.

Our Capacity to Learn

The Marvelous Human Brain

Barring the effects of physical damage to the brain, each human being has an almost limitless capacity to learn. Our brains can store and retrieve vast quantities of information. Just as important, the human brain allows us to make complex language with which to communicate our experiences—our learning. We are the "learning and languaging animal" without equivalent.

Ordinary persons learn and can use more than fifty thousand words. In many countries, people learn several languages besides their native tongue. We not only absorb language but also read and write with it and measure and perform complex calculations. We acquire complicated mental-physical skills like driving a car, typing, tying our shoes, dancing, or weaving. Generally we are not aware of how much we really do know and the complexity of the apparently simple skills we have learned.

We learn because our senses send messages to the brain, which remembers these messages and stores the information. Our memory, through conscious thought and even dreams, helps us to retrieve what we know. All of our actions—except the most automatic, like breathing and digesting—require learning. Clearly the brain is a marvelous gift.

Another interesting facet of the brain is that it functions in two modes. Developmental psychologists have discovered that the right side of the brain functions differently than the left side does. Furthermore, each of us has developed one side more fully than the other side. These differences in development also account for our unique ways of learning.

Left-brain thinking: The left side of the brain controls the motor functions of the right side of the body. In addition, it processes information in a logical, linear way—one piece of information at a time. The left side gives us our sense of time and our capacities to use language and perform mathematical functions. Logical and analytical thinking are centered in the left side of the brain. Much of formal schooling is dedicated to developing the left side.

Left-brain Thinking
logical
linear
temporal
linguistic
mathematical
analytical

Right-brain Thinking
imaginative
synthetic
spatial
conceptual
artistic
intuitive

Right-brain thinking: The right side of the brain directs the motor functions of the left side of the body. In terms of perception, the right side of the brain grasps the big picture, synthesizing many ideas, images, and pieces of information into a whole picture. The perception of space is a right-brain function. Our gestures, facial expressions, tone of voice, and other aspects of body language originate there. Right-brain thinking is intuitive and conceptual. Passions and dreams have a home in the right side. Artists, musicians, and craftspersons have highly developed right-brain functions. The right side of the brain is given less emphasis in schools—except in art, music, drama, and a few other classes (like religion).

Learning with both sides of the brain: To be whole, fully alive learners, we need to develop the capacities of both sides of the brain. For instance:

- In writing a composition, Kathleen, a primarily left-brain thinker, starts with a logical outline of the topic and works through it, systematically filling in each point. But Roy, who is mostly a right-brain thinker, lets creative ideas about the topic just flow out of his pen onto the paper, without regard to logical order. Kathleen's thinking is more controlled; Roy's is more spontaneous. Consequently, they will write two very different papers.
- Jose, who can operate equally well from the left and the right sides of the brain, uses this approach: He first allows the spontaneous flow of ideas and images onto paper, giving full dominion to the creative, intuitive side of his brain. Then he organizes these ideas and images into a logical order, discarding what doesn't seem to fit and adding new ideas as they relate to the logical outline.

Kathleen and Roy could learn a lot from Jose about using the potential of both sides of the brain.

Saying Yes to Our Unique Potential

We are wonderfully gifted with a whole gamut of ways to think and learn. However, to use these gifts we first need to acknowledge our almost limitless capacity to learn. John W. Gardner, an internationally known educator and psychologist, made this comment about the tendency to ignore our potential:

> It is a sad but unarguable fact that most human beings go through their lives only partially aware of the full range of their abilities. As a boy in California I spent a good deal

Which of your thinking processes is more developed, the right brain or the left brain? Write an assessment of your thinking, focusing on the side that needs encouragement and what you might do to encourage it.

Write your reflections on what Gardner says about potential as it relates to you personally. Do you have potential that is untapped?

of time in the Mother Lode country [the location of a principal ore deposit], and like every boy of my age I listened raptly to the tales told by the old-time prospectors in that area, some of them veterans of the Klondike gold rush. Every one of them had at least one good campfire story of a lost gold mine. The details varied: the original discoverer had died in a mine, or had gone crazy, or had been killed in a shooting scrape, or had just walked off thinking the mine worthless. But the central theme was constant: riches left untapped. I have come to believe that those tales offer a paradigm [model] of education as most of us experience it. The mine is worked for a little while and then abandoned. (*Self-Renewal,* pages 10–11)

Learning, as Gardner suggested, begins with an acknowledgment that we can learn. Some students, because of poor performance in school, give up on themselves as learners. They believe that they have no potential to grow, thus abandoning their gold mine.

Ironically, though, some people who do not believe in themselves as learners in a school setting may be wizards in other settings—in the school of life. Perhaps the high school environment simply does not give them enough room to take off. A person may finally progress once he or she identifies a passionately loved interest, whether that is in college, technical school, or a nonacademic setting. Consider this quite realistic conversation from the twentieth reunion of the high school class of 1968:

"How about that? Maureen Fitzgerald as a department store manager! Remember how she would sit in the back of our history class and never speak to anyone? Who would have thought she would go on to be a manager?"

"Yeah, it's amazing. She said she took a Dale Carnegie speaking course that made all the difference for her. But listen to this miracle. Remember how Al Johnson scraped through basic business math? Now he's a millionaire!"

Real-life examples of such surprises are people like Saint Thomas Aquinas, the most influential Catholic theologian, and Albert Einstein, the great physicist. Aquinas, who would later write huge volumes about all aspects of theology, was dubbed the Dumb Ox as a schoolboy. Einstein barely graduated from a university because he had a hard time passing the life science classes. Each of us, like these brilliant people, has a unique, perhaps not always smooth, path to learning. We need to affirm that fact and not needlessly compare ourselves to other people.

Learning: Our Own Task

Just as our dream and the quest to fulfill it are unique to each of us and ultimately are our own responsibility, so too is learning. No one else can learn for us. Parents and the courts can force young people to go to school until a certain age, but they cannot force them to learn.

Here are some guidelines for taking responsibility for your own learning:

*   *Form habits of learning.* Listen and read carefully, develop self-discipline, and foster a curiosity about the whys and hows of things.
*   *Set goals.* Decide on a purpose for your life, whether it is a career goal or simply a skill that you want to have, and relate your learning to that purpose. Having a specific goal can motivate you to do even the most tedious practice drills or endless study and research.
*   *Take the initiative.* Take the opportunities available for learning, whether through new experiences, formal education (evening and Saturday college classes or job-training programs), or resources in the community (club and church workshops, museums, libraries).
*   *Be open.* Be receptive to the people and events around you; just as important, do not be afraid to look inward at your own world of emotions, fears, fantasies, virtues, and vices. Do not *pre-judge* by settling for first impressions of people or situations (this is prejudice). Be willing to dig deeper.
*   *Be flexible.* Be ready, if necessary, to change your way of thinking, to tolerate the ambiguity of venturing from the secure known to the insecure unknown. Remember, if scientists years ago had remained content with the cathode-ray tube, today we probably would not have the microchip or any of its related computer inventions.
*   *Have courage.* Recognize that learning is open-ended. It may lead you to a place you had not anticipated; it may take you into interests that people close to you do not share. Learning may cause you to ask questions that make others uncomfortable because you see the gap between what is and what could be. Be willing to go where the learning leads you.

Learning begins with an acknowledgment that we can learn.

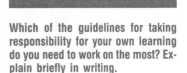

Which of the guidelines for taking responsibility for your own learning do you need to work on the most? Explain briefly in writing.

The Christian View: Learning to Be New Persons

In the Christian perspective, human beings are called to develop the full range of their potential, including their intelligence and talents. Saint Paul affirmed the importance of developing the gifts that God gave us:

> ... Lead a life worthy of the vocation to which you were called. With all humility and gentleness, and with patience, support each other in love. ...
>
> On each one of us God's favour has been bestowed in whatever way Christ allotted it. ...
>
> ... And to some, his "gift" was that they should be apostles; to some prophets; to some, evangelists; to some, pastors and teachers. ...
>
> *Your mind was to be renewed in spirit so that you could put on the New Man that has been created on God's principles,* in the uprightness and holiness of the truth. (Ephesians 4:1-2,7,11,23-24 [emphasis added])

In Paul's vision, our gifts were given for a purpose—the building of a loving and faithful community. Developing our potential, in his view, meant that *we become new persons,* with renewed minds in the spirit of God's holiness and truth. Learning—growth in knowledge, insight, and skills—is thus elevated beyond the mere acquisition of useful information, job skills, or sophistication. Learning is intended to transform us into Jesus' disciples.

Three questions can help us to recognize whether our learning is enabling us to become new persons. When we consider the kinds of learning that we are engaged in, we can ask ourselves whether the learning meets any of these criteria:

• Does the learning help me to value creation?
• Does the learning help me to serve humankind?
• Does the learning help me to gain wisdom?

Valuing Creation

Creation reflects the glory of God. Any learning that leads us to value creation more deeply is a way of praising God.

As an immediate example of this notion, try this exercise for a minute or two:

• Contemplate the knuckles of your right hand. (This may sound silly unless you realize what a miracle your hand is.)

Wiggle your fingers and then knot your hand into a fist. Imagine those knuckles working—the tendons stretching, the cartilage protecting the bones and preventing friction, the nerves sending messages from the brain to tell the hand to move, and the skin stretching and wrinkling to cover the knuckles. Even though scientists have become much more adept at making artificial joints, few professionals, if any, would boast that their products are better or more perfectly designed than your natural knuckles. Now, if you accept that God created your knuckles, and if you are truly struck with how wonderful they are, you probably appreciate God just a bit more.

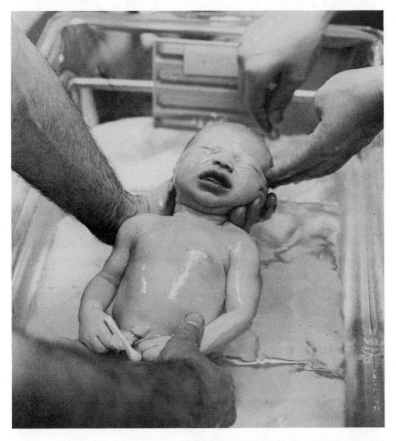

Learning that leads us to appreciate the wonders around us is ultimately praise to the creator of those wonders.

Learning that leads us to appreciate the wonders around us is ultimately praise to the creator of those wonders. Examples of formal learning in the sciences immediately come to mind: biology, chemistry, physics, anatomy, psychology, sociology, geology, astronomy, and so on. But informal learning that enables us to value creation might be such things as learning to canoe, carve wood, or plant a garden.

Christian faith beckons us to develop our potential, to praise God by valuing creation and serving humanity in wisdom.

Serving Humankind

It is quite possible for highly educated people to use their knowledge for evil purposes, to destroy rather than to serve humankind:

- Educated professionals built the gas chambers in which millions of people were killed during the Nazi era in Germany.
- Nazi medical doctors performed ghastly experiments on prisoners in concentration camps.
- The atomic bomb and chemical weapons were developed by educated people.

In other words, learning in itself does not guarantee that the knowledge gained will be used for the good of humankind.

In the Christian worldview, learning is for the service of humankind, whether it is learning that will affect masses of humanity or learning that will help one life. So a doctor studying and researching to develop a cure for AIDS and a young parent learning the skills of parenthood through experience and the wisdom of other people are both developing their knowledge, insight, and skills for the benefit of human beings. Learning is aimed at love, not at destruction.

Gaining Wisdom

In the Judeo-Christian tradition, learning should also help us to gain wisdom. For the Israelites, wisdom was knowledge of how to act, a skill in acting consistently with God's Law. As a consequence of this belief, the people of Israel were encouraged to pursue wisdom. This pursuit is depicted well in this passage from Ecclesiasticus, in which wisdom is described in feminine terms:

> Blessed is anyone who meditates on wisdom
>   and reasons with intelligence,
> who studies her ways in his heart
>   and ponders her secrets.
> He pursues her like a hunter
>   and lies in wait by her path;
> he peeps in at her windows
>   and listens at her doors;
> he lodges close to her house
>   and fixes his peg in her walls;
> he pitches his tent at her side
>   and lodges in an excellent lodging;

he sets his children in her shade
    and camps beneath her branches;
he is sheltered by her from the heat
    and in her glory he makes his home.
                    (Ecclesiasticus 14:20–27)

The people of Israel realized acutely that achieving wisdom is a lifelong process that requires dedicated pursuit. Searching for God's ways and living wisely by those ways took continual study of God's word and of creation. However, wisdom is well worth pursuing; it is protection, comfort, and glory.

The Christian tradition flows from the Jewish tradition. Wisdom for Christians is not just passive receptiveness to the truth. A wise Christian is one who not only *thinks* wisely but *acts* wisely, that is, in obedience to God's law of love. As Jesus said, ". . . 'My mother and my brothers are those who hear the word of God and put it into practice' " (Luke 8:21). Likewise, Paul told his friend Titus, "All [Christians] must also learn to occupy themselves in doing good works for their practical needs, and not to be unproductive" (Titus 3:14). Christian wisdom leads us right back to service to humankind.

Christian faith beckons us to develop our potential—to become new persons, disciples of Jesus who praise God by valuing creation and who serve humanity in wisdom. The call to develop our skills is deeply imbedded in the Christian tradition.

List two of the most significant or memorable learning experiences that you have had and explain what made them so. In addition, answer this question:
- Have these experiences helped you to become wiser?

Catholic Christianity has a rich tradition, and the Scriptures are an endless source of wisdom. Are there areas of religion that you would like to explore in your lifelong learning? If so, which areas?

Developing Skills for Life

Career-Content Skills

As a high school senior, naturally you may be thinking in very specific terms about the skills you will need in order to make a living and to use your potential in satisfying, contributing ways. You are probably focusing on **career-content skills,** that is, those skills that belong to a specific job. For example, you might be thinking about the skills involved in auto repair, computer programming, nursing, sales, personnel management, music education, physical therapy, electrical engineering, forestry management, and so on.

Such skills are learned in technical schools, colleges and universities, and on-the-job training. Finding a particular career-content area and mastering its skills will probably occupy a good deal of your time and energy over the next few years.

Transferable Life Skills

Knowledge that may be less obvious to you is that of **transferable life skills**. These are the skills that we carry with us from one job to another or from one situation to another—such things as organizing time, carefully observing, cooperating in a group, manipulating objects with dexterity, analyzing, persuading, listening, making decisions, and creating. Transferable skills help us to manage our lives productively. We may develop them in the process of formal schooling or in the context of other experiences.

In a world that witnesses a technological revolution every decade, the crucial nature of transferable life skills becomes apparent. Those persons who have acquired many transferable skills are in the best position to adapt to a changing world. They bring a wealth of applicable skills with them wherever they go; they can flex with the changing opportunities for employment, with new personal situations and demands, and with evolving challenges for service in their communities.

Study your local newspaper. List all of the learning opportunities that are described there: for example, announcements about workshops.

Persons who have acquired many transferable skills are in the best position to adapt to a changing world.

Transferable Skills: Building Blocks of Career-Content Skills

The significance and broad applicability of transferable skills does not discount the importance of career-content skills. Pursuing a particular field of interest and developing a certain expertise in that field are highly advisable. However, consider this: Every career-content skill can be broken down into its component parts, which are transferable life skills. So by developing transferable skills (in the context of school, volunteer activities, a hobby, or a job), you are actually creating the building blocks of career-content skills. Take a part-time job as an example. A high school student who has an after-school job in a fast-food restaurant is developing these skills:

- memory (recalling orders, how much lettuce to put on a double burger, and how long to let the french fries cook)
- listening (paying attention to instructions and requests)
- organization (figuring out how to accomplish all of the tasks that need to be done during a rush period)
- teamwork (pitching in to get the work done rather than sticking only to individually assigned tasks)
- manual dexterity (quickly and efficiently assembling twenty-five burgers on demand)

That student's transferable skills of memory, listening, organization, teamwork, and manual dexterity are likewise the building blocks for a host of extremely diverse career-content areas.

Similarly, required college courses that seem irrelevant to a future career often offer the opportunity to build transferable skills necessary to that occupation. For instance, biology can be seen as relevant to a future career in sales. A biology student develops these transferable skills:

- cooperation (doing lab exercises with a partner)
- comparing and contrasting (distinguishing a paramecium from an amoeba)
- analysis (determining the composition of cells under a microscope)
- communication (writing accurate answers on a test or giving an oral report in class)
- memory (memorizing lists of names or species)

If you think about it, each of these skills can be applied to a career in sales.

We need to look at the experiences ahead of us as chances to develop transferable life skills—not only for their usefulness in a future career but also for their value in enabling us to become competent, well-rounded persons. It might be interesting to conduct an inventory of ourselves to determine which transferable skills we have already acquired to some degree and which ones we would like to develop or improve on. On this page is a partial listing of such skills.

Transferable Life Skills

organizing
reading critically
writing clearly
speaking articulately
decision-making
creating
listening
giving feedback
initiating relationships
remembering
observing
eye-hand coordinating
setting priorities
evaluating
empathizing
praising
questioning
imitating
playing
manipulating physical objects
cooperating
analyzing
comparing
tolerating ambiguity
persuading
negotiating
leading

Which of the transferable life skills listed here have you already developed to some degree? List them, and next to each one, write several situations in which you might need to use that skill.

Key Skills: Decision-Making and Creating

Two skills stand out from the list of transferable life skills as deserving special emphasis in a course on lifestyles—decision-making and creating. As skills that are essential to fulfilling a person's dream, they need to be learned and cultivated by all of us. But we can also use the processes of decision-making and creating to learn even more.

Decision-Making

Dilemmas present themselves to us every day. Some are simple, like deciding what to wear to school. Others are far more complex, like whether to break up with a girlfriend or boyfriend or whether to change jobs. Often we make decisions about difficult dilemmas without knowing how we make them:

- We simply go with our gut reaction.
- We muddle through and somehow come to a decision that may or may not feel right.
- We remain paralyzed and never do decide—which is a decision *not* to decide.

Developing a conscious approach to making difficult decisions is a crucial life skill. In the midst of the conflicting pushes and pulls of a dilemma, we may not have a clear head and may fall into a decision without weighing all of the factors carefully. Following a deliberate process is a way for us to stay in charge. Also, difficult decisions inevitably involve questions of values. So the wisdom of Christian values—the central value being love—also needs to be brought into the decision-making process.

To see a conscious process of **decision-making** in a concrete situation, consider Sandy's dilemma:

Sandy is confused about whether she should buy a car to use at college next year. Finally she comes upon an article in a magazine that outlines the steps for decision-making. Over the next few weeks, she goes through each of the steps. Here are Sandy's thoughts at each point in the process.

1. Define the dilemma and the issues involved.

- This is the situation: I'm going to be on a campus in a small town. The town's public buses don't run very often and not at all on the weekends. There's no way of getting to the city

Developing a conscious approach to making difficult decisions is a crucial life skill.

thirty miles away for entertainment or shopping without a car. I can't guarantee that I will find rides home with other people, either. I sure could use a car to give me some freedom.

- On the other hand, buying a car means that I need *money*. If I use my savings now for a car, that means I have to take a bigger loan for tuition. Plus, a lot of my expense money for college, the money I earn in my work-study job, will go right into car repairs and gas.

2. Gather information about the dilemma.

- I've looked at the prices of used cars and talked to my friends and my parents about how much it costs to keep up an older

Decision-Making Process

1. Define the dilemma and the issues involved.

2. Gather information about the dilemma.

3. Get in touch with the values you most cherish.

4. Seek advice.

5. Propose a range of options.

6. Pray; ask for God's wisdom in making your decision.

7. Make the decision.

8. Take the action and evaluate the results.

car like I could afford. I've also talked with people who live at the college to see how they get around. The students with cars can go where they want to go when they want to, but most of them have to have an extra part-time job besides work-study to afford the use of a car.

- The students without cars say that they wish they had a car but that they manage without one. They walk a lot and catch rides by paying for gas, and they've discovered a lot of things to do on campus. As for getting home, they can't always go when they want to. Sometimes those students have to take a Greyhound bus. They say they don't feel so pressured for money, though. They don't need an extra job.

3. Get in touch with the values you most cherish.

- I really treasure my freedom, but I also value being able to go to college without so much pressure for money. I guess it comes down to what is going to be best for me and for my relationships with other people.

4. Seek advice.

- I talked with my brother Aaron, who went without a car during his first three years of college. He thinks that if I can possibly manage without a car, I shouldn't buy one. Aaron said that he got almost no sleep during his senior year because he worked two jobs to afford a car. He had freedom but no time to enjoy it.

5. Propose a range of options.

- If I buy a car, I could do this:
  a. take a bigger student loan each semester and have larger payments later
  b. work an extra job at school besides my work-study job and take a lighter course load
  c. work an extra summer job besides my regular one to earn more money
- If I don't buy a car, I could do this:
  a. go home when I can find a ride and take a Greyhound bus now and then
  b. catch rides around town or to the city and chip in for gas
  c. take my bike to college and start walking more often

6. Pray; ask for God's wisdom in making your decision.

- God, I am really pulled both ways on this. Please give me the wisdom to decide what to do. Help me to love myself as much as you love me and to do the thing that's going to be best for me.

7. Make the decision.

• After all of this thinking, it's really clear to me that I'd rather not buy a car. Freedom is important to me, but I think that if I had a car, I'd be more independent but very hassled. I'm going to manage without a car, using all the ways that I've thought of already and maybe some other ways that I'll think of when I get to college.

8. Take the action and evaluate the results.

• After a semester at college without a car, I can see that it's a mixed situation. The people who have cars have it good—especially if their parents are paying for the car! But I am more independent than I thought I would be. I can go anyplace around here by bike when it's warm, and walking is great; it's good for me. I get to the city only occasionally, but there are loads of things to do on campus. I'm not so busy that I have no time for fun. In my senior year, when I have an internship, maybe I'll need a car, but for now I'm fine without it.

Sandy's choice is not necessarily the decision that everyone would, or should, make. Each person's situation is unique. Each one's answer to the question, "What is going to be best for me and for my relationships with other people?" will reflect different needs and personal circumstances. The issues are not black and white but gray. Going through the process of deliberation helps to clarify the issues and discover what is really most important in a person's life. Such a conscious process is a learning experience in itself.

Write about one decision that you are having difficulty making. Using the eight steps for decision-making, try to arrive at a decision. Make notes about your thinking as you go through each step.

Creating

Many of us might not think of ourselves as creative, but we all have that little spark in us somewhere that wants to bring something new into being. Finding a new unity in things is exciting, whether you are composing a song for a rock band, writing an insightful paper for a class, or dreaming up a new game to use with the young kids at the recreation center where you are a summer counselor. The ability to create is a skill that transfers into personal satisfaction, interesting employment, and a sense of contribution to the world.

"Wonders with Nothing"

The award-winning science-fiction and fantasy writer Ursula K. Le Guin said that "the open soul can do wonders with nothing." One of the great myths about creativity is that an innovator, artist, or musician must be highly educated, well traveled, and widely experienced. Many of the greatest writers of the twentieth century were just the opposite. Among the Nobel prize winners for literature, John Steinbeck, William Faulkner, and Ernest Hemingway never finished college. Emily Dickinson, the very influential American poet, hardly ever left her house after she was twenty years old. These people had open souls and minds. They were learners because they were sensitive to every experience and saw all of life as their school.

Creative people seek to know as much about life as possible. They have inquisitive minds that are never totally satisfied with what they already know, so they ask a lot of questions. Creativity begins with openness to external reality and to a person's own feelings, ideas, intuitions, or images. Creative people also develop appropriate skills necessary to their field. For instance, a would-be sculptor may envision beautiful statues in her or his mind, but if she or he cannot use a chisel, weld, cast bronze, or mold plastic, she or he will never be a creator.

Creative people are sensitive to every experience and see all of life as their school.

Steps in Creating

Certain steps can be observed in most creative enterprises. These steps do not necessarily occur in the order in which they are listed below, and they may be repeated at different points in the process. With that in mind, this outline of steps in creating gives us a way to sort out what happens in the usually untidy (but productive) process of **creating**:

1. *Preparation to innovate or create,* during which a person gains the factual knowledge and skills needed to deal with the problem or idea
2. *Concentrated work* on the problem or idea (creativity is at least 90 percent work)
3. *Rest and retreat* from the problem or idea—a time to clear the mind and emotions, which usually ends up as a period for incubating new strategies
4. *An "aha" experience,* during which sudden new insight is gained, accompanied by exhilaration
5. *Trying out* the insight or approach that is the result of the previous steps to see how it works, appears, or sounds

Russian composer Peter Tchaikovsky described composing in this way:

> Generally speaking, the germ of a future composition comes suddenly and unexpectedly [step 4]. If the soil is ready [step 1]—that is to say, if the disposition for work is there [step 2]—it takes root with extraordinary force and rapidity, shoots up through the earth, puts forth branches, leaves, and, finally, blossoms [step 5]. . . .
>
> We must *always* work, and a self-respecting artist must not fold his hands on the pretext that he is not in the mood.

Whether the effort is by a young woman struggling to come up with a rock song for her band or by a genius like Tchaikovsky—the creative process essentially requires openness, preparation, leisure, insight, and work.

Out of the Rut: Tips to Foster Creativity

Some practical ideas can encourage creativity. Use these ideas with the knowledge that each person's approach to creativity is uniquely her or his own.

Give your intuition and imagination room to function. Many of us distrust our intuition and imagination, but creative thinking is not possible without them. To give intuition and imagination room means to use leisure time that is not crowded with things to do. Creativity grows in the quiet, unhurried space of a walk in the woods, a quiet sit in a rocking chair, or some other uncluttered moment.

Have a creative space. Most creative people set aside a definite time and space in which they are most productive. Some writers have their creative peak early in the morning. Many authors have a special chair or desk at which they discover their best ideas.

Interact with innovative people. Stimulating companions can give a charge to your work. People who get enthusiastic about their ideas will usually get you excited, too. Listening to mindless chatter can stifle creative thinking.

Ask questions. If you can gather enough courage to make inquiries, especially of other creative people, you can learn a lot that might be useful for your own projects. Practice openended questions that cause people to talk. Questions like, "What

Think about your friends and acquaintances. List the five or six people who most stimulate your creativity when you are with them. Then brainstorm, writing down your ideas about how you can spend more time with these people. If you have a hard time naming such people, write about what you can do to be around more creative people.

do you think of . . ." are better than "Did you like . . ." The first question gives the respondent room to talk; the second calls only for a yes or no answer. Most people like to share their ideas when they feel others are interested, so asking other people about their ideas is a form of compliment to them.

Break out of ruts. Eating two slices of bread with peanut butter and jelly for breakfast every morning, parting our hair in the same place forever, and coming home from school the same way every day are examples of the ruts we can fall into. Some small ways of stretching our imagination would be to try old-fashioned oatmeal with honey and raisins for breakfast, comb our hair differently some morning, or go down new streets on the way home from school. All we accomplish by walking in a rut is making the rut deeper and deeper.

Set and keep deadlines for yourself. A deadline helps to push you along to get things done. Creative people make things happen. Talking about a project is not creativity; doing it is. Without deadlines, our energies tend to drain away too easily.

Focus your attention and dig deeply. To be a creator, you have to know more about your particular project than the average person. You have to develop a keen relish for learning in your special area of interest. Innovators focus their attention and are constantly picking up new information and insights. Many creative people have whole files of notes and ideas that they have collected about their interests.

See problems and conflicts as opportunities for creativity. Too many times we tend to view problems and conflicts as things to be avoided. Many creative people are actually spurred to action by questions and adversity.

A creative person dares to be an adventurer, willing to risk new concepts and questions. However, he or she is also a disciplined worker. As with decision-making, the skill of creating provides the tools for further and deeper learning.

A creative person dares to be an adventurer but must also be a disciplined worker.

Next Year: Opportunities and Adjustments

For many high school graduates, the first year after high school is one of the most challenging, interesting, traumatic, and growthful years of their lives. Legally and psychologically, by choice or by necessity, the graduate quickly assumes a much greater degree of independence and responsibility than she or he has ever had.

If you continue your schooling next year or take a job, you will be faced with tremendous opportunities for growth, both from added responsibilities and from the changed circle of people with whom you will interact. Because the next chapter focuses on work, most of the discussion here will center on being a student next year at an institution of further learning.

Becoming a First-Year Student Again

If you attend a nursing or technical school, a community college, or a state university, you will be a first-year student again. You will have the chance to direct your learning along new pathways and to escape ruts that now dissatisfy you.

Consider the opportunities for new learning. At a large state university, you may have as many as 350 majors from which to choose. Even at a smaller technical school, you will be able to select from a wide array of fields of study. Having a reasonably clear sense of your talents, your skills, and your dream can help you to focus your energies. However, one exciting aspect of further education is that you have the opportunity to satisfy your curiosity about many subjects.

Further schooling gives you a chance to direct your learning along new pathways and to escape ruts that now dissatisfy you.

Flexibility About Majors

Standard advice for first-year college students is to be flexible about choosing a major and to avoid locking in to a major right away.

- Roughly 70 percent of all college students change their major at least once.
- About 20 percent of all first-year students change their major from the time they apply to a college until the time they register for courses.
- Nearly 50 percent of all college graduates change their career plans almost immediately after college and enter fields that have little apparent relationship to their major.

These figures point out that college can be much more than job training. It is a time to deepen basic skills like reading and communicating (writing, speaking, using computers and other media) and a time to explore many of life's important questions (in subjects such as theology, philosophy, literature, art, music, psychology, sociology).

Becoming fixed in a major before you really know what you

want and where your talents lie can have detrimental effects. When you finally do switch to a major that suits you, you may lose credits from specialized courses in your previous major. Also, prematurely jumping into a major may mean that you must take courses for which you have little talent and less interest. As a first-year student, enjoy the opportunity to dip into a wide array of general courses that can help you to build skills and choose your future.

The best way to choose a major is to study a subject that gives you the most energy and about which you are most enthusiastic. Later, you can explore the application of your skills in summer jobs or internships. Most college professors can give examples such as English majors who are outstanding salespersons for steel or pharmaceutical companies and physics majors who end up as lawyers. Thinking and communication skills, rather than knowledge of a particular subject area, are perhaps the most important outcomes of further education.

New Responsibilities

Different responsibilities in the first year of college or technical school provide other learning experiences. Because further education is voluntary and because most programs do not follow an eight-to-five schedule, many decisions are placed with the student. Below is a list of some decisions that students—especially those living away from home—have to make every day:

- when to get up in the morning
- whether to eat or skip breakfast
- whether to attend or cut classes
- when and how much to study
- whether to drink alcoholic beverages
- whether to exercise
- how much sleep to get
- whether to keep the room clean
- whether to have premarital sex
- what courses to choose
- whether to see an adviser
- whether to drop or add courses

Some of these decisions may seem trifling and simple, but with less parental supervision, many students have a hard time managing them. Coping with more responsibility is a wonderful learning experience, but it can be difficult for those unsure of who they are and what their goals are.

Interview a first-year technical school or college student. Find out about the adjustments, new responsibilities, valuable lessons, and frustrations connected with his or her experience of further schooling. Put the interview in written form.

A Widening Circle of Friends

The new relationships that you will form next year will provide vivid learning experiences, too. In fact, friends, reference groups (clubs, organizations, teams), and general student culture have a major impact on personal development. You will learn more about who you are and what you can do as your circle of relationships widens. From one relationship, you might enter into the world of canoeing and hiking, conservation, or politics. Others might involve you in discussions of values and religion or help you to understand yourself as a communicator. Still other friends might be card players who show you the ins and outs of cribbage or poker. You can learn from all relationships.

Essential to making further education a complete learning experience—socially, intellectually, physically, and emotionally —is an openness to people and ideas, questions and conflicts. Along with this openness, knowing your goals will help you to have a security that can allow you to be flexible.

On the Job

If you begin a job next year rather than go to school, that choice likewise provides great opportunities for learning.

The most obvious opportunities are new job responsibilities, which can be very demanding. For instance, you may be responsible for operating extremely expensive equipment. Developing technical competence or increasing communication skills can

Essential to making further education a complete learning experience is an openness to people and ideas, questions and conflicts.

make you feel miles ahead of where you were in your senior year of high school. Your willingness to learn challenging skills at work will probably have a major influence on your job satisfaction.

If you move out of your family's home and become financially independent of your parents, other responsibilities will greet you—the pressing realities of monthly rent and other bills, cooking, shopping, cleaning, doing laundry, and providing for all of your needs. You may find yourself buying cookbooks and cooking for the first time, budgeting household expenses, or mastering the fine points of sewing curtains.

As with college students, your circle of friends will probably change next year, and with that will come new ways of thinking, relating to people, and enjoying life.

So if your path takes you to a new job next year, you will continue learning about people, ideas, and values. Your learning will, again, depend on an open and inquiring mind and a sense of what your goals are.

Fully alive persons are full-time learners.

The Adventure of a Lifetime

Life is full of chances to learn. In fact, scarcely an experience exists that cannot be turned into learning if we are open to what the opportunity has to offer.

The key to lifelong growth is to value our own unique potential to grow and then to take charge of our learning. The conscious development of knowledge and skills is an adventure worth the effort. Learning is life-giving and invigorating, and fully alive persons are full-time learners.

Psychologist John Gardner expressed this need for conscious dedication to becoming all that we can be through lifelong learning:

> Exploration of the full range of our own potentialities is not something that we can safely leave to the chances of life. It is something to be pursued systematically, or at least avidly, to the end of our days. We should look forward to an endless and unpredictable dialogue between our potentialities and the claims of life. . . . And by potentialities I mean not just skills, but the full range of our capacities for sensing, wondering, learning, understanding, loving and aspiring. (*Self-Renewal,* page 11)

Review Questions

1. What is learning?

2. What is meant by the school of life? Why is learning in this school important?

3. List and describe four things that learning does for us.

4. Cite two examples listed in the chapter that illustrate how marvelous the human brain is.

5. Describe the differences between left-brain and right-brain thinking.

6. As suggested by Gardner's quote on pages 143–144, where does learning begin?

7. What aspect of learning do the examples of Saint Thomas Aquinas and Albert Einstein illustrate?

8. List and explain the six guidelines for taking responsibility for your own learning.

9. From a Christian perspective, what three questions can help us recognize whether our learning is helping us to become new persons?

10. What are career-content skills?

11. What are transferable life skills? Summarize one example from the chapter of how we can develop transferable skills in an activity.

12. List the eight steps for decision-making.

13. Describe the characteristics of creative people.

14. What are the five steps in the creative process?

15. Describe the eight tips that foster creativity.

16. What attitude about a major in college is recommended for first-year students?

17. In what ways can having a job after high school be a positive learning experience?

7 Work: Creating a New World

PEOPLE generally spend forty to fifty years of life working at various jobs and pursuing one or more careers. That represents about one hundred thousand hours of employed work. But work is significant for us not only in terms of the time it occupies in a lifetime but also in terms of the major role it plays in shaping our identity, forming significant relationships, and fulfilling our life dream.

Selecting a career is one of the key developmental tasks for young adults. If you go on to college after graduation from high school, a career choice may still be some years away. If you choose to study a job specialty in technical school or plan to get a job directly after high school, work issues are more immediate. Regardless of which path you will be taking next year, time spent now on thinking about the role of work in your life is time well spent.

A Place in the World

Many working people would probably agree with the following comments from Barbara, a woman in her thirties who has been a saleswoman and a market researcher. Her words convey the significance that work can have in human life:

> "To be occupied is essential. One should find joy in one's occupation. . . . Work has a [negative] sound. It shouldn't. I can't tell you how strongly I feel about work. . . .
>
> "Work has a dignity you can count upon. . . . There's quite a wonderful rhythm you can find yourself involved

Think of some people you know who love their work so much that it is a source of renewal for them. Write a brief description of each person.

in in the process of any kind of work. It can be waxing a floor or washing dishes. . . .

"Everyone needs to feel they have a place in the world. It would be unbearable not to. I don't like to feel [useless]. One needs to be needed. . . . Everyone must have an occupation.

"Love doesn't suffice. It doesn't fill up enough hours. . . . I don't think [we] can maintain [our] balance or sanity in idleness. Human beings must work to create some coherence." (Studs Terkel, *Working,* pages 422–424)

Purpose is what gives life coherence. **Work** is sustained effort that has a purpose; it typically involves something that *has to* be done. To the extent that our work is something we *love to* do and *want to* do, it becomes—like leisure—a source of renewal.

The purpose of work might be to produce a car, assist the elderly to get social-security benefits, design a lamp, wait on customers, teach English composition to high school students, or audit a company's financial books. Although the concept of work, in a broad sense, includes unpaid but purposeful effort (a parent caring for a child, a son doing the family dishes, a woman organizing a neighborhood crime watch, a child studying), in this chapter we will discuss work that is a person's usual means of earning a living.

Work has a purpose, so, in the words of Barbara, it "has a dignity you can count upon." Work generally enables people to "feel they have a place in the world" because they are needed to accomplish the purpose of their work.

Why Work?

We long for work that has dignity, even if we do not necessarily express ourselves in those terms. However, our motives for working are as varied as any other aspect of our personalities. Usually some combination of the following motives gives an individual reason to work:

- to earn money
- to fulfill ambitions
- to develop a sense of identity
- to do what one loves to do
- to build the earth
- to answer a call

Write about what you think each of the following people expects of you in terms of your future career:
- mother
- father
- grandparents
- closest friend (same sex)
- closest friend (other sex)
- two of your teachers (past or present)
- a brother or a sister

Look over your list of other people's expectations about your career, and write a brief reaction to each expectation. Write as if you were talking honestly and openly to these people about their views.

To Earn Money

Most of us work to earn money so that we can meet our basic needs. We must clothe and house ourselves and buy food and other fundamental goods and services. Though many people have dreams of wealth, most of us just hope to have enough money to live comfortably. Income is not a bad motive for work; it is a reality. Even when money is our primary motive, work can be fulfilling for other reasons as well. This is evident in the comments of Delores, a waitress:

"I became a waitress because I needed money fast and you don't get it in an office. My husband and I broke up and he left me with debts and three children. My baby was six months. [I needed] the fast buck, your tips. . . .

"I have to be a waitress. How else can I learn about people? How else does the world come to me? . . . Everyone wants to eat, everyone has hunger. And I serve them. . . .

"People imagine a waitress couldn't possibly think or have any kind of aspiration other than to serve food. When somebody says to me, 'You're great, how come you're *just* a waitress?' *Just* a waitress. I'd say, 'Why, don't you think you deserve to be served by me?' It's implying that he's not worthy, not that I'm not worthy. It makes me irate. I don't feel lowly at all. I myself feel sure. I don't want to change the job. I love it." (Terkel, *Working,* pages 294–295)

Delores needs to make money, but she enjoys her work and sees it as a service. Her job has meaning for her.

To Fulfill Ambitions

Many people see work as a way to fulfill their ambitions.

- An engineer who has always wanted to work in the space program and finally has the chance to do so after college finds work meaningful and energizing.
- A young man who has desired since childhood to be just like his third-grade teacher begins to fulfill this ambition in his first year of classroom teaching.

The ambition to do some particular work may be part of a life dream.

Do you have an ambition that you have always wanted to fulfill? If so, write about that ambition and how you might fulfill it through work.

To Develop a Sense of Identity

Work is one way that we clarify who we are. Work gives us an arena within which to answer these questions:

- What specific talents or skills do I have or could I develop?

Interview two people who have had a minimum of five years of full-time working experience. Ask them these two questions:
• What have you learned about yourself as a person through your work?
• What have you learned about the workplace and what it means to be a worker?

• What characteristics do I possess that are particularly appreciated or admired by other people?
• How will I react in a given situation?

A job enables us to develop a sense of identity. For instance:

• A month ago, Wanda began her job as a medical clerk in a busy, understaffed emergency room of a major metropolitan hospital. She has been observing the reactions of other emergency-room staff members when patients or families approach them to get information, complain about a long wait, and so on. Some of the employees resent these "intrusions" and want to "put those complainers in their place." Other staff members stay calm and are helpful. Wanda herself has developed a real knack for soothing patients and family members when they are upset by taking a genuine interest in them and their concerns. It is a part of herself that she had never realized before this job.

To Do What One Loves to Do

People who love their jobs tend to work with a special outlook. They bring to their tasks a joy and commitment not found in individuals who feel constrained to work by circumstances. People who enjoy their jobs are renewed by their work. Someone once said, "Happiness is being paid to do what you would do anyway."

Unfortunately, love of work does not exist for everyone. Delores, the waitress, said that she loved her work, but all of us probably have been served by waiters or waitresses who clearly did not. Perhaps their curt answers or bored expressions were clues that they were not happy. The problem might have been the conditions of the work itself, the attitude that the worker brought to the job, or a poor match between the job and the talents of the worker.

To Build the Earth

The desire to build the earth—that is, to build conditions for a better life for the earth and its inhabitants—is another motivation for working.

• A veterinarian who helps farmers keep their animals healthy clearly does something good for society.
• A chemist who researches new, low-pollution fuels for cars performs an important service to the planet and to all life.
• A friendly and efficient nurse's aide in a retirement center meets patients' physical and emotional needs.

People in such positions frequently are very conscious that their work is contributing to a better world, and they find that awareness motivating.

In the above examples, it is easy to see the connection between the work and the building of a better world. However, service professions are not the only jobs that build the earth. All jobs performed with a dedication to quality can contribute to a better world (provided, of course, that the results of the work are not detrimental to life):

- Workers on an aircraft assembly line build the earth by doing their work carefully. If rivets are installed sloppily, the lives of future passengers could be endangered.
- Accountants who are honest and competent ensure that the government receives the taxes it needs to function and help their employers to run efficient businesses that employ people and provide goods and services.

When assembly-line workers and accountants do their jobs, they may not think of their work as contributing to a better world. However, to the extent that these individuals are dedicated to quality, their work does help to build the earth.

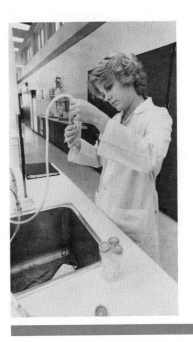

Jobs performed with a dedication to quality can contribute to a better world.

To Answer a Call

Some people see their work as more than a job. They see it as a vocation, or calling. They feel that some need in the world is calling to their very depths for a response and that this work is very specially *theirs* to do. These people may be in the helping professions—occupational therapists, nurses, social workers, teachers, religious, priests, or youth ministers—or they may be writers, park naturalists, or restorers of old buildings. What is important is the passionate conviction that these people have that they are *meant* to do this work.

Pat, the administrator of a school for dropouts, described his sense of calling in this way:

> "[I] drifted until '67. Suddenly I had the urge. At one time, I'd have said I had the calling. I started teaching. . . .
>
> "My work is everything to me. . . . I'd rather die for my work life than for my personal life. I guess you can't really separate them. . . .
>
> "I run into people who say how much they admire what I do. It's embarrassing. I don't make any judgments about my work, whether it's great or worthless. It's just what I do best. It's the only job I want to do. . . . This is my life."
> (Terkel, *Working*, pages 489, 491, 493)

Pat found it hard to neatly define how or why he received his calling, but his sense of vocation was very real and compelling.

Quoting one of the dozens of working people from his interviews, author Studs Terkel concluded, " 'I think most of us are looking for a calling, not a job. Most of us . . . have jobs that are too small for our spirit. Jobs are not big enough for people' " (*Working,* page xxiv).

We may debate Terkel's conclusion, but it is probably true that the human heart yearns for more than a paycheck from a job. Although we may work because of financial necessity, what keeps us happy and productive in a job is more complicated than money. Job satisfaction has to do with meaning.

On any given day, our motives for picking ourselves up and going to work may be quite mixed. What is essential for a high school senior is to consider which motivations will lead to joy, hope, service, and personal growth. This consideration can help when deciding on further studies or when beginning a job search.

A Christian Vision of Work

The Dignity of Work

In simplest terms, work has dignity and value when it meets some aspect of human need, when its purpose is to contribute to the common good. Society would not exist without work.

Work as Co-creation

The Christian tradition has long been concerned with the meaning and dignity of work. Work was one of the first topics of the Bible. The creation account given in Genesis describes God's commanding the newly formed humans:

> . . . "Be fruitful, multiply, fill the earth and subdue it. Be masters of the fish of the sea, the birds of heaven and all the living creatures that move on earth. . . . to you I give all the seedbearing plants . . . and all the trees with seedbearing fruit; this will be your food. . . ." And so it was. God saw all he had made, and indeed it was very good. . . . (Genesis 1:28–31)

Later, after sin had entered the human scene, being fruitful and taking on the role of caretakers of the earth became more difficult. Humankind had to work harder to survive. God said, " 'By the sweat of your face will you earn your food . . .' "

Write your reactions to each of the following statements:
- It is human nature for people to do as little work as they can get away with.
- People work primarily for money; recognition and satisfaction are much less important.

(Genesis 3:19). We are still charged with the same task by God, but the writers of Genesis explained that we work hard because of the disharmony in creation caused by sin. Yet creation itself is very good.

If we believe that all of creation is God's work, building the earth becomes a form of co-creation, a co-working with God. By working for the good of humankind and nature, of which we are a part, we become involved in the process of creation.

- Swimming instructors co-create when they teach children to swim. The instructors not only impart a survival skill but also help the children to better enjoy water, one of God's wonders. God created the water, and the instructors help kids to appreciate it.
- Plumbers who insulate pipes in newly constructed homes co-create when they ensure that the pipes will not burst in the hard freeze of winter. Their responsible work aids the physical and psychological well-being of the residents.

Jesus the Worker

Jesus was a model for working. As a young man, he probably became quite used to hard work. After all, he was raised in the household of a carpenter. If Jesus lived like other boys and young men of his era, he learned Joseph's trade and practiced it until he began his public ministry.

When Jesus' work became preaching the Good News, healing, and counseling his followers, his work probably seemed even harder. In three short years, he journeyed by foot throughout his country. Crowds gathered to hear him. Jesus not only gave spiritual nourishment to the people but in several instances also fed their physical hunger. He summarized the motivation for his lifework when he said, " 'I must proclaim the good news of the kingdom of God to the other towns too, because that is what I was sent to do' " (Luke 4:43). Jesus, a man of action, felt the urgent demands of his lifework because he was *sent* by God to do that work.

Building the earth becomes a form of co-creation, a co-working with God.

Neither Jesus nor the Apostles lived in luxury. For example, wherever Saint Paul was preaching, he usually sought work in order to feed himself. He did not want to be a burden on anyone. Paul was convinced that by working, Christians build the kingdom of God.

The Church's Affirmation of Work

The dignity of work has been a part of the Christian tradition from Saint Paul to Pope John Paul II. In his letter *On*

Human Work, Pope John Paul II commented that through work, people become more human. He added that work has dignity because through it, we are co-creating with God. Affirming the value of human work, John Paul II quoted one of the documents of Vatican Council II, *On the Church in the Modern World:*

> Christians are convinced that the triumphs of the human race are a sign of God's greatness and the flowering of [God's] own mysterious design. For the greater [humankind's] power becomes, the farther [our] individual and community responsibility extends. . . . People are not deterred by the Christian message from building up the world, or impelled to neglect the welfare of their fellows. They are, rather, more stringently bound to do these very things. (*The Church in the Modern World,* no. 34)

In the Christian worldview, work has the potential to contribute to the building up of the world and to the welfare of humanity. In other words, work can be an act of love.

Work and Loving

We can love through our work with an occupation that gives direct service to people in need; the works of mercy—feeding hungry people, clothing poor people, and so on—are clearly opportunities to love. Nursing, teaching, counseling, and social work fall into the same category. But what about other kinds of work, those jobs that do not provide direct service?

Our Choice of Work

Most jobs can be loving—that is, they can foster the good of other people—even if the work does not involve direct service to people in need.

- A contractor who builds solid, decent houses fosters the good of the people who will live in those houses.
- A medical lab technician who is careful about doing tests accurately serves the patients who depend on the results.

Unfortunately, not all work promotes the good of others; some work is destructive.

- The work of abortionists is not loving; it is killing.
- Scientists who develop weapons for biological warfare participate in what could become the future destruction of a population.

Most jobs can be loving, even if the work does not involve direct service to people in need.

List at least four types of work that you consider fundamentally evil, and write a brief explanation of why you think as you do.

- Managers of pharmaceutical companies that send dangerous or untested drugs to Third World countries cause potentially grave harm to people there.

Workers may face difficult moral dilemmas in their decisions about employment. Bishop Leroy Matthiesen of the Diocese of Amarillo, Texas, has dealt with that dilemma because his diocese is the site of a plant that is the nation's final assembly point for nuclear weapons. The bishop issued a plea in 1981:

> We urge individuals involved in the production and stockpiling of nuclear bombs to consider what they are doing, to resign from such activities, and to seek employment in peaceful pursuits.

Besides issuing this appeal to the conscience of assembly-line workers, the bishop also set up a fund to help those plant workers who, for reasons of conscience, had decided to resign but could not yet afford to leave their jobs. The fund provided them with immediate financial assistance and help in finding and paying for job placement counseling. As in this case, the Christian community needs to be particularly supportive of those faced with moral dilemmas about their choice of work.

The Way We Work

As mentioned earlier, working with a concern for quality is a way of caring. An auto mechanic who competently performs a wheel alignment shows care for another person—the customer. A careless alignment can cause problems for the car owner—tires may wear unevenly, steering may become difficult, and ultimately an accident could result. Working competently and responsibly is a form of caring.

Our Treatment of Co-workers

Workers also show care by the way that they treat co-workers. The basic principle of treating our neighbors as we ourselves wish to be treated applies in the workplace. We cannot be intimate friends with everyone at work, but we can be courteous and helpful. We can also show care for other workers by doing our jobs right. If an airline representative writes up a plane ticket correctly, the customer is well served; but in addition, other representatives or flight attendants will not have to handle an irate passenger whose flight arrangements have been mishandled.

Working competently and responsibly is a form of caring.

We are challenged to find work that truly expresses who we are and who we want to become.

The Promotion of Justice and Safety

Care for co-workers can be demonstrated in another way—through a concern for just and safe practices in the company.

- In 1984, a U.S.-owned chemical plant in Bhopal, India, had a disastrous leak of toxic gas, killing 1,757 people, sending more than 2,000 people to the hospital, and leaving 60,000 Bhopalis unable to do a full day's work for the rest of their life.
- In 1986, the space shuttle *Challenger* exploded, killing seven astronauts.

In both instances, human error, faulty design, and the cover-up of major problems caused disaster.

Each year, other tragedies on a smaller, less public scale are caused by negligence or by looking the other way in order to cater to deadline or profit pressures. A worker who points out or protests conditions that might lead to accidents has courage and great caring.

Promoting justice in wages and conditions for co-workers is also essential to caring. The church has long been a leader in this matter of justice. Pope John Paul II said this about worker solidarity:

> In order to achieve social justice . . . there is a need for ever new movements of solidarity of the workers and with the workers. This solidarity must be present whenever it is called for by the social degrading of the subject of work, by exploitation of the workers and by the growing areas of poverty and even hunger. The church is firmly committed to this cause for [it] considers it [to be the church's] mission, [its] service, a proof of [the church's] fidelity to Christ, so that [it] can truly be the "church of the poor."
> . . . In many cases [the poor] appear as a result of the violation of the dignity of human work . . . especially the right to a just wage and to the personal security of the worker and his or her family. (*On Human Work*, no. 8)

Solidarity with co-workers in the cause of justice and safety is seen by the church not only as a right but also as a duty.

We will find no scarcity of ways to love through our work, but the challenge is to find work that truly expresses who we are and who we want to become.

Toward a Life's Work

Making an informed decision about what work to choose can save us the tremendous pain of being in the wrong job. Sometimes people must take a job simply to make a living, and people rarely find a job in their youth that they stick with until retirement. In fact, most workers change not only jobs but also careers several times. So seniors should prepare themselves to find work and a career that fits them at their present stage in life, with the understanding that they will probably change jobs and maybe careers throughout their lifetime.

Below are some suggestions about career selection that can be helpful when considering future work.

> Making an informed decision about what work to choose can save us the tremendous pain of being in the wrong job.

Assessing Yourself

The best way to begin thinking about possible careers is to assess your interests, personality, and skills to see how these aspects of yourself might relate to future work.

Interests: Each day you are involved in a wide variety of activities. Over the last seventeen or eighteen years, you have done some things that you liked and other things that you found disagreeable. Try to describe what you like to do. Consider jobs you have had, extracurricular activities, hobbies, courses in school, and so on.

Personality: One way to define your personality is to consider whether you prefer working with *things, people,* or *data.* If you like to work with things, maybe you should consider truck driving, engineering, diesel mechanics, or computer programming. If you prefer working with people, you might gravitate toward teaching, sales, ministry, or entertainment. If you like data, you might consider accounting, proofreading, or statistical analysis. All of the occupations listed here are worthwhile, but their appeal to you depends on your personality.

Skills: You must consider the skills that you have or ones that you can develop. After all, some people who like playing basketball, are absorbed by it, and dream of making a career of it may lack the skill to play professionally. You need to be realistic about what you can do or have the capacity to learn if you are going to successfully choose a life's work.

Looking Beyond Stereotypes

You must choose a career that *you* want rather than one that society considers appropriate for a man or for a woman.

- A respected judge can be a woman or a man.
- Nursing is not strictly women's work.
- College teaching is no longer the sole preserve of men.
- Computers do not know the sex of the programmer.
- Children respond marvelously to male as well as female day-care workers.
- For many years, the fastest typist in the world was a man.
- Today women are opening small businesses by the thousands.

In other words, when you consider career options, be open to *all* possibilities. Be as free as you desire to be in your search.

Considering Work Environments

Certain work environments suit each of us best. Some of us work best alone; others hate to be alone. Working outdoors has an appeal for some; for others, having an artificial houseplant in an air-conditioned office is as close as they want to come to nature. Some people enjoy an on-the-road job; others see travel requirements as very disrupting to life. The work environment is an important consideration.

Looking at Clusters of Work

Some examples of clusters of work are agriculture, health care, social services, the arts, home economics, marketing, and

Write your reflections on the following questions:
- Do you prefer to work with data, people, or things?
- How does your preference show itself?

Write about the kind of work environment that would suit you best.

public relations. Each of these clusters includes many occupations. It is best to look at whole clusters before becoming focused on a specialty.

For example, the cluster of health care includes such occupations as physical therapy, rehabilitation counseling, nursing, dietetics, dental hygiene, medicine, radiology technology, medical lab technology, speech therapy, occupational therapy, and respiratory therapy. Each of the listed occupations also has its own specialties.

Researching One or Two Clusters

Research in some detail the one or two clusters that most interest you. You can seek printed material from school counselors or the public library (reference librarians can be particularly helpful in pointing out the best sources). This procedure will help you to narrow down the possibilities to more specific occupations that you want to research in more depth.

Contacting People in Your Fields of Interest

Once you have narrowed your focus to a few occupations, interview people working in those fields and, if possible, spend some time observing them at work. Too frequently students are convinced that they want a certain line of work because the pay seems good or because there are many openings in the field. Once they have interviewed and observed people in those careers, they either will be more convinced or will realize that the field is not for them. Either way, the students will be able to make a realistic assessment about the career.

Trying Out Careers

You can get firsthand experience in a given field. Find work now in jobs related to your interests. High school and college jobs can be excellent opportunities for gathering information about work and particular careers. Whether you are interested in a liberal arts area or in engineering, electronics, or cosmetology, if you can find summer, holiday, or part-time employment in your field or a related area, you will learn many valuable lessons.

Most colleges offer internships for students. For example, a marketing student may gain useful skills by taking a semester away from campus to work as an intern in a marketing firm. The student receives credit toward the marketing major as well as invaluable job experience.

List all of the clusters or fields of work that you can think of. Study the want ads and count the number of job openings in each cluster. If salaries are given in the ads, try to estimate the entry-level pay for the various jobs.

Search the want ads for all jobs that relate to the career cluster that most interests you—for example, in the health-care cluster, a nurse anesthetist and a radiologist. If you come across a specialty of that cluster that you are unfamiliar with, do some research to find out what that specialty entails.

Interview someone who does the type of work that you would like to do. Make up your own questions in addition to these:
- How did you get into this line of work?
- What do you like most and least about your job?
- What do you see as the purposes, goals, and values that this work serves?
- Would you encourage someone to go into this work? Why or why not?

Some colleges and universities have co-op programs, most often for students in the sciences, engineering, or business. In a co-op program, a student might work for a cooperating company during one quarter and go to school during the next quarter, alternating quarters of work and school until she or he finishes the degree. A co-op student receives a salary while working, gains valuable experience, and many times can move immediately into a position with the cooperating company. In choosing a college or technical school to attend, you might wish to find out if the school has internships or co-op programs.

These suggestions may help you to begin the adventure of discovering the thrust of your life's work. No single job, probably no particular career, will encompass your life's work. However, we all must make our beginnings.

Caution: Problems and Hazards at Work

No examination of jobs and careers would be complete without pointing out some of the problems and hazards that people encounter as they work.

Work Addiction

When work becomes the only way that we measure our worth, then all of life becomes work, and our opinion of our worth becomes fragile indeed. We suffer from work addiction when our sense of our own value and our happiness comes to depend completely on how hard we are working and how successful we are in our work. This addictive tendency goes beyond an admirable pride in our work and a dedication to doing a good job. It is the work ethic gone to extremes.

In Arthur Miller's play *Death of a Salesman*, Willy Loman is plagued with this very tendency, and it proves to be the death of him. For years, Willy has lied to himself about how successful he is as a salesman, convincing himself that he is better at sales than he really is, because success is everything to him. After years of working for the same company, at age sixty-three, Willy is put on straight commission (his only income is a percentage of his sales, which at this point are very meager). To Willy, this is like being fired. He is so tied to his illusory image

If you plan to attend college or technical school, find out if the schools that you are considering have internships or co-op programs.

We suffer from work addiction when our sense of our own value depends completely on how successful we are in our work.

of himself as a successful salesman that he despairs. The fact that Willy has a wife who loves him does not prevent him from taking his own life, crashing his car so that it looks like an accident.

At Willy's funeral, his friend Charley seems to share Willy's notion that work equals a person's worth. Charley says this of Willy:

> "Nobody dast blame this man. . . . Willy was a salesman. And for a salesman, there is no rock bottom to the life. He don't put a bolt to a nut, he don't tell you the law or give you medicine. He's a man way out there in the blue, riding on a smile and a shoeshine. And when they start not smiling back—that's an earthquake. And then you get yourself a couple of spots on your hat, and you're finished. Nobody dast blame this man. A salesman is got to dream, boy. It comes with the territory."

People may become fixated on work for some of the following reasons:

- From childhood on, people are praised for what they *do* rather than appreciated for who they *are*. Personal qualities are valued insofar as they help a person to perform more successfully.
- People are told that if they work hard enough, they can do *anything*. They then assume that if they do not achieve their goals, something is very wrong with them.
- People are subtly convinced that "an idle mind is the devil's workshop." Even play becomes work-oriented as people scramble to fill their leisure time with achievements—a fantastic tan or a tennis victory, for instance.

Some symptoms of work addiction include working more hours than necessary, spending weekends or off hours doing one chore after another, feeling guilty when not doing anything, neglecting exercise or a balanced diet. Work addicts can find vacations and periods of illness unbearable. Likewise, unemployment and retirement can be emotionally devastating to someone who equates self-worth with work.

In the Christian vision, work has dignity, but it does not define who we are. Human beings do not have to work to prove their worth to God. People are saved because of God's unconditional love for them, not because of their personal achievements. One who is work-addicted has difficulty realizing that he or she is inherently good and deserving.

Referring to the three reasons for work addiction, assess how vulnerable you are to this problem. Write your reflections.

Competition

Capitalism is built on competition. Two companies selling luncheon meat may constantly improve their products, introduce new lines, have special sales, and spend bundles of money in order to outsell each other. If one company drives the other out of business, it will have a corner on the luncheon meat market, and its profits will go up. In our economic system, that is success.

Within companies, competition for positions can be just as fierce. Two bright salespersons might vie for a district manager position that has just opened up because the last district manager was fired due to poor profits. This sort of competition may raise productivity in the short run, but it does not produce a healthy atmosphere for work or cooperative relationships among employees. One successful business executive remarked:

> "You get enemies in business, especially if you're successful. Ones that have grown up and started with you. You want to be liked and you want to help people. I've found out you can't. It's not appreciated. They never thank you." (Terkel, *Working*, page 463)

The problem with competition is that there are always winners and losers. Winners relish the struggle. Losers suffer. In the process, enemies are made. In contemplating a career, you might ask yourself how much competition you want to tolerate.

Conformity

Every organization has rules to follow. Working with any company, or even alone, demands that we conform to some policies and procedures. Some policies—such as quotas for the amount of work to be done—may be obviously necessary; others may seem arbitrary and purposeless. For instance, some businesses have strict or outdated dress codes. Women might be told to wear dresses. Men might have to have their hair cut in a prescribed way.

Some issues around conformity have to do with informal norms, not with company policies. For example:

- Cindy begins her new job as a counselor's aide in a group home for retarded adults. The work can be trying, and sometimes the residents are extremely hard to handle. At coffee breaks, staff members who have been at the home

The problem with competition is that there are always winners and losers.

longer make fun of some of the residents—out of their ear-shot, of course—to lighten the mood. Cindy feels that such behavior is unkind and unprofessional, but she wants very much to be accepted. If you were Cindy, would you conform to the patterns of the other staff members, joining in on the jokes that poke fun and reasoning that "we need a break"? Would you ignore the comments? Or would you let the others know in a tactful way that such joking seems hurtful to the residents, even though they are out of earshot?

We need to decide how much and what kind of conformity is tolerable for us. Our integrity is at stake.

Repetition and Dullness

Many kinds of work are repetitious. A typical example of this is assembly-line work. New technology, especially robotics, has eliminated some jobs that demand machine-like activity. However, many types of work still seem as if they could be done by machines.

Such routinized work can become boring and mindless. Satisfaction in the job decreases. Women and men simply become replaceable parts in a large operation. One worker talked about his job in this way:

> "You come in each day: you're timed on this job. . . . All right; today's output: 240. And that's your number; and you think of the 240 until you've done it; and you're number-minded; and when you go home the boredom is there with you." (Alasdair Clayre, *Work and Play,* page 176)

The danger in this kind of work is that it dulls the spirit. Soon a split widens between work and the rest of life. For eight hours a day the person feels that she or he is not living.

Moral Conflicts

Having a well-defined set of values is important as we enter our work. If we are not clear about where we stand on moral issues, we may find ourselves more easily compromised. Take Greg's situation as an example:

- Greg works for a grocery store as a cashier. Yesterday a customer complained to Rick, the cashier at the next register, that she had been shortchanged. Rick then apologized and gave the customer the correct amount. Today Greg sees that

Routinized work can become boring and mindless; the danger is that it dulls the spirit.

the same kind of incident is happening again. He can't be sure, but he has a strong hunch that Rick is regularly short-changing customers and pocketing the difference. When customers complain, Rick simply apologizes and corrects the error. Greg knows that Rick has been gambling lately because he talks openly about some of his winnings. Greg wonders if he should tell the boss or let the situation go.

This kind of moral dilemma and other ones of greater magnitude happen regularly in many occupations. For instance, some companies that supply the government with equipment have knowingly lowered prices on bids and then had huge cost overruns. Other companies have doctored reports about the performance of equipment so that it could pass government standards. By remaining silent, employees who know about deceitful practices in effect allow cheating, and this cheating brings about government overspending and, worse, potentially dangerous equipment failures. When the truth is revealed, employees usually tell government investigators that they had to keep quiet about the wrongdoing or lose their jobs.

We need to work, but no job is worth tossing out our moral values. It is important to consider your values as you enter the workplace.

Discrimination

Despite progress made in the legal system to combat discrimination based on gender, race, religion, or age, it still exists. Women still make less money than men for the same work. In the early 1980s, women earned about sixty-six cents for every dollar earned by men in comparable jobs. Frequently, people in a racial minority are the last hired and the first fired.

Another problem that plagues the workplace is sexual harassment, a form of discrimination. Instances of sexual harassment range from the very obvious to the very subtle. The situation of a supervisor who threatens to fire a subordinate unless he or she grants sexual favors is one of overt harassment. More subtle is the comment that a male executive might make to a female employee that she should wear something a bit more "feminine" to impress a major client to whom the company is making a sales pitch. In effect, the executive is asking her to use her sexuality to raise company profits.

In searching for a job or in planning a career, you need to ask yourself some searching questions about your own attitudes

Knowing your moral limits is important. List five things that, for moral reasons, you would not be willing to do as part of a job.

toward groups that are often victims of discrimination. The Christian principle of treating others as we wish to be treated can be a helpful guideline to follow in order to avoid discrimination against others. In addition, you should consider these questions:

- Will I work for a company that discriminates?
- Will I be silent about discrimination if I see it in the company that I work for?

If we think that we are being subjected to discrimination or harassment, we need to remember that the legal system has established complaint, or grievance, procedures to aid victims. We have a duty to protect our dignity as human beings, God's creations.

Rapid Changes

The amazing changes in the workplace due to technological developments have been chronicled in the media. Robots assemble automobiles, computers displace telephone operators, and so on. Additionally, technological advances have created new jobs for people in telecommunications and other fields. What is constant is change—rapid change. A person cannot assume that the way she or he performs a job today will still be the same next year.

Consequently, today's workers must be flexible, ready for retraining, and aware of the advances being made in their particular fields of work. This implies lifelong learning, as was discussed in the last chapter.

Unemployment is frightening because of what it can do to a person's self-image and sense of purpose.

Unemployment

For someone who is employable, willing to work, and needful of work, unemployment is a fearsome possibility. It is frightening not only because of the obvious financial consequences but also because of what it can do to a person's self-image and sense of purpose. As mentioned earlier, unemployment is especially difficult for someone who is work-addicted, whose whole sense of identity and self-worth is bound up in work. Developing our self-image around relationships, our faith, our interests, and so on, as well as around the work we do is one way to prevent the devastating psychological impact of being jobless.

Unemployment is a social evil that tears at individuals and at the fabric of a culture. Commenting on the problem of

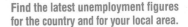

Find the latest unemployment figures for the country and for your local area.

unemployment, the U.S. Catholic bishops, in their 1986 pastoral letter on the economy, said:

> Full employment is the foundation of a just economy. The most urgent priority for domestic economic policy is the creation of new jobs with adequate pay and decent working conditions. . . .
>
> Employment is a basic right, a right which protects the freedom of all to participate in the economic life of society. . . . Jobs benefit society as well as workers, for they enable more people to contribute to the common good and to the productivity required for a healthy economy. *(Economic Justice for All,* nos. 136–137)

In the bishops' view, unemployment is not simply an individual problem but a social evil. Decision-makers in government and business must hold the dignity and the needs of the worker as the uppermost concern in formulating policies and strategies that affect job opportunities.

A Dream Being Realized

Compose a prayer that shares your thoughts, fears, hopes, or beliefs about work.

We need to work not only to support ourselves and our families but also to have purpose, to accomplish things, to realize our potential, and to contribute something of value with our lives. In the Christian worldview, work is co-creation with God; work has immense nobility.

During young adulthood, choosing what type of work you will do is a challenge. You must follow a careful process to determine what field of work to pursue so that the "have to" of work can come as close as possible to the "want to" and "love to" of a dream being realized.

Review Questions

1. Define work.

2. Explain each of the six motives for working that are discussed in this chapter.

3. How is work a form of co-creation with God?

4. What part did work play in Jesus' life?

5. In what four ways can people love through their work?

6. What three personal aspects should be assessed before an individual attempts to select a career?

7. Following self-assessment, what are the next six steps in selecting a career?

8. What is work addiction, and what are some of its symptoms?

9. How might competition create problems for workers?

10. Explain how conformity and repetition are difficulties in the workplace.

11. What are some moral conflicts and types of discrimination that some workers must face?

12. Why is unemployment such a devastating event for workers?

8 Money and Possessions: The Need for Perspective

IN North American society, no aspect of existence seems to cause as much stir as money and possessions. Think of TV shows that have gained popularity by depending on the public's fascination with wealth, for instance, game shows and most soap operas. Cruising up and down a giant indoor shopping mall is a major social event in many towns. Scandals involving huge sums of money wrack government and business. Marriages end because of differences over money and possessions. The society we live in seems quite preoccupied with money and possessions.

A Sense of Perspective

We need a certain **sense of perspective**—a healthy, objective distance—about money and possessions. We must be able to sort out what is *enough* and what is *excess*. Without such a perspective, we could begin to expect more of material things than they can possibly deliver; we might expect them to satisfy our deepest yearnings—in short, to make us happy. Coming to a sense of perspective about money and possessions and cultivating the wise use of money are integral to the developmental tasks of young adulthood, especially these:

- becoming autonomous
- constructing and living out a value system
- selecting a career
- taking part in the broader community

The young couple in this example have worked at developing a healthy perspective about money and possessions:

Nancy and Les were looking forward to a free evening out. The invitation they had received in the mail read, "You have been selected to be our guests at a prime rib dinner at the Sterling Motel Restaurant on Friday, October 9." In small print at the bottom, it said, "Courtesy of Over the Rainbow Investment Corp., Phoenix, Arizona."

Nancy and Les did not get much of a chance to appreciate the dinner, however, because at their table of three couples was seated a salesman from the Over the Rainbow Corporation. His hard-sell pitch for undeveloped real estate in Arizona began with the salad course and persisted through dessert. After the meal, he began a slide show about "the investment opportunity of a lifetime." Having indulged in the meal, all of the couples were a captive audience—no sneaking out the back door.

Nancy and Les noticed that some of the other couples were warming to the idea of taking out substantial loans to finance the purchase of land two thousand miles away that was "absolutely certain" to triple in value in two years. Some couples were ready to take the next step, an "all-expenses-paid" trip to Arizona to see the land. But Nancy and Les had come for the meal and were not interested in the land deal. It sounded kind of shady, anyway.

After a pep talk to the whole group, the property salesman took Les and Nancy aside (by this time, they had given the impression of being uninterested). Fifteen minutes of pitching passed, but the salesman could not break this couple's resistance to investing in an "obvious" real estate gold mine. Showing his frustration, the salesman finally blurted, "What's the matter? Don't you *want* to make money?"

"We just want to make a living, not a killing," Les said simply. "We're not really interested in getting rich quick, even if this deal could make us rich. There are lots of other things in life to be interested in. Money isn't really what makes people happy."

"Well, of course not," responded the salesman, relieved to finally be able to agree with Les and Nancy on a point. "It's not the *money* that makes people happy; it's the *things* that money can buy—vacations in the Bahamas, a sports car, a pool, a beach house, designer clothes."

"All of that is nice, but we're not so convinced that those things are going to make us happy, either," answered Nancy. "We're not against money or having things. It's just that all we want is enough to meet our needs and have a decent life."

Think about someone you know who seems to have a healthy perspective toward money and possessions. Write about how that person shows this perspective.

"That's what I'm talking about—a decent life," hissed the almost frantic salesman through clenched teeth.

"I guess we've got a different idea of what a decent life is," Les reacted calmly.

The now worn-out salesman sighed, "I don't understand you two. I give up."

The Need for Money

In order to survive and to lead dignified lives, human beings need money and the things that money can buy. Food, shelter, clothing, and medical care are obvious survival needs. But in order to live beyond the level of sheer survival, money is also needed for education, transportation, some forms of entertainment, provision for the future—contributions to social security, retirement plans—and so on. These elements of a dignified life beyond sheer survival have become so taken for granted in our society that we see them as basic needs. They are what Les and Nancy had in mind when they talked about "a decent life."

Practicality and responsibility require that somewhere on the way to adulthood, we begin to provide for our own needs.

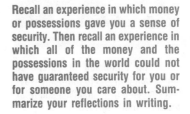

Recall an experience in which money or possessions gave you a sense of security. Then recall an experience in which all of the money and the possessions in the world could not have guaranteed security for you or for someone you care about. Summarize your reflections in writing.

Not to recognize the need for money is to be foolish. Most of us can see the wisdom in the familiar saying, "You can't live on love." Practicality and a sense of responsibility for our lives require that somewhere along the way to adulthood, we begin to provide for our own needs, to support ourselves.

So money and possessions in themselves are not evil. However, the issue in learning to live happily, justly, lovingly, and freely with money and possessions is developing a sense of balance and proportion. We need money to live a dignified life, but what constitutes a dignified life—or in Nancy and Les's terms, a "decent life"—can be interpreted in varying ways. Even the basic survival needs of food, shelter, clothing, and medical care can be defined in radically different ways. To a Peruvian peasant and a Haitian factory worker, for instance, North America's suburban version of an "adequate shelter" would be considered a mansion in their societies. In the story at the beginning of this chapter, Les and Nancy probably would offer an idea of "adequate clothing" very different from the salesman's notion.

List the elements that constitute what you envision as a dignified life.

Beyond Necessities

In addition to meeting survival needs and the requirements of a modestly dignified life, money offers some extras:
- choices
- pleasure
- power

Choices

Discretionary income, that is, income over and above what will cover necessities, implies choices. A person who has extra money can use discretion in deciding what to do with that money. He or she can decide whether to buy a used car or a new car, take a vacation at home or in Europe, go to a private college or a state college, save the money or spend it. The feeling of having options is a good one.

Choices, whether or not they involve money, give people the opportunity to decide what their values are. In fact, a person's spending patterns give a very useful indication of that person's values.

Pleasure

Discretionary income enables us to purchase many things that give us a feeling of well-being and pleasure. It is nice to have enough money to escape the winter doldrums for a week or two, to wear the latest fashions, or to hear the sounds we like to hear pouring out of a compact disc stereo system. These kinds of pleasure can give real enjoyment and can also offer comforting distractions from problems.

Becoming immersed in purchased things can blind us to the many ways that we can enjoy ourselves and relax without spending money.

It is that distracting quality of "pleasure for sale" that can also be its great pitfall. The immersion in purchased things and experiences can continually take us away from facing reality. Besides, pleasure for sale can blind us to the many ways that we can enjoy ourselves and relax without spending money. Finally, we need to be cautious about constantly turning to purchases to create happiness in our lives; the kind of happiness that material things can provide very quickly fades.

Power

Beyond giving increased choices and offering pleasure, discretionary income brings a certain kind of power—not necessarily the power of a political tyrant or a corporate tycoon but the "able to" kind of power. Power enables us to do many things, for instance, to make more money. Capital enables us to start organizations that further our goals or to invest in a worthy community cause. Political power usually requires money. Few "mere folks" are elected to major political offices.

Sometimes money gives us the power to impress others and to run with influential crowds. For instance, a high school senior with money can gain a certain kind of status by always having an available car, by treating friends to snacks, and so on.

The power that money can bring must be handled with great caution. The old adage "Power corrupts and absolute power corrupts absolutely" contains more than a grain of truth.

Choices, pleasure, and power are the usual motivators for having plenty of money—more than enough to take care of necessities. Like money, these benefits in themselves are not bad. However, they need to be treated with a healthy distance and perspective because their appeal can be strong enough to create all kinds of illusions for people—the chief one being that our deepest dream, the good life, can be bought. People under this illusion fall prey to an insatiable desire for money.

Find an article in a magazine or newspaper that shows how people can use money to achieve or exercise power. Prepare to explain in class the significance of the article.

Greed:
Money in the Driver's Seat

An insatiable desire for money or for anything else is **greed**. To people who are greedy for money, there is never enough. Illustrations of this abound. In recent years, Wall Street executives have been caught and punished by government authorities for trading inside information about mergers and other business deals. By selling what was supposed to be secret information, the stock-market executives had allowed their cohorts to make enormous sums of money—millions of dollars. Ironically, many of these investors were already immensely rich, but they had an insatiable desire for more.

Haunted by Greed

The root of all evil is not money in itself but people's value systems that make money and possessions the ultimate goal of their lives. In effect, money becomes their god. Few people will admit that money drives them, but their actions often reveal the truth. In the story "The Rocking-Horse Winner" by D. H. Lawrence, the insatiable desire for money is an unfriendly ghost that haunts a family, although the parents will never admit its power:

The root of all evil is not money in itself but people's value systems that make money and possessions the ultimate goal of their lives.

> Although they lived in style, they felt always an anxiety in the house. There was never enough money. The mother had a small income, and the father had a small income, but not nearly enough for the social position which they had to keep up. The father went into town to some office. But though he had good prospects, these prospects never materialised. There was always the grinding sense of the shortage of money, though the style was always kept up.
>
> . . . The [mother's] failure made deep lines come into her face. Her children were growing up, they would have to go to school. There must be more money, there must be more money. The father, who was always very handsome and expensive in his tastes, seemed as if he never *would* be able to do anything worth doing. And the mother, who had a great belief in herself, did not succeed any better, and her tastes were just as expensive.
>
> And so the house came to be haunted by the unspoken phrase: *There must be more money! There must be more money!* The children could hear it all the time, though nobody said it aloud. They heard it at Christmas, when the expensive and splendid toys filled the nursery. Behind the shiny modern rocking-horse, behind the smart doll's house, a voice would start whispering: "There *must* be more money! There *must* be more money!"

Even people who feel they are struggling financially, like the parents in the story, can let the ghost of greed take over their household, seizing control of the minds and hearts of those within.

The Buy-on-Credit Mentality

If D. H. Lawrence's family of characters had lived in our era, they would have had credit cards. A great deal of our retail economy is built on credit purchases. Many luxury items—such as stereos, color televisions, cars, appliances, furniture—are bought over several years by making monthly payments. Interest charges generally raise the actual price of the item dramatically. Even so, instead of saving money until they can pay for an item free and clear, people are willing to go into serious debt to have what they want immediately.

According to many psychologists, one mark of a mature person is the ability to *delay gratification*—to wait for pleasure if necessary. Mature individuals are not trapped by the childish attitude, "I want what I want when I want it." Yet the phenomenon of increasing consumer debt in our society because of credit purchases seems to indicate that immediate gratification, not delayed gratification, is typical of our culture.

One reason that people are willing to dive into debt for quick gratification is that they are influenced by advertising that preaches the ease of miraculous ownership. The goal of some of the most sophisticated brand advertising, after all, is to create insatiable desires in people to buy and possess. We are taught to be greedy. Ads tell us that all we need for bliss is a recliner, a trip to Hawaii, a fancy blender, a high-powered personal computer, exorbitantly expensive perfume, fashions by XYZ, a new recreational vehicle, a red sports car, and so on. Every day we learn of new products—possession of which is absolutely imperative if we are to "have it all." So people buy these items on credit. The combination of advertising and credit has made new levels of greed possible for greater numbers of North Americans.

Corporate Greed as a Virtue

Greed in our society is not confined to individuals; it extends throughout the social structure to many institutions. In fact,

How much pressure do you feel to have more money? Do you ever hear a subconscious voice within you saying, "There must be more money"? If so, where does this voice come from? If not, why do you think that you do not feel driven to have more money? Write about your reflections.

List five things that you feel you need and would buy if you had the money. Then write all the reasons you can think of for why you need each item.

in much of the corporate world, greed is seen as a virtue, not only accepted but welcomed as a guiding principle of action. As a result, the profitable and efficient operation of a corporation becomes more important than the lives of individuals who depend on it for jobs or the quality of the products.

Searching for cheap locations: A company that wishes to increase its profits may decide to move its operations to another part of the country, where labor and fuel costs are cheaper. If workers wish to follow the company, they can, but that means uprooting families, taking cuts in pay, disrupting relationships, and so on. Also, more and more companies are moving their plants to Third World countries, where the price of labor is so cheap (and frequently the working conditions are so poor) that profits soar. For larger corporations, exploitation yields increased profits. In fact, many manufacturers are claiming that they cannot afford to run plants in North America anymore.

Sacrificing quality: In the quest for economic progress, companies may also sacrifice quality for profit margin. For decades, many U.S. car manufacturers showed huge profits but skimped on research into and development of higher-quality automobiles. After all, the higher the quality of the cars, the less often they would have to be replaced. But foreign imports began biting into U.S. automakers' profits because the imported cars were better designed and built, more reliable, and fuel-efficient. In this situation also, the effects of the decline in the U.S. auto industry have been felt by many North Americans—increased unemployment not only among autoworkers but also among steelworkers, tire makers, and component assemblers.

Selling death: Some companies have given jobs to many people, made huge profits, and manufactured high-quality products, but their greed has exacted a human toll in other ways. For example, many arms manufacturers sell death to almost anyone who can pay for it, and some makers of pesticides and other toxic chemicals have built unsafe factories where accidents have taken lives.

When corporate greed becomes a virtue, compassion, love, and care for nature in the corporate context may be seen as vices, unnecessary luxuries that efficient, profitable companies cannot afford to indulge in. Greed, whether individual or corporate, runs directly counter to the Gospel.

A day at the stock exchange: Wealth can fool us into thinking that we have control of life and give us the illusion of ultimate security and freedom.

Christianity on Greed

The Hazards of Pursuing Wealth

It is no wonder that the Christian Testament offers so many warnings about the dangers of pursuing riches. Saint Paul, writing to his friend Timothy, talked about the personal hazards of living a life devoted to the accumulation of wealth:

> We brought nothing into the world, and we can take nothing out of it; but as long as we have food and clothing, we shall be content with that. People who long to be rich are a prey to trial; they get trapped into all sorts of foolish and harmful ambitions which plunge people into ruin and destruction. "The love of money is the root of all evils" and there are some who, pursuing it, have wandered away from the faith and so given their souls any number of fatal wounds. (1 Timothy 6:7–10)

In his Epistle, Saint James used colorful and tough language to warn those who grew rich at the expense of their workers that their rewards would not last forever:

> Well now, you rich! Lament, weep for the miseries that are coming to you. Your wealth is rotting, your clothes are all moth-eaten. All your gold and your silver are corroding away, and the same corrosion will be a witness against you and eat into your body. It is like a fire which you have stored up for the final days. Can you hear crying out against you the wages which you kept back from the labourers mowing your fields? The cries of the reapers have reached the ears of [Yahweh]. (James 5:1–4)

The Christian Testament conveys a deep distrust of a preoccupation with money and possessions. Although riches in themselves are not evil, they very readily can get in the way of what is important and valuable in life. Wealth can fool us into thinking that we have control of life and give us the illusion of ultimate security and freedom. In addition, riches often are gained at the expense of poor people.

Freedom or Slavery?

One of the lures of money is the notion that it brings freedom. An income does give us options and choices, but sometimes we can deceive ourselves about how much and what kind

List five factual instances in which the love of money was the root of evil. Then list five examples of instances in which money itself, as opposed to the love of money, was used to contribute to the common good.

of freedom we really are getting by pursuing money. Consider this story:

> Jeff quit the cross-country team to get a job. His coach and some of the other team members had been counting on him to help them have a winning season, but Jeff simply could not see spending so much time for so little tangible gain. Besides, he wanted to make some money so that he would have the freedom to buy the things he wanted. So Jeff began working at a fast-food restaurant. He learned to deep-fry potatoes, rapidly cook and assemble twenty varieties of hamburgers, make change, smile at customers, mop floors, and so on.
>
> When Jeff told his parents that he had found a job, he had assured them that he would save some money for college. But his paycheck never seemed sufficient to buy all of the things that he felt he needed. New clothes, records, shoes, and other purchases kept soaking up the money Jeff made, and still there were more things to buy. He tried to work more hours, but even so, his money was always gone before he could reach the bank with it. This frustrated Jeff.
>
> Jeff also found himself bored stiff with the job. The management could assign him any hours that it pleased, sometimes making him work a late-night shift followed by a day shift. If Jeff complained, the management would cut his hours. He began to realize he was being taken advantage of—making terrible wages in a company that made billions of dollars through underpaid workers like himself.
>
> Even though Jeff disliked his job and was usually behind in his schoolwork, tired, and grumpy from working too many hours, he was continually broke. Jeff felt that he had no choice but to keep working.

Jeff's longing for the freedom to buy whatever he wanted and his inability to control his spending matched very well with the company's policy of hiring and exploiting cheap labor. He was caught in a tight trap, not free at all. He felt like a slave.

Just as we can become addicted to work, we can become enslaved by money and the pursuit of it. This is perhaps the most insidious aspect of money: it can end up owning us. Lack of money can stifle us, but the desire for money and possessions can do the same. The Christian message is that we should be free of slavery to material things. Jesus understood the trap that made Jeff feel like a slave: " 'No one can be the slave of

Do you know anyone in a situation similar to the one in which Jeff found himself? If so, describe the situation in writing. Then answer this question:
- What are some of the forces that cause us to want to make more and more money?

two masters: he will either hate the first and love the second, or be attached to the first and despise the second. You cannot be the slave both of God and of money' " (Matthew 6:24).

The U.S. Catholic bishops, drawing their inspiration from Jesus, recognize how enslaving the pursuit of wealth can be. In their pastoral letter *Economic Justice for All: Catholic Social Teaching and the U.S. Economy,* they called Christians to a different kind of freedom than the freedom to buy: "Americans are challenged today as never before to develop the inner freedom to resist the temptation constantly to seek more" (no. 75). The Christian Scriptures and the tradition of the Church ask us to be wise enough to resist the slavery that masquerades as freedom.

The Christian Alternative: A New Attitude Toward Ownership

The Christian view of money and possessions calls for an attitude toward ownership that departs decisively from the prevailing attitudes in our society. In fact, Christianity presents an alternative view of economic life that is based on the biblical vision of creation.

In the biblical vision, *everything on earth belongs first and foremost to its creator.* The earth and all that it contains are God's, and in the words of the early church father Saint Cyprian, "Whatever belongs to God belongs to all." In his letter *On Human Work,* Pope John Paul II echoed Saint Cyprian when he wrote, "The right to private property is subordinated to the right to common use, to the fact that goods are meant for everyone" (no. 14). This notion of ownership—that the goods of the earth really belong to all of us—has profound implications:

- No *absolute* right to private property exists; what we own is lent to us by God so that we may tend it for the good of all. We are not free to use our possessions in ways that hurt other people or the earth.
- The accumulation of wealth and resources by a minority of the world's population betrays the gift of creation.

Given this biblical vision that the goods of the earth are for everyone's use, the Christian attitude toward ownership of

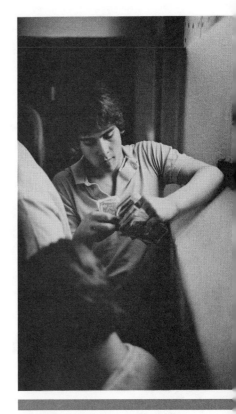

The most insidious aspect of money is that it can end up owning us.

money and possessions is characterized by these elements:
- sharing
- simplicity
- equality
- justice

Sharing

The early Christian communities practiced a life of **sharing** quite literally. The Acts of the Apostles records, "And all who shared the faith owned everything in common; they sold their goods and possessions and distributed the proceeds among themselves according to what each one needed" (Acts of the Apostles 2:44–45). As a consequence of this policy, the Acts of the Apostles later states, "None of their members was ever in want..." (Acts of the Apostles 4:34).

A Model for the World Community

Although the Christian community in Jerusalem was small, its communal sharing of goods provided a model of loving behavior for all Christians to follow. No one lacked basic necessities because everyone shared.

The same cannot be said of our world community today, where a minority of the world's population has amassed most of the wealth. In general, the right of a relative few to own and control the earth's resources is seen today as an absolute, not as something subject to considerations of what is best for the wider human community; however, the right to private property, in the Christian vision, is not absolute.

Lazarus and the Rich Man

Jesus preached that sharing was not optional but required of his followers. One of his more colorful stories was the one about Lazarus and the rich man (Luke 16:19–31):

Lazarus, a poor man, begged to eat the crumbs from the rich man's table. Admittedly, Lazarus was not very attractive; he was covered with sores and was dressed in rags. But the rich man had a massive banquet each night and could afford to throw poor Lazarus a few crumbs. Instead he ignored Lazarus.

Eventually both men died. Lazarus went to heaven, and the rich man burned in hell. The rich man looked up and saw Lazarus with the prophet Abraham in heaven. The rich man begged for a drop of water from Lazarus, but it was too late.

Do you agree or disagree with this statement?
- Generally, poor and middle-class people give a greater percentage of their income to charity than do rich people.

If you agree, why? If not, why not?

Abraham told the rich man that the gulf was too wide between him and Lazarus. In addition, Abraham reminded the rich man that he had ignored all of the warnings of the prophets about greed, so he was getting what he deserved.

The rich man suffered an eternity of torment not because he had been wealthy in life but because he had refused to respond to the needs of others.

The obligation to share exists not only on the individual level but also on the global level. Pope John Paul II, in his address to North Americans at Yankee Stadium in 1979, drew a parallel between the gospel story of Lazarus and the contemporary global economy in which a minority of the world's countries own most of the wealth. Pope John Paul II went on to say:

> We cannot stand idly by, enjoying our own riches and freedom if, in any place, the Lazarus of the twentieth century stands at our doors. In the light of the parable of Christ, riches and freedom mean a special responsibility. ("Special Sensitivity Toward Those in Distress," no. 7)

"We cannot stand idly by, enjoying our own riches and freedom if, in any place, the Lazarus of the twentieth century stands at our doors."

A Fair Balance

Jesus taught that sharing is an obligation for his followers, so Christians might ask, How much giving is proper? Saint Paul gave Christians a guideline to follow when he talked to the community of Corinth—a rich and powerful city where the church prospered. He was writing to the Corinthians to ask for donations to the community in Jerusalem, which was literally on the verge of starvation due to a famine. After complimenting the Corinthians for their previous acts of generosity, Paul said:

> It is not that you ought to relieve other people's needs and leave yourselves in hardship; but there should be a fair balance—your surplus at present may fill their deficit, and another time their surplus may fill your deficit. So there may be a fair balance; as scripture says: No one who had collected more had too much, no one who collected less had too little. (2 Corinthians 8:13–15)

Fair balance—these two words were the key to Paul's advice.

Later in the same letter, Paul added another piece of advice for the Corinthians:

> Each one should give as much as he has decided on his own initiative, not reluctantly or under compulsion, for God loves a cheerful giver. (2 Corinthians 9:7)

Just as love cannot be forced out of someone, neither can true sharing of resources be forced; it is, after all, an aspect of loving. If we give, we should do so freely and cheerfully.

Neighbors in Need

In just about any direction that we look, people are in need. The U.S. Catholic bishops described some of these neighbors in their pastoral letter on the economy:

> Homeless people roam city streets in tattered clothing and sleep in doorways or on subway grates at night. Many of these are former mental patients released from state hospitals. Thousands stand in line at soup kitchens because they have no other way of feeding themselves. Millions of children are so poorly nourished that their physical and mental development are seriously harmed. (*Economic Justice for All*, no. 172)

Most of us could give examples from our own communities of people in need of economic help.

Jesus called his followers to share with their neighbors so that everyone would have enough to live, not simply to survive but to live in dignity.

Simplicity

Another characteristic of the Christian attitude toward ownership is **simplicity**. A simple life does not imply poverty or starvation; it does not mean that we go about in rags. Simplicity means that we live close enough to the limits of our resources that we can rely on God's love for us.

Neither Too Much nor Too Little

One of the best descriptions of simplicity comes from the Book of Proverbs:

> . . . Give me neither poverty nor riches,
>   grant me only my share of food,
> for fear that, surrounded by plenty, I should fall away
>   and say, "Yahweh—who is Yahweh?"
> or else, in destitution, take to stealing
>   and profane the name of God.
>
> (Proverbs 30:8–9)

Too many rich people tend to act as if God were not in charge of the universe, puffing themselves up with the feeling

Simplicity means that we live close enough to the limits of our resources that we can rely on God's love for us.

Recall a time when you shared something you owned with someone else.
• Why did you share?
• How did it feel?
Write about your reflections on the benefits of cheerful giving.

of security that comes with money. On the other hand, having too little can drive people to desperate acts. Having just enough money is satisfying and does not push people to any extreme.

Enjoying Life's Goodness

Simplicity is described well in the short story "Neighbour Rosicky" by U.S. writer Willa Cather. Rosicky was a Czech immigrant who had come to the Nebraska territory to plant his crops in the rich soil and to raise his family in the clean air. He struggled and never had a lot of money, but his family was happy and wholesome. In this passage, the town doctor reflected on why the Rosickys were such a happy family:

> Sometimes the Doctor heard the gossipers in the drug-store wondering why Rosicky didn't get on faster. He was industrious, and so were his boys, but they were rather free and easy, weren't pushers, and they didn't always show good judgment. They were comfortable, they were out of debt, but they didn't get much ahead. Maybe, Doctor Burleigh reflected, people as generous and warm-hearted and affectionate as the Rosickys never got ahead much; maybe you couldn't enjoy your life and put it into the bank, too.

What Cather described was simplicity: having enough, being generous and warmhearted, and enjoying the goodness of people instead of fretting about acquiring more possessions.

Simple living is not simple to do. Considerable thought is required to sort out what is necessary, what is luxury, and what is just plain silly. Additionally, simplicity demands that we have enough strength of personality to act generously and deliberately instead of being dragged along by our every whim or by every advertisement. Like the Rosicky family, maybe we cannot enjoy life and put it into the bank, too.

If you decided to simplify your life—streamline ownership of things and depend less on money for happiness—how would you do it? Try to outline a "simplicity of life" plan:
- What would you give away?
- What would you keep?
- What are all of the ways that you could have fun without spending money?

Equality

Another characteristic of the Christian attitude toward ownership is the notion of the fundamental **equality** of all persons in God's sight. Certainly no preferential treatment based on class distinctions should exist among Christians. In Saint James' letter, he said:

> . . . Do not let class distinction enter into your faith in Jesus Christ, our glorified Lord. Now suppose a man comes into

your synagogue, well-dressed and with a gold ring on, and at the same time a poor man comes in, in shabby clothes, and you take notice of the well-dressed man, and say, "Come this way to the best seats"; then you tell the poor man, "Stand over there" or "You can sit on the floor by my foot-rest." . . .

The right thing to do is to keep the supreme Law of scripture: you will love your neighbour as yourself; but as soon as you make class distinctions, you are committing sin and under condemnation for breaking the Law. (James 2:1–3,8,9)

Once again, the central principle for Christians—loving our neighbors as we love ourselves—gives us guidance on how to live our lives.

Justice

". . . Private charity and voluntary action are not sufficient. We also carry out our moral responsibility to assist and empower the poor by working collectively through government to establish just and effective public policies" (*Economic Justice for All,* no. 186). This statement by the U.S. Catholic bishops in their pastoral letter on the economy summarized an essential characteristic of the Christian attitude toward ownership of money and possessions—justice. Their point was that although private charity and sharing are imperative, individual good works will not counterbalance the harm done by the unjust and oppressive laws and practices that are allowed by society. **Justice** demands that Christians address and reverse these laws and public practices.

As an illustration of this point, reflect on the increasing numbers of homeless people referred to in the bishops' statement on page 200. The causes of the increase in homelessness are many:
- a nationwide policy of discharging patients from state mental hospitals without adequate community support systems to care for them
- unemployment
- cuts in government funding for public welfare programs
- cuts in government funding for public housing programs

Charitable individuals and groups have helped thousands of street people to find shelter and food, but ultimately changes that address the *causes* of homelessness are needed to solve this

Although private charity and sharing are imperative, such good works will not counterbalance the harm done by unjust and oppressive laws and practices.

Research this week's newspapers and news magazines to find three areas in which changes need to be made in our social system so that needy people are better served. Write about those areas.

plight. Working toward such changes is the task of Christians, cooperating with other people of goodwill. Christianity does not stop at charity but moves on to work toward justice in public policy.

Six Guidelines

The following six guidelines summarize the Christian attitude toward ownership:

1. *Celebrate the creator's gift.* All of the earth is God's. We are simply guardians and helpers in tending creation. God has given us the earth to provide for our needs. All of life is a gift to be celebrated and cherished—not to be possessed and hoarded as if we will own it forever. Besides, loving and caring are far more important than material possessions.

2. *Remain free.* We need not be taken in by advertisements that tell us that happiness consists of owning a certain car, wearing just the right jacket, or having the ultimate sound system. We do not have to be possessed by possessions. Instead, we need to love ourselves enough to know that we are valuable and lovable just as we are.

3. *Share generously and cheerfully.* Sharing our surplus with others is one way of living joyfully, without the burden of excessive wealth. God promises innumerable blessings to those who give to help their neighbors.

4. *Live simply.* To live simply means to consume only what we need. It means that we may have more to share with other people and that we are not shackled by owning a lot of things that have to be protected. In the words of Saint Elizabeth Ann Seton, "Live simply, so that others may simply live."

5. *Advocate change.* Exercising our power to advocate change in public policy is one way of helping poor and powerless people. By using what influence we have for the common good—supporting consumer protection, human rights, and a just economic system—we build up the Body of Christ.

6. *Manage resources responsibly and knowledgeably.* In order to follow the first five guidelines, we need to responsibly and knowledgeably manage the resources entrusted to us by God. Most of us find it easy to engage in chaotic spending habits. We may spend spontaneously and then have to borrow money to take care of necessities. Even sharing generously can cause serious problems if we do it thoughtlessly. So learning to budget money and take proper care of

All of life is a gift to be celebrated and cherished.

possessions is essential to having adequate resources to meet our needs and to help other people in need.

Wherever Your Treasure Is . . .

We are economic beings, needing financial and material resources to survive. But we need to put our economic needs into a healthy perspective, one that sees their value and importance but does not make them the be-all and end-all of existence. We need to see our economic decisions as having the potential to contribute to the creation of a loving community, where everyone's needs are met simply because they are human beings who have dignity.

We need to see our economic decisions as contributing to the creation of a loving community.

Our decisions about money and possessions tell very powerfully who we are and what we value. In the Sermon on the Mount, Jesus spoke of the decisions that form our very hearts and souls:

> "Do not store up treasures for yourselves on earth, where moth and woodworm destroy them and thieves can break in and steal. But store up treasures for yourselves in heaven, where neither moth nor woodworm destroys them and thieves cannot break in and steal. For wherever your treasure is, there will your heart be too." (Matthew 6:19–21)

In our quest to fulfill our life dream, we need to ask ourselves if the treasure that holds such promise for us—our dream—is one that can be destroyed by moths or taken by thieves. We need to question whether our dream is primarily a material one or one that can never perish.

Review Questions

1. What is the issue in learning how to live with money and possessions?

2. How does discretionary income allow some measure of choice, pleasure, and power?

3. Using two examples from this chapter, describe how greed can affect people.

4. How is the buy-on-credit mentality created?

5. Describe three examples from this chapter of the effects of corporate greed.

6. Using two examples from the epistles of Paul and James, summarize the Christian attitude toward greed.

7. How can desire for money and possessions be a kind of slavery, and how did Jesus warn against it?

8. What is the biblical vision of creation as it relates to ownership and property?

9. How did the early Christians practice a life of sharing?

10. How does the story of Lazarus and the rich man relate to the contemporary global economy?

11. Describe simplicity from a Christian point of view.

12. How are equality and justice aspects of the Christian attitude toward money and possessions?

13. List and explain the six guidelines that summarize the Christian attitude toward ownership.

9 Leisure: Re-creating Yourself

IF we look at the amount of time, work, and planning that goes into our leisure time, we come to the strange conclusion that for most people, leisure is a serious matter. Most of us complain that we do not have enough leisure, so when each Monday comes around and we return to school or to work, we begin the long wait until Friday. We feel, sometimes acutely and even desperately, the need to renew ourselves through leisure.

The irony is that North Americans have more time for leisure today than any other generation in our history has had. The relative abundance of free time is a rather recent phenomenon:

- In 1860, the average North American worker put in sixty-eight hours on the job each week. Computed on the basis of a five-day work week, that was almost fourteen hours a day.
- A century later, the average worker was on the job for only thirty-seven hours each week—somewhat over seven hours a day.

These figures show that today, about *half* as much time is devoted to employed work as one hundred years ago, and the trend toward further shortening the work week is growing. In addition, time formerly spent on chores is now freed by laborsaving devices—microwave ovens, vacuum cleaners, washing machines and dryers, lawn mowers, snowblowers, and so on.

Unfortunately, the additional hours of leisure that we have available do not necessarily translate into more renewal and refreshment. Consider, for example, the dilemma in which Dee found herself:

Dee sat on the bar stool, glaring at Rosie, Larry, and Brian, who were drunkenly trying to play pool. "It's a good thing

North Americans have more time for leisure today than any other generation in our history has had.

the felt is already torn up," she muttered to herself angrily as Larry jammed his pool cue into the tabletop, making the cue ball hop wildly. Dee's companions laughed outrageously.

"Hey, Dee. Come on and play some pool!" Larry yelled through the smoke and clamor that surrounded the patrons of Kelly's Bar. "And bring me another beer."

This command further infuriated Dee. "That jerk. He can get his own beer," she fumed to herself. Her eyes stung from the smoke. "This is great. I can just imagine how smelly my sweater's going to be if we ever get out of here."

When Rosie had asked her to go out, Dee had not dreamed that she would be spending Friday night in a bar watching three drunk acquaintances play pool. All she wanted to do was to go somewhere to relax after a hard week of classes. She would have enjoyed sitting someplace comfortable, instead of on a wooden bar stool, and simply talking—getting to know Larry and Brian better. She wondered if such a thing as a sober social life existed around the university.

Dee's mind drifted to thoughts of what the next day at brunch in the student union would be like. Of course, the main topic of conversation would be how awful everyone feels from drinking so much. Dee groaned inwardly, "I suppose I'll have to speak in whispers at brunch because, as usual, the people at my table will all have hangovers."

Dee was distracted momentarily from her daydream when Larry lurched into her as he ordered another beer. "How come you didn't get me a beer?" he charged. But as soon as the sweating bottle was in Larry's hands, he forgot to wait for Dee's answer and stumbled back to the pool table.

Dee returned to her daydreaming, thinking now with a frown about her short-lived intramural career. She had believed that intramural sports would be a good way of getting to know people and simply relaxing, but the first tag football game had ended that illusion. Her dorm team had played the women from a sorority. After several plays, the teams had begun yelling at each other and at the referee who had called players from both sides for illegal blocks. Dee remembered how she had stalked off the field after being elbowed in the neck intentionally.

Now, looking at her watch, Dee wondered how much longer she would have to wait before arguing with Larry

Leisure is a time when we are allowed to not work; we are not pushed to do anything.

about not letting him drive home. "This is a terrible way to have fun and relax," Dee grumbled to the face that stared back at her from the mirror across the bar.

Dee's kind of dilemma is certainly not unusual. Obviously Larry, Brian, and Rosie had a different notion of what constitutes leisure than Dee had. Dee thought that surely there were better things to do with her leisure time than drinking or knocking heads in tag football. Perhaps Larry, Brian, and Rosie also wondered the next day why they had become so drunk on Friday night.

Many young adults turn to recreational activities for relief from stressful lives, but like Dee, many people begin to wonder what kinds of activities will really bring relaxation. Excessive drinking and competitive games that are taken too seriously do not have good track records for relaxing people. One of the tasks of this phase of your life, using leisure time for re-creating, entails examining how and what kinds of leisure can renew you.

Does the story about Dee seem realistic to you? Do you ever feel like Dee? If so, describe in writing a situation you have been in that parallels the situation in this story.

Time for Renewal

Leisure is a time when a person is free from the demands of work or other duties. This definition reflects the origins of the word *leisure,* which comes from the Latin word *licere,* meaning "to be permitted." Leisure is a time when we are allowed to not work; we are not pushed to do anything.

The Creative Power of Emptiness

Leisure has the potential to re-create us, to give us new life and freshness, to form us anew. The word *recreation* contains such a meaning. This ancient saying by the Chinese sage Lao-tzu seems to recognize this creative power of "emptiness," of time unstructured by demands and obligations:

> We put thirty spokes to make a wheel:
> But it is on the hole in the center that the use of the cart hinges.

> We make a vessel from a lump of clay;
> But it is the empty space within the vessel that makes it useful.

> We make doors and windows for a room;
> But it is the empty spaces that make the room livable.

Thus, while existence has advantages,
It is the emptiness that makes it useful.

Leisure is like emptiness. Just as the space in a vessel is essential for the vessel to be useful, so is leisure necessary for us. We need empty times—times when we have no projects to complete, no homework to do, no deadlines breathing down our necks. We need empty times to open our heads and hearts to listen, to think, to breathe freely, and to be in touch with ourselves.

Periods of leisure can be empty of demands and obligations but also very active. For example, four friends who spend ten days together on a canoe trip may be kept quite active. They paddle their way across lakes, carry canoes and packs overland, collect wood for fires, cook, set up tents, spend a lot of time applying mosquito repellent, and so on. With all of this "work," camping is still considered to be leisure because the element of duty is missing, the sense of "having to."

So leisure can involve plenty of exertion, or it may be much more restful, like simply lying on the ground while watching the clouds pass lazily overhead. What is essential to a leisure activity's power to re-create us is that it be something we want to and love to do, something we undertake because we enjoy it.

When Play Is Really Work

Some leisure activities are goal-oriented; that is, at the same time that they are enjoyable, they also produce an outcome:
- making a quilt
- building bookshelves
- performing in a community theater production
- taking a course on local history

However, **play** is a type of leisure activity that involves mental or physical exertion but produces no particular outcome other than the enjoyment of the activity itself. Its purpose is simply to enable people who are playing to have fun. The spirit of freedom and spontaneity that characterizes play is something that modern human beings seem to have particular problems with.

For many people, the joy of play has been left behind with the activities of childhood. Yet, like children, adults need to play. Consider this example:

I know a man who cannot play with his children. He says that they make him impatient. When they sit down to play

Do some brainstorming to come up with a list of objects that require emptiness to be useful. Then write your reflections on this question:
- What experiences of emptiness—times when you have been free of demands and tasks—have had great value to your development as a worker, a student, or simply a human being?

Create a list of active leisure activities that require a great deal of effort but are still enjoyable.

Considering the definition and description of leisure given in this chapter, answer this question in writing:
- Were Dee's friends experiencing leisure?

a game of cards the children keep changing the rules! "How can you play if you keep changing the rules?" He does like to play tennis on Sunday mornings. "There you have definite rules and something to accomplish." I think that the fellow is a fixated worker and does not know it. The fact that he cannot play with his children is consistent with the way that he lives his life. He is a worker at everything. He tells me that he plays tennis; I suspect that he is "working" at something he enjoys. (Martin C. Helldorfer, *The Work Trap,* page 17)

Even competitive sports, the primary attempts that adults make to play, can themselves be work if undertaken with a spirit of having to win. They can be draining rather than renewing, tension-building rather than relaxing.

Describe a time when what should have been play became work for you. Write about the circumstances that caused this change.

Even for God, a Day Off

In the Book of Genesis, we are told that even God rested after working for six days to create the world:

> Thus heaven and earth were completed with all their array. On the seventh day God had completed the work he had been doing. He rested on the seventh day. . . . God blessed the seventh day and made it holy, because on that day he rested after all his work of creating. (Genesis 2:1–3)

The message of this excerpt from Genesis is that if God took a rest, we certainly can, too. God is not like human beings, who physically and mentally wear out. Rather, the wisdom of this passage is that it is a godlike practice to contemplate the wonders of creation, to rest in and appreciate God.

The Practice of the Sabbath

The Judeo-Christian practice of observing the Sabbath (literally, "rest") as a day of rest and worship dates from the earliest days of Israel's history as a people liberated from slavery in Egypt:

> " 'Observe the Sabbath day and keep it holy, as Yahweh your God has commanded you. Labour for six days, doing all your work, but the seventh day is a Sabbath for Yahweh your God. You must not do any work that day, neither you, nor your son, nor your daughter, nor your servants—male

or female—nor your ox, nor your donkey, nor any of your animals, nor the foreigner who has made his home with you; so that your servants, male and female, may rest, as you do. Remember that you were once a slave in Egypt, and that Yahweh your God brought you out of there with mighty hand and outstretched arm; this is why Yahweh your God has commanded you to keep the Sabbath day.' " (Deuteronomy 5:12–15)

Moses reminded the Israelites that God had saved them from slavery in Egypt and that God intended that no living creatures, even the animals, should ever become slaves to work again. Thus the Sabbath, with its detailed laws to guarantee that a spirit of work would not creep into this sacred day, was required.

For the most part, Jesus kept the laws of Sabbath observance, but he spoke out against the Pharisees' legalistic interpretation that put the laws above the needs of human beings: "The Sabbath was made for man, not man for the Sabbath" (Mark 2:27).

Jesus understood his own need for leisure that would bring him refreshment and new strength for his mission. Repeatedly, the Gospels cite instances when Jesus, either alone or with his disciples, withdrew to pray and meditate. He is also pictured enjoying companionship at many banquets, even making wine for the guests at a wedding feast. Jesus knew the importance of leisure.

Among the early Christians, the practice of the Sabbath was transferred from Saturday, the Jewish day of rest, to Sunday, the day of the Resurrection. The celebration of the Eucharist—a feast of love, gratitude, and remembrance—became the highest form of leisure for the early Christians.

Worship as Leisure

The Eucharist—in fact, all worship—can be seen as the model of leisure. Many experiences of worship combine to bring renewal to worshipers:
- celebration
- gratitude
- rest
- realization of life's meaning and purpose

In almost every culture, certain days are set apart for worship. Work is put aside. Special ceremonies are conducted, and feasts are shared. What we currently consider leisure once had

Recall the ways in which you spend a typical Sunday. List each activity that you might do and the amount of time that you might spend on each one. Then write a response to this question:
- How do you assess the quality of your Sunday leisure?

its roots in worship. For instance, the Greeks held festivals to the gods, during which the great tragic dramas like *Oedipus the King* and *Antigone* were performed. The main point of the plays was to illustrate the relationship between the gods and human beings. Parts of the pageantry of the plays were prayers and songs to the gods. Drama is still considered a form of leisure, even though its roots in worship have been forgotten by most people.

Most cultures have recognized the need not only for rest but also for definite times to worship and to celebrate God's action in their lives. Worship is recognized by many of the world's people as offering the kind of renewal that leisure brings.

In our contemporary world, families particularly need to rediscover a sense of worshipful rest and peace together. One mother described her family's method of calming down, a ritual that they call their Sabbath:

> "It is planned for a time when we're all tired and tense. We prepare ahead of time to keep ourselves from being caught up in schedules. No one works that day. After turning off our phone, we sleep in or have a quiet morning and some family activity in the afternoon—maybe a hike, a picnic, or a movie. We avoid driving far or spending much money. We rediscovered local streams and parks we'd ignored for years. Driving slowly we talk and explore, relaxing to recharge mental energy. We visit others only by consent of everyone in the family. Sometime during the day we include devotions. Our five-year-old son particularly likes to turn out the lights, light a candle, pop corn, and listen to religious music. This is amazingly calming, like a campfire.
>
> "Our Sabbath does wonders for our entire family. It is a way of saying we come first to each other and to God, and that there are times when no one may make demands on us." (Quoted in Longacre, *Living More with Less*, pages 220–221)

Worship can be a model of leisure; it combines celebration, gratitude, rest, and realization of life's meaning.

The Benefits of Leisure

Whether our leisure pursuits are solitary or done with other people, whether they have certain goals or no goal but enjoyment itself, these activities have the effect of re-creating us. In other words, they help us to pull together our scattered or worn-out selves, find fresh energy, and go on to cope and grow. A given leisure activity might re-create us by offering one or more of the following benefits:

- personal space
- reduction of stress
- physical health
- learning
- creative expression
- social growth

Personal Space

Leisure can give us room to cope with emotional, spiritual, and other issues that come up in the course of living. Sometimes we need to have some personal space in order to open our eyes and see things in new ways. The poet Robert Frost described this need for drawing back in his poem "Birches":

> It's when I'm weary of considerations,
> And life is too much like a pathless wood
> Where your face burns and tickles with the cobwebs
> Broken across it, and one eye is weeping
> From a twig's having lashed across it open.
> I'd like to get away . . . awhile
> And then come back . . . and begin over.

When we are worried and cannot seem to find our way, when we just cannot think straight and have been hurt, we need to pull back for a time, regroup, and prepare to begin over.

Personal space might be an afternoon at home listening to music, a walk alone or with a friend in a park, or just about anything that allows us time to think or to let go of pressures from the roles that we have as students, workers, teachers, or parents.

Sometimes we need to have some personal space in order to open our eyes and see things in new ways.

Recall a stressful period of your life. Try to describe in writing the factors that caused the stress and how you attempted to cope with the stress.

Reduction of Stress

One of the most helpful benefits of leisure is that it can reduce stress, which has a growing number of causes and manifestations in our society. Sources of stress for young adults range from external causes like financial pressures, deadlines, or bureaucratic regulations to internal causes like high or unrealistic expectations of oneself, guilt, conflict with others, or loneliness.

Of course, some stress is part of every life and can be expected to come our way even daily—such good things as the challenge of meeting new people. So we must cope with stress before its effects build in us to the point that we are overly stressed, manifesting any of the following characteristics:

- loss of commitment or energy
- cynicism or negativity
- sloppy work habits
- frequent absences
- alcohol or drug abuse
- withdrawal
- easily triggered anger
- rigid (strictly by-the-rules) action
- frequent illness
- depression
- lack of concentration
- chronic overwork

Whenever a cause of stress, such as a conflict with a roommate, can be identified, it needs to be addressed directly, and the wise use of leisure time helps us to identify and find the strength to confront that source of stress:

- If we are working too long, we need to cut back.
- Regular exercise, at least three times a week, is a great aid.
- Balancing work with periods of play and time with friends is very important.
- Sometimes we can find relief from stress simply by talking about it with someone.
- Spending time in private, "doing nothing," can be our most valuable antidote to stress. During such times, we can listen to what our inner voice is telling us.

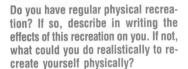

List some antidotes to stress that you could build into your lifestyle. For instance, more sleep, exercise, or realistic personal expectations.

Physical Health

Closely related to leisure's ability to reduce stress are leisure's benefits to physical health. In recent years, the relationship between physical and emotional wellness has been studied actively. Although all of the precise relationships are not understood, physical wellness can contribute to emotional health, and the ability to cope with stress can contribute to physical health. People in good bodily shape tend to have more energy for all of their tasks, and they seem to feel better about themselves, too. Likewise, people who are able to cope well emotionally are less likely to become ill.

So by reducing stress, almost any kind of enjoyable leisure promotes physical well-being. In addition, some forms of leisure—such as swimming, racquetball or tennis, aerobics, or yoga—promote physical health directly.

Do you have regular physical recreation? If so, describe in writing the effects of this recreation on you. If not, what could you do realistically to recreate yourself physically?

Learning

After twelve years of formal education, many seniors do not automatically think of learning as a benefit of leisure or even as connected to leisure. Learning seems instead to be more the product of toil. The ancient Greeks looked at learning differently. In fact, the Greek word for leisure is *schole,* from which we derive the word *school.* For the ancient Greeks, learning and leisure were synonymous; learning was freely chosen because it led to enjoyment. School was not compulsory (no one took attendance), and the curriculum flexed with the interests of the students. North Americans need to recover the ancient Greeks' sense of the intimate connection between leisure and the pleasures of learning.

The learning that comes from reading an interesting article or book, talking with someone new, or listening to someone in a new way is a pleasurable benefit of leisure. Traveling in a leisurely way can be a wonderful learning experience. As long as we are open but not striving under some compulsion to learn, we will find all kinds of learning in leisure experiences.

Describe in writing one instance in which you experienced enjoyment while learning.

Leisure permits us the time and the atmosphere to lower our guard and to give full sway to the creative side of ourselves.

Creative Expression

Some forms of leisure offer us the benefit of creative expression not frequently found in the workplace. Amateur musicians, artists, and actors abound, along with gardeners and just plain funny people. Leisure permits us the time and the atmosphere to lower our guard and to give full sway to the creative side of ourselves, using our right side of the brain. (See the discussions right-brain and left-brain thinking on pages 142–143 and on creating on pages 155–158).

Social Growth

Although relationships can begin at work, the intimacy of friendship typically grows during times away from work. Relationships require time and freedom to be nurtured, and leisure offers the fertile soil of time that is free from demands and obligations.

Going with friends to games or movies, eating together, and simply talking are essential to our growth as social beings. The feedback that we receive helps us to establish a sense of identity and gain self-confidence.

Overcoming Barriers to Leisure

Most of us do not have to be convinced that leisure provides many benefits. After all, people almost universally crave leisure, recognizing intuitively that they need its renewing effects—even if they are not quite sure what to do with leisure time once they have it.

Relationships require time and freedom to be nurtured.

With increasing amounts of leisure time, North Americans in the closing decades of the twentieth century have the potential to re-create themselves and to grow in unprecedented ways. However, a number of common barriers stand in the way of such growth and renewal:

- boredom
- equating leisure with consumption
- difficulty in balancing work and leisure
- lack of leisure for mothers at home

We need to overcome these barriers if the leisure time increasingly available to us is to deliver the renewal that it promises.

Boredom

- The weekend was a real drag. The dance was boring and so was the game. And wasn't my date blah? Conversations with him are as much fun as watching paint dry. Nothing was on TV! Some boring old movie from the sixties was on late Saturday night. Then on Sunday I had to do homework. Yuck! I hated that novel for English class. It was so slow-moving. Tell me what happened because I just could not get through it. When I took a break in the afternoon, my family was watching football. Why they sat there watching when

Does this complaint of boredom sound familiar to you? List two or three times in recent weeks when you felt bored. Then answer these questions in writing:
- Why were you bored?
- How could you have turned those situations into leisure?

the score was 42–0 is beyond me. When I asked them that, they just stared at me like I was crazy. So that was my fun weekend. Boring, boring, boring.

Most of us have probably caught ourselves complaining like this. Boredom seems to be a major complaint against life.

One hundred years ago, only a fraction of the population had time to be bored, but shortened work hours and once unimagined laborsaving and timesaving devices have changed all that. Now boredom—a weariness and restlessness caused by a lack of interest—seems to plague many people's leisure time.

Engagement: The Key to Renewal

People who are chronically bored seem not to invest themselves in life. They tend to settle for extremely limited goals, making trivia the focus of their leisure time. They might not even be conscious of how bored they are. Passive, repetitious activity fills their free time, activity like watching soap operas, sporting events, and game shows on television or driving around for hours on end.

Bored people may try to escape their boredom by repeating the same passive activities, but they fail to realize that becoming *engaged* in life, unlike passively watching life or TV mockups of life, is the key to overcoming boredom and being re-created by leisure. Taking a community education course, exercising, attempting something creative, socializing, enjoying a concert—these require personal involvement, and they yield many of the renewing benefits of leisure that we discussed earlier. Going to school, an activity that is the focus of boredom for many students, can actually be experienced as leisure if the student invests herself or himself in learning and does not feel compelled to learn.

Even doing nothing, recommended earlier as a source of renewal, implies an involvement of mind and emotions or it becomes boring. Take this situation, for example:

- On Sunday afternoon, Denise goes to the park and sits in the shade of an ancient oak tree. After a few minutes she thinks to herself, "Well, what am I going to do now? I can't just sit here. It's boring." While she is thinking about how bored she is, huge white clouds are sailing overhead. The tree's branches are quivering in the breeze. Children are swinging and laughing. And the busy week she just finished has gone unexamined, including the reasons for the fight she had with her boyfriend.

If watching television seems to promote passivity in us, it is not offering the refreshing leisure that we need.

Denise correctly realizes that she will be bored if she does not become engaged in some way, but she thinks that she has to *do something external* in order to be engaged and to overcome boredom. Denise does not realize that engaging her mind in enjoying the scenes around her or in examining what is going on in her life is exactly what she needs to do. Doing nothing implies internal engagement, but people may bypass that involvement in their inner world in favor of external activity. Thus, they lose out on the refreshing benefits of simply doing nothing.

Watching Television: Leisure or Boredom?

Is watching television really leisure? The answer to this question is *maybe*. Some programs engage us, challenging us to think, to feel strongly, or to learn. However, when watching television is only an attempt to escape from life by passively observing the antics of others, it leads to boredom.

Unfortunately, many TV programs satisfy us like a steady diet of white bread might. The first several bites would be satisfying enough, but soon we would become bored and want something more exciting—peanut butter, cheese spread, or cream cheese with dill—anything to add spice to the drab bread. TV addicts keep hoping to find the spice that they are looking for in the next show.

If watching television seems to promote passivity in us, we can be sure that it is not offering the refreshing leisure that we need. In addition, the inactivity of sitting for hours can actually impair our health and increase, not decrease, our level of stress.

Equating Leisure and Consumption

Another barrier to getting the refreshment that we need from leisure is the notion that leisure is synonymous with consumption, with spending money on consumer items. However, leisure is not the same as having things—even enjoyable things like a recreational vehicle, a powerboat, membership in a health club or spa, a swimming pool in the backyard, or a vacation at a fancy resort. Unfortunately, many people go into debt to buy such things, which means that they have to work harder and worry more about paying for their leisure.

Vacations, for instance, can be wonderful opportunities for refreshing ourselves if they free us of stress, give us space, allow

The notion that leisure is synonymous with spending money on consumer items is a barrier to leisure.

Do some daydreaming. Imagine that you have three days free of all work and other obligations. You also have whatever money you will need. Outline in detail how you will use this leisure time:
• Where will you spend this free time?
• What will you do?
• Who will be your companions—if you invite any?

Imagine that you have three days of free time and that you have *little* money to spend. Outline in detail how you will use this time.

Write about what the ideal vacations you described above say about who you are and what your dream is.

for creativity, and offer chances for fun and enjoyment. But sometimes vacations lead to work because, in an attempt to buy two weeks of sun and sand, people have to skimp and save during the other fifty weeks of the year to pay off a loan for the vacation.

Besides the work and stress of paying for big-ticket leisure items, many possessions used for enjoyment require maintenance. Boats, cars, lake cabins, and swimming pools can take a lot of energy out of us. For example, consider owning a swimming pool. Unless we have enough money to hire a company to do such work, we have to vacuum it, check the water purification system regularly, and drain and clean it periodically. Surely owning a pool has advantages. Swimming is great exercise. Floating on an air mattress is relaxing on a hot afternoon. But the responsibilities can be burdensome and may end up turning leisure into work.

Some leisure activities that have been listed in this chapter are inexpensive, even free. The key point is that spending money on leisure does not guarantee that we will be refreshed. In fact, consumption for leisure can have the opposite effect, making us work for and worry about our possessions.

Work and Leisure: A Difficult Balance

As we discussed in chapter 7, many people become addicted to work. It becomes their reason for existence—the all-absorbing focus of life. Whether people are obsessed with work in order to make more money (often so that they can purchase leisure items) or in order to feel worthy, responsible, or important, the result is the same: work addicts do not have time to receive the renewal that they need from leisure.

Balancing work and leisure can be a very difficult task. The rewards of working can seem to far outweigh the less tangible benefits of relaxation. People inclined to think that way need to realize that leisure aids their ability to work. Many of our most creative ideas occur when we are relaxed—when we are being leisurely. Employees who approach their work day refreshed by leisure are much more productive on the job. So companies that require workers to put in unusually long hours can actually hurt their own interests in addition to hurting their employees.

A person's commitment to a healthy balance between work and leisure may be a hindrance to promotion in a career if the company that he or she works for does not see the value in such a balance. Consider Susan's situation:

Susan works as a salesperson for a pharmaceutical company. The company managers are so pleased with the way she has developed her sales territory that they want to move her to another state to open up a new territory. The move will bring a substantial raise for her.

Three years ago Susan accepted her present territory after successfully building up business in what had previously been a very weak area for the company. She has proven her value to the company in both of these territories through extremely hard work and long hours.

But recently Susan has found a balance in her life. Because her sales territory is secure, she has turned more of her attention to her personal life—making friends in town, buying a house, and enjoying the nearby national park, where she frequently hikes or cross-country skis in winter. Susan is not interested in moving and starting all over again, working herself to exhaustion and foregoing a personal life.

Susan is worried, though. Two other salespeople who refused to relocate for the company now have dead-end careers. Their pay raises have been meager; one of them needed more money later and asked for a change in location but was passed over. Susan knows that by turning down the move, she is jeopardizing her chances for advancement in the future.

When Susan tells her supervisor of her decision, she is treated coldly and basically is told that the company will not take her decision lightly.

Susan thinks that the price of moving again is too high when measured against the satisfying balance of work and leisure that she has found. She has opted for that balance even at the risk of decreasing her future financial success. Ideally, companies should respect employees' decisions to lead balanced lives, recognizing that in the long run, such decisions will promote the employees' health and productivity.

Mothers at Home: A Lack of Leisure

One group of people who seem particularly blocked from the leisure time that they need are women with young children. (Increasingly, men are taking on some of the caretaking tasks that

Many of our most creative ideas occur when we are relaxed.

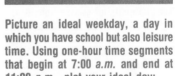

Picture an ideal weekday, a day in which you have school but also leisure time. Using one-hour time segments that begin at 7:00 *a.m.* and end at 11:00 *p.m.*, plot your ideal day:
• What would you do?
• Who would you be with?
• Would there be a balance between work and leisure?

"The 'letting be' and 'letting happen' may turn out to be the most significant thing one can do."

Set two goals for yourself about using leisure better, and write them down. Try to be specific. For instance, I will go swimming at the YMCA at least three times a week. Then write some practical strategies for meeting your goals. For example, I will check on a YMCA membership this afternoon.

Write a short prayer that talks with God about your use of leisure and asks for help in meeting your goals for leisure.

traditionally have been done by women. The considerations here could also apply to fathers who take full responsibility for child care.) A woman who stays at home to care for her young children may find herself worn out and depleted. Because she is at home, she gets the message that she is not "working," but in fact, she is always on the job. She has little privacy; recreational activity is almost impossible; and she cannot leave her young children while she goes outside for exercise without hiring a sitter.

Caring for children is a twenty-four-hour-a-day job with little recognition. Although attitudes have changed somewhat, many men still feel that when they come home, their work is done. So instead of helping with children and household tasks, husbands feel that they have a right to leisure.

The burden on an employed mother whose husband recognizes only his own need for leisure is even worse. In such cases, the woman is expected to shoulder full responsibility for cooking, cleaning, and child care in addition to bringing home a paycheck. This is a recipe for physical and emotional exhaustion.

In thinking about a possible marriage, both individuals need to take a hard look at their mutual expectations about child care and household responsibilities. A balance between work and leisure is important in each individual's life, and married partners have to be willing to negotiate that balance in their own relationship.

The Value of "Wasted" Time

Making a welcome space for leisure in our lives is not a luxury but a necessity. Renowned psychologist Rollo May summed up the re-creating potential of leisure in his words about "wasted" time:

We can use [leisure] for random thinking, reverie, or for simply wandering around a new city for a time. Yes, the time may be wasted. But who is to say that this "wasted" time may not bring us our most important ideas or new experiences, new visions, that are invaluable? The "letting be" and "letting happen" may turn out to be the most significant thing one can do. (*Freedom and Destiny,* page 177)

Review Questions

1. What is leisure, and why is it necessary?

2. What distinguishes play from other types of leisure? How can play become work?

3. In Genesis 2:1–3, why did God take a day off after creating the world?

4. How did the Jewish tradition affirm the importance of leisure in the Jewish laws? How did Jesus' life affirm leisure?

5. What is the relationship between leisure and worship?

6. List and describe the benefits of leisure.

7. How do many people try to escape from boredom? How is engagement in life the key to overcoming boredom?

8. In what ways can television viewing increase boredom? When can television viewing be considered leisure?

9. Consumption is sometimes equated with leisure. How can this be a false equation?

10. Why is it sometimes difficult to balance work and leisure?

11. What are some of the special problems with leisure that can be experienced by women with children?

10 Single Life: A Path to Fulfillment

MOST people lead the single life for some part of their lives, and in that sense, being single is quite common. What is not so common is an appreciation of living singly as a path to fulfillment and happiness, just as the other lifestyles—marriage, religious life, and ordained ministry—can lead to fulfillment. Being single is not simply a state of being *not* married, *not* a religious, or *not* a priest. It is that but also more than that: the **single life** is a lifestyle in its own right with its own unique opportunities and problems.

A Variety of Situations

Statistics demonstrate a dramatic rise in the number of single people living in the United States:

- Three times as many people under thirty-five years of age lived alone in 1980 as compared to 1970.
- One out of four households was composed of a single person.
- One out of ten adults never married.

Many situations account for the single status of millions of adults:

- Some people are single because of the death of a spouse.
- Other people delay marriage for further education or a career or because they have not found a person that they would want to marry.
- With the divorce rate at about 50 percent (that is, about half as many divorces as marriages occur in a year), a large percentage of singles are divorced people.
- Some people choose to remain single, and the number of singles in this category seems to be increasing.

The single life is a lifestyle in its own right with its own unique opportunities and problems.

The following remarks represent various situations of the single life:

- *Ruth:* I never thought Charlie would die so suddenly and so young. He was only sixty-three. We had talked a lot about things we would do when he retired. After three years, I've adjusted pretty well. Lucky for me, I had been working at the same job for fifteen years. Just having to get up and go to work helped me during those first months after he died. Since I quit work last year, I've gotten involved in the local senior citizen activities. Next week, my good friend and her husband and I are going to an Elderhostel program in New Mexico [Elderhostel is a summer program for older persons that consists of short courses offered by many college campuses]. We attended one last year and took courses on assessing property value, the flowers of Virginia, and the Gospel of Mark. The program is only a week long, and the price is reasonable. I learn a lot, and it's a nice chance to meet other older folks. I still miss Charlie, but he wouldn't want me to mope around. He would want me to enjoy life.

"I'm coping, but I'm also realizing all the stuff that I don't know about being a parent."

In writing, describe your reactions to Jan's comments.

- *Dave:* If I couldn't use a can opener and there weren't any frozen dinners, I'd be in big trouble. No, really I'm coping, but I'm also realizing all the stuff that I don't know about being a parent. Ever since my wife and I separated, I've come to appreciate all the work that she did. After four months of being a single parent, I still mess up the wash cycles on the laundry, occasionally forget what time Scottie gets out of day care, and on and on. The worst thing—I'll never forget it—was when I came home from work, still ticked off at one of the accountants, and I started dinner and completely forgot to get poor Scottie. I still get real emotional when I think about how I got there and found him sitting on the steps, crying his eyes out. I'll never forget to pick him up again. Like I say, things are rotten sometimes, but I'm much closer to my son now, and that's great.

- *Jan:* I've been single ever since college. I've dated a lot and even came close to becoming engaged once, but then the decision came down to whether I liked the way my life was going or whether I wanted to change it by marrying. I had to admit that I liked being able to travel as much as I do without feeling that I was neglecting kids or a husband. And now I am next in line for a promotion. If I get it, I'll have to move to Pittsburgh. The promotion is a great opportunity that I might not have had if I had gotten married. Sure,

I get lonely sometimes, and I may get married someday. But I'm just not ready to take on that type of responsibility. Maybe, because I'm thirty-three, I'm fooling myself that I might get married someday. For right now, though, I'm really happy with my life as it is.

Whether chosen or the result of circumstances, the single lifestyle can be rich in experience, purposeful, and fulfilling.

The Calling to Single Life

A Life of Loving

For those persons who choose to remain single because of a conviction that that lifestyle represents the best way for them to grow and to make a contribution to the world, the single life is a vocation—a calling. Other persons who are single by force of circumstance and who do not wish to embrace the single life permanently still need to value their singleness as a lifestyle to which God may be calling them, even if only for a short time. They need not consider this phase of life as merely a "holding pattern" until something better comes along. The story of a life's unfolding can be mysterious indeed, with events and circumstances eventually bringing forth unimagined fruits. By valuing the opportunities and challenges of singleness, a single person can make a valuable contribution to humankind and can develop his or her own life, too.

Central to the call for all Christians is the command to love God and neighbors. As was discussed in chapter 3, love is essential to happiness and to a sense of meaning in life, and love can be given and received whether a person is single, married, religious, or ordained. The single life is as much a call to love as the other lifestyles are. The person who taught us most dramatically and effectively about the centrality of love was Jesus—a single person. Within a single lifestyle, Jesus answered the call to love, giving Christians for all time a model of how the single life can be a life of love.

Many single people contribute their time, money, and energy to loving in some of the following ways:

- their jobs—both in their dedication to the work itself and in the ways that they treat their co-workers
- volunteer work in parishes, soup kitchens, programs for the handicapped, and so on
- commitment to a cause such as world peace or environmental issues

Many single people contribute their time, money, and energy to loving through volunteer work, for example, helping in a soup kitchen.

- generous, supportive friendship with others
- work in foreign countries where people are in need—for example, through the Peace Corps or the Maryknoll Lay Missioners

Jean Donovan: A Call to Serve in El Salvador

In the late 1970s, a young single woman from Cleveland, Ohio, found herself pulled from a rather comfortable life by a sense that she was meant for something more. At twenty-four years of age, *Jean Donovan* had a master's degree in economics, an executive position with one of the largest accounting firms in the United States, a nice apartment, her own car, and a motorcycle. She had close friends and a caring family. Yet she also had a belief that she was called to work with the poor people of El Salvador. So Donovan left the security of job, relationships, and possessions to join a team of Catholic missionaries who were distributing food and clothing to Salvadoran victims of the civil war that was tearing the country apart. She explained why she went into this dangerous situation:

> I have been thinking about this vocation for many years. Actually I think, that for a number of years, Christ has been sending various people into my life, that through their example and actions I saw a calling to missionary work. I have a gut feeling that my main motivation to be a missionary is a true calling from God. (Ana Carigan, *Salvador Witness,* page 67)

Death squads were killing anyone who showed the least sign of opposition to the Salvadoran government and the very rich people who wanted to stay in power there. Some priests and religious had already been killed. Donovan knew this before she went to El Salvador and wrote:

> There's one thing I know, that I'm supposed to be down here, right now. Not that I'm going to be able to do anything, or contribute to anything, but it's just a feeling I have. And maybe—maybe I *will* be able to. . . . I read a very interesting article . . . about Tom Dooley hospital [Dooley, a single man, was a doctor who served in Laos in the 1950s and 1960s during a civil war]—and two of the things that really hit me in it were: first, that you can contribute a lot and make a big difference in the world if you realize that

Jean Donovan, a lay missioner in El Salvador, said yes to life, found meaning in caring for other people, and gave up her life for them.

the world you're talking about might be very small—maybe one person, or two people. And the other thing it said was that if you can find a place to serve, you can be happy. I think, they're both really true. (Carigan, *Salvador Witness,* page 96)

Because of their work with poor people and other victims of the civil war, Donovan and three U.S. women religious were targeted for execution. Donovan knew that she was in danger; anyone who helped needy Salvadorans or showed the slightest objection to the military was at grave risk. Death came in December 1980 when Donovan and the other three women were returning from the airport to the town where they worked. Their van was stopped by Salvadoran national guardsmen. The women were raped, murdered, and buried in a shallow grave.

Jean Donovan said yes to life, found meaning in caring for other people, and gave up her life for them. She would have felt that she was answering her call to serve even if she had contributed to the lives of only one or two persons. But Donovan could not have anticipated the inspiration that her life and death would give to thousands of North Americans who for the first time would open their eyes to the injustices being done in El Salvador and would become involved in the U.S. religious movement for justice.

Christians are called to live out the mission of love in unique ways. For Jean Donovan, the way to live out that mission was as a single woman and lay missioner. A person who wants to discern his or her distinct call needs to ask the question, How is God calling me to grow, to develop, to love, and to serve? For some people, the vocation will be to a single life. From a Christian point of view, single persons can make a difference and be happy if they care for others—even if the world they care for is very small.

Misunderstanding the Single Life: Barriers to Hearing the Call

Discerning a genuine call is not an easy matter. It requires a radical openness to possibilities that a person may not have considered before as well as rigorous honesty with oneself. Unfortunately, the single life is frequently misunderstood and clouded by societal prejudices. These barriers to understanding can make it even more difficult for a person to discern a clear call to that way of life.

Do you agree with this statement by Jean Donovan? Think of instances when you have made a big difference in the world—even if that world consisted of only one or two persons. Describe one instance in writing.

Research Jean Donovan's life. Write about how she arrived at her decision to serve the people of El Salvador.

The chief prejudice about the single life is the presumption that marriage is the normal way of life; so by implication, being single is assumed to be abnormal. For instance:

- Courses like this one for high school seniors used to be (and in many places still are) called "marriage" courses.
- Formerly, men who were not married were dubbed as "old bachelors"; single women used to be called "spinsters" (recall the card game "Old Maid": nobody wants the Old Maid card).
- Today's myth of the "swinging single" as a pleasure-seeking female or male desperately looking for a temporary partner is no improvement on the old images.
- Church activities are usually directed toward children and married adults—schools and religious education programs, sacramental preparation programs for children and their parents, dances for couples, and so on. Activities for single people are scarce in the churches.
- When screening job applicants for high-level positions, many major corporations assume that a single person may not have the stability and maturity necessary for corporate responsibility.
- Dinners and parties both inside and outside the business world are often geared toward married couples. A single person may feel that like it or not, he or she must bring a date or stay away.

Is the image of the "swinging single" a myth or a reality? What are some common misconceptions about the single life other than those mentioned in this chapter? List as many as you can think of and your reactions to them.

Today's myth of the "swinging single" is no improvement on former images of single persons.

An individual who sincerely seeks to know whether her or his call is to the single life must sift through such evidence of prejudice and misunderstanding, putting it aside in favor of a realistic assessment of the opportunities and problems of being single.

Being Single: Opportunities and Problems

Each opportunity in life seems to carry with it a corresponding problem. Opportunity entails risk. The single life, like every lifestyle, has unique opportunities and problems. Whether a person is single permanently or temporarily, by choice or by circumstance, considering these opportunities and problems can help that person to consciously shape his or her decisions about how to live.

Freedom or the Danger of Egocentrism?

The Opportunity: Freedom

A single person has **freedom** to make decisions based on her or his convictions, needs, or goals. Take Jack's situation, for example:

- For several years, Jack has been eager to move out of a major city to the mountains. He wants to hike, fish, hunt, and breathe the clean air—not only on vacations but all year round. Jack knows that he can quit his job as a mechanic at the airport and support himself on less money with a highway maintenance job. He realizes that if he were married and had kids, the decision would have to take into account his wife's desires and job and their children's needs. This decision is easier for Jack than it would be for a married person.

Single people have the freedom to choose for themselves— from simple choices like where to go for dinner to complex decisions like cross-country moves or career changes. They can involve themselves in unpopular causes or take on volunteer tasks that might seem impractical or risky to some observers. For instance, Jean Donovan put her life in danger. A married person with young children would need to evaluate her or his decision to take such a risk against a very different backdrop of responsibilities and concerns.

Dorothy Day, founder (with Peter Maurin) of the Catholic Worker Movement, lived her single life with the freedom that she believed all Christians are called to have. In the 1930s, she began a newspaper that advocated peace and justice (which still sells for a penny a copy), and she started a network of houses of hospitality (staffed largely by single people), which continue

List five single people over the age of twenty-two with whom you are acquainted. Interview one or two of them to find out what they see as the advantages and the disadvantages of the single lifestyle. Then summarize the results of each interview in a report.

Dorothy Day, co-founder of the Catholic Worker Movement, lived her single life with the freedom that she believed all Christians are called to have.

to shelter homeless people and feed hungry people. Although arrested many times in protests against U.S. involvement in three different wars, in marches for voters' rights, and in support of strikes by migrant farm workers, Day kept speaking out in print and in person, spreading the gospel message.

What Day preached was a stirring call to leave behind the false thinking of the times—a thinking that trapped people into maintaining personal security rather than living the freedom of the Gospel. These words about security, written in 1935, still have a very contemporary ring:

> Christ told Peter to put aside his nets and follow him. He told the rich young man to sell what he had and give to the poor and follow Him. . . . He spoke of feeding the poor, sheltering the homeless, of visiting those in prison and the sick, and also of instructing the ignorant. . . .
>
> Paul Claudel [a French philosopher] said that young people have a hunger for the heroic, and too long they have been told: "Be moderate, be prudent." . . .
>
> In this present situation when people are starving to death [although] there is an overabundance of food, when religion is being warred upon throughout the world, our Catholic young people still come from schools and colleges and talk about looking for security, a weekly wage. . . .
>
> Why they think a weekly wage is going to give them security is a mystery. Do they have security on any job nowadays? If they try to save, the bank fails; if they invest their money, the bottom of the market drops out. If they trust to worldly practicality, in other words, they are out of luck. . . .
>
> What right has any one of us to security when God's poor are suffering?

Strong challenges, tough words. They came from a woman who gave up a career in commercial journalism to do just what she challenged others to do. In her printed words and in the witness of her own life, Day called people to a freedom that is rooted in the Gospel. She intended her message for Christians in all walks of life, not only in the single life, but her own single lifestyle gave her the freedom to live without the types of guarantees that many of us want.

The Problem: The Danger of Egocentrism

At the same time that the single life offers the freedom to make decisions based on a person's own convictions, needs, and

---

Write your reactions to Paul Claudel's statement.

List and describe all of the ways that people have told you to be moderate or prudent. Then answer this question in writing:

- What do you think can happen to people who live their entire lives being moderate—never being heroic in relationships or taking a stand on principle?

desires, it presents a parallel problem—the danger of developing **egocentrism,** a self-centered or selfish outlook.

Particularly if a single person lives alone, he or she may not have the constant opportunity for give-and-take relationships that are part of a community whose members are committed to one another, such as a family or a religious community. Such relationships rub off some of the rough edges of an individual's personality, enabling a person to adjust to other people's needs and ways of living.

The single life presents a problem— the danger of developing egocentrism, a self-centered or selfish outlook.

In the extreme, a lack of give-and-take relationships can lead to an inability to commit oneself to anything or anyone. The freedom to choose may become so distorted that an individual is absorbed only in choices that imply no involvement or commitment. When love is possible, an egocentric person might push away, saying that she or he does not want to be tied down. She or he will not take responsibility in a group endeavor because she or he "just cannot plan that far ahead." Some egocentric individuals literally wander from job to job, city to city, and even country to country, continuously moving away from commitment.

A writer conducted a series of interviews with some "WTs" —world travelers—a nickname given to drifters who inhabit beaches on sparsely populated islands in the Philippines. Many of the drifters were in their twenties and thirties, and most had

Do you have any rough edges in your personality that might become exaggerated if you lived alone? If you are unaware of any, ask your parents, brothers or sisters, or close friends.

dropped out of universities and out of society. Helga, a Swiss woman, was typical of the drifters:

- Well, I am a secretary for a year in Zurich. I make a lot of money and save everything, and then I go somewhere far away for as long as my money goes. Here it is cheap to live okay. I like the beaches, and Filipinos are very friendly. I may stop soon, though, because my life is going nowhere. I mean, I have no one to depend on, and my mother died last year. My brother and father could not find me because I was on an island with no phones. I found out about the funeral a month later. I do not know, but this may be my last trip. My life does not have any—well—*shape* to it.

Flexibility and freedom are advantages of single life, but Helga was right: when a person makes no commitments and is rootless, life can lack shape. Establishing a career and stable, intimate relationships does not become easier later in life.

> Can you think of any other examples of people without commitments, whose lives are shapeless? Write your reflections on how you think their lives became this way.

Solitude or Loneliness?

The Opportunity: Solitude

Some people assume that being alone is the same as loneliness, an emotionally painful condition. They fear being alone and dread being single if it means coming home to an empty apartment every night. Actually, time spent alone can be full and renewing. **Solitude**—being alone for thought, creative pursuits, rest, learning, or prayer—is necessary for growth as a person. The single life generally offers more opportunity for solitude than the other lifestyles because a single person typically has more control over his or her time and space.

Many creative persons have had the solitude to develop their talents because they were single. Among such persons was *Flannery O'Connor,* one of the most original and respected U.S. fiction writers of this century. For many of her productive years before her death in 1964, she suffered from a disease that handicapped her. Nevertheless, O'Connor used the time that she had to be creative. Her letters show her to have been feisty, witty, committed, and largely content with who she was. Of special importance is the fact that O'Connor learned to live with her illness and to use the solitude of her single life to think, write, and be creative. In one of her letters she wrote:

> In a sense sickness is a place, more instructive than a long trip to Europe, and it's always a place where there's no company, where nobody can follow. Sickness before death is

a very appropriate thing and I think those who don't have it miss one of God's mercies. Success is almost as isolating [as illness] and nothing points out vanity as well [as illness does].

O'Connor did not readily express her emotions about her illness and the anguish that it caused her. But as she indicated in the same letter, her inner emotional world gave thrust to her creativity:

But the surface hereabouts has always been very flat. I come from a family where the only emotion respectable to show is irritation. In some this tendency produces hives, in others literature, in me both.

On another occasion, O'Connor wrote wryly about herself as a person of faith:

I am not a mystic and I do not lead a holy life. Not that I can claim any interesting or pleasurable sins (my sense of the devil is strong) but I know all about the garden variety, pride, gluttony, envy and sloth, and what is more to the point, my virtues are as timid as my vices. . . .

However, the individual in the Church is, no matter how worthless himself, a part of the Body of Christ. . . . [But] I distrust pious phrases, particularly when they issue from my mouth.

Single people have the space and time to encounter themselves and to reflect on their experiences.

O'Connor's words show that she was involved with her faith, in touch with who she was, and witty. Her aloneness gave her time and space to write and to live fully despite her chronic illness. O'Connor's letters also point to another advantage of being single: To live in a healthy way, we all must come to grips with who we are and accept ourselves. Single people have the space and time to encounter themselves and to reflect on their experiences. By living alone, they may have a harder time running away from themselves than do people who are surrounded by family.

Aloneness or solitude that is chosen has other benefits. Being in touch with ourselves and our convictions can give us the courage to stand up for things that we believe in or to endure the social isolation of making an unpopular decision. Such courageous stands in turn can strengthen us even more. Solitude can strengthen our spirit. In addition, solitude can urge us to appreciate our relationships more. Sometimes we can see the beauty of good friends and family only when we have been away from them for a while.

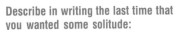

Describe in writing the last time that you wanted some solitude:
• What made you want time and space to be alone?
• If you were able to be in solitude, were you helped by the experience?

"Pray that your loneliness may spur you into finding something to live for, great enough to die for."

The Problem: Loneliness

Being alone is not always experienced in a positive way, as solitude. It may be experienced instead as **loneliness,** a feeling of sadness from being alone. Even when we are physically with people, we can feel lonely if we are psychologically isolated or alienated from them. Loneliness can exist in any walk of life, including marriage. It is part of the human condition.

Single life perhaps presents more obvious occasions for loneliness. One experience that single people frequently recount is the difficulty of coming home after a splendid day. No one is there to talk with about a great success, so the victory seems flat, perhaps meaningless. Or after a bad day, a single person needs a willing listener to help make sense of a failure, but no one is there to talk with, and the trouble seems to grow even worse. Eating meals alone, especially in restaurants, can feel particularly awkward and lonely.

As a single person grows older, the fear of being alone in old age also grows. Not having children or a community to take care of him or her during periods of illness can burden a single person with worry, physical distress, and loneliness. Knowing that a caring person is within earshot lightens the load of illness for anyone—young or old.

Loneliness can be heightened for divorced or widowed people. After years of living intimately with someone, they are suddenly deprived of companionship, affection, and the challenges of living closely with another person. A huge gap exists in their lives. Even if a relationship had been a difficult one, it nevertheless provided shape and form to life, and the absence of that relationship leaves a person feeling disconnected.

Although loneliness can be a painful problem of being single, it can also be an opportunity. Painful experiences are not always to be avoided; sometimes they are the path to growth. Psychologist Clark E. Moustakas, who has done extensive studies on loneliness, drew this conclusion:

Loneliness keeps open the doors to an expanding life. In utter loneliness one can find answers to living, one can find new values to live by, one can see a new path or direction. Something totally new is revealed.

. . . It is not loneliness which separates the person from others but the terror of loneliness and the constant effort to escape it. . . .

Loneliness is as much a reality of life as night and rain and thunder, and it can be lived creatively, as any other experience. So I say, let there be loneliness, for where there is loneliness there is also sensitivity, and where there is sensitivity, there is awareness and recognition and promise. (*Loneliness,* pages 102–103)

These may seem like strange words from a psychologist because the common belief is that loneliness should be escaped at all costs. But the pain of loneliness is also the pain of being human. *Dag Hammarskjöld,* a Swedish man who served as secretary-general of the United Nations from 1953 to 1961, understood this aspect of loneliness from his own life as a single person. This dedicated peacemaker wrote his personal reflections in a journal. After Hammarskjöld's death, his notes were published as *Markings* and inspired millions of people around the world. On loneliness, Hammarskjöld wrote:

What makes loneliness an anguish
Is not that I have no one to share my burden,
But this:
I have only my own burden to bear.

. . . .

Pray that your loneliness may spur you into finding something to live for, great enough to die for.

(Page 85)

The challenge of turning the problem of loneliness into an opportunity involves using the loneliness, as Hammarskjöld did, to experience a deeper level of being human. Loneliness becomes hazardous when a person cannot grow by it but instead becomes paralyzed by it, falling into a downward spiral of depression and negative thinking.

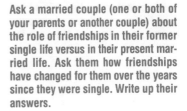

Is there anything that you believe in right now for which you would be willing to die? Write your reflections on this question.

Wider Friendships or Not Belonging with One Special Person?

The Opportunity: Wider Friendships

For a single person who has no children or the kind of intense involvement that family requires, the possibility of a wide network of friendships opens up. Certainly married people, religious, and priests have friends, but the particular commitments of their lifestyles tend to focus their relationships more on family, the religious community, and their ministry, respectively. A single person may have the time and space to pursue a much broader range of friendships and types of intimacy—recreational, intellectual, aesthetic, spiritual, work, common-cause, and so on. Because the single lifestyle does not

Ask a married couple (one or both of your parents or another couple) about the role of friendships in their former single life versus in their present married life. Ask them how friendships have changed for them over the years since they were single. Write up their answers.

provide ready-made relationships, a single person must exert a great deal of initiative to create a network of friends, but the rewards of those relationships can be great.

Doris is an example of a woman who has taken the initiative in friendships during her single life, since her husband left her twenty-five years ago. An admiring younger friend commented about Doris' life:

> When I was growing up, Doris was the most exciting person I'd ever known. I would go to the big city to stay with her for a few days, and she would treat me like a princess, showing me the sights, buying me a new dress. Then we would pop in on her friends or bump into them on the street—what an incredible variety of human beings!
>
> There was the old woman from Italy who made spaghetti for her, the security guard she became good friends with while serving on a jury, the priest she met in Vatican City who turned out to be the pope's assistant, the fatherless little boy whom she was teaching to ice skate, the nuns who had served with her in Vietnam in the refugee camps, the doctor from the Philippines and her elderly mother, a young Japanese couple for whom she was searching for housing. And that's only the beginning.
>
> Doris knew *everyone,* not just casually but at some very significant level. Her friends seemed to look to her for a special grace. I think she brought a kind of magic into their lives. I know she brought it into mine. Her life has been all about friendship.

The Problem: Not Belonging with One Special Person

Even if a single person has a wide variety of friends, she or he is not immune to the feeling of not belonging in a special way with one person. Ted, a thirty-eight-year-old electrician, expressed this feeling:

> You know, sometimes I come home and wonder what I'll be like when I'm seventy, if I live that long. Most single men die earlier than married men do. That's a sobering thought, eh? Anyway, what bothers me is that with all my good friends—and I really am lucky to have such good friends—I still don't have anybody who is there all the time for me. Sundays or days when I'm feeling lousy are the worst. It's not just loneliness but more—Who cares for me in particular? focuses their attention primarily on me?

"What bothers me is that with all my good friends, I still don't have anybody who is there all the time for me."

Ted asked a question that many single people ask, especially as they approach the age of forty, when they begin to confront their own aging process. Although Ted has friends who care for him, he knows that no one of them can be as responsible to and for him as a spouse would be. Many married older people do lose their spouses; thus marriage does not guarantee companionship in old age. But that fact does not quite satisfy the doubts from which Ted's concern originates.

> Have you ever had the desire to belong with one special person? If so, in writing, describe the feeling and why you felt the way you did.

Professional Commitment or the Trap of Expectations?

The Opportunity: Professional Commitment

Some people make the decision to stay single because they truly want to focus more on their work than on relationships with a spouse and children. In fact, given heavy professional responsibilities, a single person's decision to delay marriage or not to marry at all may be a wise one. Remaining single also gives the individual the flexibility to relocate for a new job or a promotion, perhaps even across the country, if such a move seems desirable. A cross-country move with a family is much more difficult. Consider this situation:

• Stan is a dedicated young lawyer who works in the consumer advocacy movement. His work involves bringing lawsuits against national corporations that produce unsafe, unreliable, or ineffective consumer products. Of his decision not to marry, Stan says, "I am married to my work. I love what I'm doing. With the kind of schedule I keep, it would be irresponsible for me to marry. I'm constantly traveling, and my hours are completely irregular. Besides that, my salary as a consumer advocate is barely enough to feed myself, let alone anyone else."

If Stan were to assume the responsibilities of marriage, he would have to divide his energies between his family and his work. The single life gives him the opportunity to commit himself to his profession as he feels called to do.

The Problem: The Trap of Expectations

In the situation described above, the young lawyer feels married to his work; it is the major focus of his life. Employers and other workers certainly cannot and should not expect that kind of dedication from all, or even most, single professionals, yet sometimes single people end up feeling trapped by that exact expectation. Ann, an assistant dean of students at a college, is immersed in her career and enjoys it. But she described the problem of dealing with others' expectations:

> . . . I think [my career] takes up a greater portion of my time as a single person than it would for someone who is married. . . . A good 80 percent of what I do is job-related. I think that's one of the myths about the single lifestyle . . . that it must be nice because you can go home and don't have the family there; you don't have "responsibilities." But if you are a single person in a career, particularly a career where you are with people a lot or people look to you for leadership, people tend to think that you are never off duty. Consequently, you can many times be much more taken up by projects and by people than if you aren't single. (Mary Judd, *Love and Lifestyles*, page 88)

The expectation that a single person can absorb unlimited work assignments because he or she is not married is unfair to that individual. Single people have needs for relationships and solitude like everyone else.

Employers or other workers also may assume that single persons are not as entitled to pay raises and promotions as married persons are. A complaint heard in a discrimination suit against a college uncovered this situation:

- A woman who was a basketball and volleyball coach was not promoted to athletic director because, as she was told, "Don has a family to support and needs the job more. You're single, and so it's not as important." The woman coach had been at the college longer, had led her teams to conference titles, and had received the full support of a large segment of the college community. She was discriminated against not only as a woman but also as a single person.

A Less Expensive or More Expensive Lifestyle?

The Opportunity: A Less Expensive Lifestyle

A person who is choosing a lifestyle might wonder, Is it more costly to live as a single person or as a married person? The answer, of course, depends on the standard of living that a person decides is necessary, whether or not she or he is single.

"I think my career takes up a greater portion of my time as a single person than it would for someone who is married."

Certain factors make single life potentially less expensive, and other factors make it potentially more expensive.

On the less expensive side, a single person obviously does not have to support a spouse and children. The need to feed, clothe, shelter, educate, get medical care, find recreation, and so on, applies only to an individual, not to a whole family. Furthermore, a single person can opt for a simple lifestyle that might be more difficult with a family. For example, some single persons choose to live in convenient locations without a car and major appliances like a washing machine because they can get around easily on public transportation or on foot and can wash their clothes at a nearby self-service laundry. It is much more difficult for a family to live without a car or a washing machine. Undoubtedly, life can be less cluttered with possessions when the needs and wants of only one person are at issue.

Married persons, on the other hand, must listen to the increasing chorus of children's requests for possessions as the children grow and develop their own tastes and desires, and a couple must make difficult buying decisions, often using very limited resources. Life can get materially complicated. Increasingly, families require two incomes to meet the needs and wants of their members.

So the single life, with economic decisions to be made by and for only one individual, can be a less expensive lifestyle.

The Problem: A More Expensive Lifestyle

Even though single people have a greater degree of choice about the use of their income, living alone can be expensive. Like a married couple starting to furnish an apartment, a single person needs furniture, a toaster, a radio, towels, and so on. The key difference is that a single person has to pay for these items with one income instead of two. Even if a single person shares an apartment or a house with someone else, the arrangement is usually temporary, and the person eventually must buy his or her own furnishings.

Other costs put demands on a single person's budget. Taxes often are higher for single people with no dependents. Insurance rates frequently are higher per person, too, especially for single men. Single people tend to eat out more often than married people or those living in communities, and when single people do eat at home, they tend to use convenient but expensive foods like microwave dinners and deli salads.

Although single persons can opt for a relatively simple

Certain factors make single life potentially less expensive, and other factors make it potentially more expensive.

lifestyle, sometimes, in order to meet more people, they choose to live in rather expensive singles apartment complexes, to join costly health spas, or to spend more money on entertainment than if they were married. What could be a less expensive lifestyle can turn into a high-priced way of life.

A Life Full of Possibilities

At some phase of life, most of us live the single life.

- You might wish to examine how singleness, whether permanent or temporary, could contribute to fulfillment of your dream and Jesus' dream of the peaceable kingdom, a loving community, and people who are fully alive.
- You might ask yourself how you could use the opportunities of the single life to develop as a person and to contribute to the world.
- You might reflect on some of the problems of being single and think about how you would deal with them in your life.

If being single is a temporary decision for you and you would like to someday marry or enter religious life or the priesthood, you might treat your time of singleness as a chance to learn more about yourself, establish a career, develop wider friendships, and explore life. Whether it is a temporary or a permanent state, being single needs to be thought of as a fruitful way of life, one that is full of possibilities.

Dag Hammarskjöld's personal reflection on individuality offers wisdom for all of us on how to live a fulfilling and generous single life:

> Don't be afraid of yourself, live your individuality to the full—but for the good of others. Don't copy others in order to buy fellowship, or make convention your law instead of living the righteousness.
>
> To become free and responsible. For this alone [were] man [and woman] created. (*Markings*, page 53)

Dag Hammarskjöld, the secretary-general of the United Nations from 1953 to 1961: "To become free and responsible. For this alone were we created."

Write a brief summary of your ideas about the way that being single, either permanently or temporarily, fits into your dream.

Review Questions

1. Summarize the reasons that Ruth, Dave, and Jan are single and how each person feels about it.

2. What is central to God's call for single Christians?

3. What was Jean Donovan's main motivation for becoming a single missionary?

4. What question does a person need to ask in order to discern his or her distinct call?

5. List at least three examples from this chapter of how misunderstandings or prejudice about the single life have been expressed.

6. How can being single allow a person more freedom? Give two examples of such freedom that were mentioned in this chapter.

7. What is egocentrism, and how can it be a problem for singles?

8. How can solitude be a full and renewing part of the single life?

9. What is loneliness? How can loneliness be both a problem and an opportunity for single persons?

10. How can singleness allow for developing a wide circle of friendships?

11. What is a question that many single people ask as they begin to confront their own aging process?

12. How can singleness be an opportunity and a problem with regard to one's career?

13. Single life can be less expensive in some ways and more expensive in others. Explain how this statement is true.

14. What is Dag Hammarskjöld's advice for making single life meaningful?

11 Dating and Courting: Toward Finding a Life Partner

AS a high school senior, perhaps you have been dating for several years. You probably have heard all sorts of comments about dating and courting from friends. The following comments represent some reactions that you may have heard already or that you may hear in the next several years:

- Whenever I go out with Sharon, we just enjoy being with each other. I hardly even think of us as dating; we're just friends.
- When I met Jose, it was love at first sight. We've been going out together for a year now. We'd be married, but we just don't have the money to get started yet.
- When I go out with Bill, there's only one thing he wants.
- I just want to have fun and not get too involved. I went out with this guy last year—an accounting executive. He was very nice, but when he started talking about visiting his mom and dad, I knew that he was getting too serious. I'm not ready to marry, so I broke off the relationship.
- Joni and I go out dancing because we really enjoy it. Well, if you want the truth, we are great dancers. But otherwise, we don't do much together.
- I wasn't attracted to Herm right away. In fact, our blind date was a disaster. He actually nodded off during dinner. I thought, "What a jerk." Later the woman who had arranged the date explained that Herm had just driven across Tennessee after spring break and was exhausted. As I've gotten to know him over the last ten months, I've come to love him. We just match. So we're planning to get married when he finishes going to pharmacy school.

"I just want to have fun and not get too involved."

- Right now in my life, I'm down on dating. I just cannot be bothered by all the pain and pressure of getting caught up in a romance, and then, bam, it's over and I'm alone. I have to get ready for my MCAT [Medical College Admissions Test].
- I don't like to date more than one person at a time. When I date someone, I need to know pretty quickly whether we're serious enough to start going together. If not, it's no use dating.

Eight different people equal eight different perspectives on dating and courting. Many of the above comments represent the thoughts of young adults beyond high school age. For some of them, dating is closely linked in their minds with the possibility of marriage. Dating that occurs in high school usually does not point toward marriage, but as a young adult grows, dating issues begin to turn into concerns about finding a life partner.

This chapter focuses on two areas:

- **Dating,** the broad range of social engagements that a person has with members of the other sex
- **Courting,** the specific kind of dating in which two persons begin to ask themselves, If I were going to marry, would this be the person I would choose?

Dating may or may not lead to courting. A person may date several people in the same time period, but courting usually implies that the dating relationship is exclusively between two persons.

Certainly dating and courting call on our confidence, our communication skills, our creativity in using leisure, and our sense of values. But above all, dating and courting call on us to take the opportunity, in a relaxed and unpressured way, to enjoy another person, possibly to come to know that person deeply, and to learn about ourselves. Dating can be a joy and an adventure.

If you were trying to describe the difference between a date and just being with someone, how would you do so? Write an explanation of the difference.

The word *courting* sounds old-fashioned, but we do not seem to have another word that fittingly describes this process. Try to create or identify a word to replace *courting,* and write an explanation of why your word might be better.

Dating: Motives, Pressures, and Possibilities

Why People Date

Looking at what motivates people to date is one way to gain insight into how dating can be a joy and an adventure. In any given situation, a person's motives naturally will be mixed, and some motives for dating can lead to more satisfaction than others. Any of the following motives might be combined in a particular instance of dating:

- *Sexual attraction:* We long to seek completion as persons through relationships with other people. Sexual attraction, which in its best sense is more than just physical attraction, moves us to explore relationships. This kind of attraction ignites romantic love.

- *Fun:* Some people are funny, spontaneous, and interesting. On a date with such a person, we feel comfortable, accepted, and entertained. Dating is for the fun of it.

- *Ego boost:* Sometimes going out with a certain person can boost our ego because that person is physically attractive, wealthy, or powerful. Although we may not like to admit it, we might be dating that person to draw others' attention and approval to ourselves.

- *Getting out of ourselves:* Talking with another person, actively listening to him or her, and being sensitive to his or her feelings and ideas are wonderful ways to stretch ourselves beyond our own narrow concerns and interests. It feels good to get out of ourselves.

- *"The thing to do":* Peer pressure to date can put a tremendous burden on a shy person or a person who would rather do such things as study, work, or play tennis. The individual may feel forced to date to avoid being judged as strange—taking on one form of discomfort to avoid another.

- *Companionship:* We seek someone with whom to share experiences. Talking with someone after a movie usually feels better than walking home alone. The companionship of dating overcomes loneliness.

- *The joy of give-and-take:* We may want to offer our talents, skills, and affection to another person, realizing that she or he has talents, skills, and affection to offer as well. We enjoy the adventure of a give-and-take relationship.

- *Finding a marriage partner:* Marriage may not be a strong motive for dating if a person is just recently out of high school, but as an individual reaches the late twenties and thirties, the desire to find a lifelong partner may take on an urgency that he or she had not known before.

Self-awareness about our motives for wanting to date a particular person, or for wanting to date at all, can help us to become more genuine in those relationships. We may question our own motives if they seem primarily negative, or we may

From what you have seen of the dating scene, are there pressures from your peers to date? If so, try to list the various sources of pressure. Describe in writing how you feel about the pressure to date that is put on you or on other people.

Consider someone you are presently dating or someone you would like to date. Which of the motives given in this chapter is dominant for you? Are you comfortable with this motive? How do you think this motive affects or would affect your relationship?

Few people getting ready for a first date with someone are calm and serene.

wonder why certain motives are absent in a given dating relationship. Understanding our motives also can help us to appreciate the gift that we have in a very satisfying relationship.

The Pressure to Make It Perfect

Although dating is ideally a joy and an adventure, it can put tremendous pressure on us as we try to ensure that everything about the date goes perfectly. Few people getting ready for a date—especially the first one or two dates with someone—are calm and serene. What they experience is a bit like stage fright, and they are plagued by a swarm of doubts:

- Do I look okay?
- I wonder what my friends will say about my date.
- Maybe my date is going out with me just to be nice.

The pressure to have everything turn out perfectly creates these doubts.

It is natural to want to be thought of as likable and attractive, and understandably, we may feel anxious about our image when dating someone new. The problem is that such anxiety turns our attention inward—How am *I* doing? How do *I* look?—rather than outward to the other person. What we may forget is that if we are anxious, our date is probably anxious also. Maybe if we stepped back and realized that neither of us is perfect and that both of us are somewhat nervous, we could relax and enjoy each other.

The pressure to have a perfect dating experience shows itself in two ways:

- high expectations
- concerns about being attractive

High Expectations

Having hope is not the same as having expectations. Having *hope* implies that a person is ready to respond when an opportunity presents itself. Having *expectations*, on the other hand, indicates that a person thinks a certain outcome is probable. When we *expect* something to happen and it does not, our disappointment can be great. Notice what happens to Laura when she expects too much of her date:

Laura is feeling very down. Her classes have been a drag, teachers are piling on homework, and she is worried about next week's midterm exams. Her parents are irritated with her, and her best friend has been giving her the cold shoulder.

Luckily, Laura is looking forward to a date with Eddie on Friday night. It will be her first time out with him, and he has the reputation of being a very funny guy. "Surely he'll pull me out of this depression," she thinks.

However, when Friday evening is over and Laura realizes that Eddie has *not* cheered her up, she feels even worse. She wonders: "What went wrong? Was Eddie bored with me? Why wasn't he as much fun as I thought he would be?"

Laura's high expectations invited disappointment; they put pressure on the situation and on Eddie. A sense of hope instead would have opened Laura to the kind of mutual sharing with Eddie that marks real friendship.

Concerns About Being Attractive

Besides expecting too much of our dates, another pressure may be our concern about the attractiveness of our physical appearance and our personality. We may think that having a perfect dating experience means that *we* must be perfect. This kind of thinking leads to anxiety that prevents us from enjoying the other person on a date.

We are who we are—shy or sociable, overweight or thin, imperfect but lovable human beings. Certainly we can grow and improve ourselves, but at any given point, we need to like and accept ourselves as we are today.

It is true that good looks may initially draw other people to an individual, but this quickly becomes a much less important source of attraction. The experience of married people gives evidence of this fact. A group of researchers recently asked married couples what they valued most in a mate. The ten characteristics most valued by both women and men in the study were the following:

1. good companion
2. considerate
3. honest
4. affectionate
5. dependable
6. intelligent
7. kind
8. understanding
9. interesting to talk to
10. loyal

People who have these characteristics are prized as lifelong partners. When we evaluate our own attractiveness, focusing on

List in rank order the ten characteristics that you would consider most important in someone you would wish to date. Then make another rank-ordered list of characteristics that you would consider most important in someone you would wish to marry. Are the two lists different? If so, write your reflection on why there are differences.

When deciding what to do on a date, consider mutual interests.

List as many different dating activities as you can think of. Next to each activity, describe at least one way in which it would foster intimacy.

these criteria rather than on our exterior appearance may help us to concentrate on what makes us truly attractive.

What to Do, Where to Go?

Routines are easy to slip into when dating. The old standards of entertainment are always available and do not require much imagination: movies, restaurants, games, dances, and school activities. In college, the old standards do not change much, although going to bars might be added. It is important to remember that many dating possibilities are available.

In order to make a date interesting and mutually beneficial, you need to ask, What does this person like to do? Then you should be open to new ideas. Recall the nine types of intimacy on pages 66–67. One way to plan a date is to ask yourself how your relationship with the other person can become more intimate—intellectually, recreationally, aesthetically, creatively, or spiritually. Remember, too, that being renewed by leisure requires physical or mental engagement, not passivity.

Here are some different date activities that might sound appealing:

- *An orchestra concert:* If your friend likes this kind of music, try it out.
- *A soup-kitchen date:* Maybe your friend volunteers at a soup kitchen or in some other facility. If so, accompany her or him to volunteer someday. You will get a better sense of who your friend is and will have a lot to talk about later.
- *A canoe trip:* Take your friend canoeing on a river or a lake for an afternoon. It is fun to see each other in a different light, out in the natural world.
- *A tennis match:* Any sport suitable for two will do—bowling, swimming, cross-country skiing, and so on. What can be particularly fun is to have your friend teach you a sport that you do not already know.
- *A photography expedition:* Head out across town together to capture your favorite sights on film. Put each other in the pictures.

So when deciding what to do on a date, consider mutual interests. Use some imagination. Become engaged in some mental or physical activity. Be open to new adventures. Intimacy can grow in many ways.

Dating and Sex: Decisions with Consequences

To experience dating as an enjoyable opportunity for growth, we need to be aware of why we are dating, to deal with pressures about making every date perfect, and to be imaginative and open in planning dates. But dating frequently involves more than that: it may challenge us to make decisions about sexual involvement. The following story illustrates some of the consequences of decisions about sex:

> When Mary was a junior in high school, she started dating Rob, who was a first-year student at a college in town. After their first date, Mary knew that Rob had been around. From some of the innuendos that his friends made, Mary got the idea that he had been involved sexually with several women. Mary was flattered by Rob's attention. She felt that she must be pretty special, someone worth caring about. As Rob's girlfriend, Mary also became more interesting to her classmates, and she met many other college students at the parties of Rob's friends.
>
> Eventually Rob began pressuring Mary to have sex with him. She found it difficult to say no. Mary was afraid that if she did not have sex with Rob, he would reject her, and all of the new friendships that she was making would evaporate.
>
> Saying yes to Rob did not help matters. He became possessive and demanded that she be ready to go out whenever he wanted and that she do whatever he wanted. The pressure of Rob's demands, her neglected schoolwork, and her worry about losing him made Mary feel like a slave. Even so, Mary broke off her relationship with Rob only after she saw him flirting with another woman.
>
> Mary thought that that was the end of the situation, but it was not. She did not feel well and began to suspect that she had caught some sort of sexually transmitted disease from Rob. The symptoms were there, she had to admit. Mary was petrified of telling her parents because then they would know that she had had sex with Rob, but she was equally scared about the possibility of disease.
>
> During the next two months, Mary refused dates with

Dating challenges us to make decisions about sexual involvement.

two other guys she had always wanted to go out with. Her grades suffered because she was so worried. The isolation terrified Mary, but she knew that if she told her friends, they would feel superior and might even tell others.

Finally, in addition to the symptoms of the sexually transmitted disease, Mary developed a case of bronchitis. In a visit to the family doctor, tired of the worry and fear, Mary described her other symptoms to the doctor. After some tests, her fears were confirmed. Fortunately, the disease was treatable. Mary was relieved of her physical problem, but the feelings of isolation, betrayal, guilt, and anger would not heal so easily.

Premarital sexual intercourse may not end in pregnancy, sexually transmitted disease, or bitterness—but nothing guarantees that it will not. The decision to become sexually involved with someone always carries consequences of one kind or another, so the decision must be taken seriously.

Premarital Sex: Why and Why Not?

Valid Reasons?
Consider some of the reasons that young people give for having sexual intercourse with their dates:
- I may lose him if I don't have sex with him.
- We just got carried away.
- I won't be a man [woman] until I've had sex.
- Once we start drinking, forget about self-control.
- If we're in love, why isn't it okay to have sex?
- What's the big deal about putting on the brakes? Sex is what makes life interesting.
- Most of the people I know do it.
- She'll think I'm gay if I don't have sex with her.
- Sex will prove whether we love each other.
- It's okay to have sex because we'll get married if I get pregnant.

Long-term Consequences
The trouble with all of the reasons advanced by people who want to have sex while dating, or by those who coax their reluctant dating partners to have sex, is that none of these reasons recognizes the long-term consequences of sexual intercourse before marriage.

Using current magazines and other sources, write a report on one of the following topics:
- teenage pregnancies
- teenage marriages
- AIDS
- herpes
- another sexually transmitted disease

Pregnancy: The most obvious consequence is premarital pregnancy, which affects not only the two partners but also the whole life of the child who will be born. A child needs to be raised and loved in a stable family. A teenage single parent is not well-equipped to raise a child; if the young couple should marry under the pressure of a pregnancy, the stability of their marriage would be in serious question. "Shotgun" marriages—that is, marriages under pressure—have a poor rate of success. Moreover, abortion as a solution to a premarital pregnancy carries other deeply harmful consequences.

Sexually transmitted disease: No one should be naive about the long-range effects of AIDS (acquired immunodeficiency syndrome), which at this point is fatal and incurable, and the less serious but incurable genital herpes simplex. Of course, diseases like gonorrhea and syphilis, though curable, are not what we would wish to give to or receive from someone we love. If no established commitment exists between two people who have sexual relations, it is dangerous to assume that a sexual partner has not had sex with someone else. In the age of AIDS, indiscriminate sex can be deadly.

A diminishing relationship: Frequently young people who choose to have sex while dating assume that sex will enhance and deepen their relationship. Instead, it often diminishes their relationship. Without a long-term commitment, the relationship can take on a one-dimensional, sexual character. Other types of intimacy may be crowded out of the couple's awareness in favor of sex. In addition, the emotions stirred by having sex may be so strong that they obscure the young persons' better judgment about their relationship; they may no longer be able to evaluate whether the relationship is healthy and whether they would really want to marry each other. The couple may lose the perspective that love is proved over years and through many types of intimacy.

A premarital pregnancy affects not only the two partners but also the whole life of the child who will be born.

Do you agree that premarital sexual relations can crowd out the development of other types of intimacy in a relationship? Write a rationale for your position.

The Church's Response

You probably already know the church's view on the decision of whether to have sexual relations before marriage: *no.* What frequently gets lost in the decision-making process is why the church has traditionally taken this position.

Mutual commitment: The story of Mary's unhappy relationship with Rob and the long-term consequences described above illustrate why the church cautions against premarital sexual intercourse. The absence of a firm commitment to each other means that unmarried couples like Mary and Rob are not pledged to mutually bear the consequences of sexual intercourse. The church sees sexual relations as an expression of deep love between two people—love so profound that the two individuals pledge themselves to mutual, lifelong commitment in marriage. The sexual intimacy that expresses that love should be the full meeting and sharing of body, mind, and heart; it is not to be taken lightly, as mere recreation for people who are not committed to each other.

A life-giving context: The Christian community believes in promoting the full life and love of persons. The church teaches that because of its emotional, practical, and social consequences, sexual intercourse must happen only in a context that will be life-giving, fulfilling, and loving. In the church's wisdom, that context is found in marriage.

Members of Christ's Body: Saint Paul condemned fornication—sex outside of marriage—in his first letter to the Corinthians, who certainly knew about sexual immorality. Corinth had a reputation for being a very wild city. Prostitution and all sorts of other sexual activity flourished there. Paul warned the Christians in Corinth to refrain from extramarital sex because it would tear apart the loving community that he was trying to build. In addition, he told the Corinthians:

> "For me everything is permissible"; maybe, but not everything does good. . . . The body is not for sexual immorality; it is for the Lord, and the Lord is for the body. . . . Do you not realise that your bodies are members of Christ's body? . . . (1 Corinthians 6:12–15)

As members of Christ's body who care for one another, Christians who are dating are called to do only what will promote the total good of the other person.

We are sexual beings, blessed with sexuality so that we can bring about new life—children, love between a man and woman, and other relationships that flow from creating family. Sexuality, like all fragile gifts, must be handled with care. It requires stability based on the commitment that marriage promises.

The Christian community believes in promoting the full life and love of persons.

Successful Courtship, Successful Marriage?

Even though you are, by statistical average, about seven or eight years away from marriage (if you marry at all), dating will begin to take on more meaning as you move into young adulthood. Increasingly, dating will become a way of discovering what kind of person you want to spend your life with, a means of exploring how to relate to a person whom you might someday marry.

If a person you are dating as a young adult becomes very special to you and you feel the beginnings of love, then dating may turn into courting. The term *courting* might sound quaint, but it implies that a dating relationship has moved to a deeper level and that the two individuals may each be asking themselves, Is this the person I might marry? Love requires knowledge, and mutual love requires mutual knowledge. Courting is an important step because it allows two persons the time to learn more about each other.

Courting: A Recent Tradition

Today we expect that two people who marry love each other and have a basis for that love in an in-depth knowledge of each other. Dating and courting are now accepted as part of the process of choosing a spouse, but this was not always the case.

For many centuries, marriage was looked upon as a social, economic, or political contract between families or even nations. Most marriages were arranged either formally, through marriage brokers or matchmakers, or less formally, through relatives. In fact, arranged marriages existed as common practice in the Western world until this century and in the Eastern world until recently. Such marriages are still the practice in many areas of the world.

When a couple entered into an arranged marriage, the two persons could hope for love to develop, but expectations had to be minimal. Often they did not even meet before marriage. If the two persons did meet, they were supervised by chaperones. Understandably, the system led to many abuses of personal dignity. Many touching stories have been written and

Interview a married couple whom you consider to be happy together. Use these and other questions:
- How did your relationship begin?
- How could you tell that your relationship was becoming serious?
- How long did you date before you became engaged?
- Do you think that a long period of courting and engagement helps a marriage?
- How important is it to date a variety of people?
- What advice about dating would you give to high school seniors?

Write about the results of your interview.

songs have been composed about the pain of a lover who could not marry the person he or she really wanted because of an arranged marriage or class differences.

Of course, the divorce rate for arranged marriages was extremely low, not because the individuals were terribly happy but because divorce was almost unheard of. For example, divorce in England required an act of parliament. Also, the same social, economic, and political pressures that led to marriage arrangements kept those marriages together. Certainly, people's expectations of marriage in those times were much lower than the expectations that we have today.

In our time, most North Americans expect that marriage requires hard work, fidelity, and a spirit of unselfishness, but they expect to receive as well as give. They look for marriage to bring love, personal fulfillment, and opportunity for growth. For a marriage to meet these latter expectations, the individuals must know and trust one another well before the marriage. Seeing into the mind and heart of another person takes time. A period of courting provides that time and opportunity.

Seeing into the mind and heart of another person takes time. A period of courting provides that time and opportunity.

Approaches to Courting

If you were to interview a dozen married couples about what paths the partners took in arriving at their decision to marry each other, you would probably come up with a variety along the following lines:
- the whirlwind romance approach
- the childhood sweetheart approach
- the "I want it all" approach
- the late-blooming approach
- the open exploration approach

Each approach implies a different kind of courtship, and as you might expect, some approaches have a better chance of leading to a happy marriage than others do.

The Whirlwind Romance Approach

The *whirlwind romance approach* is well-described by the name itself: whirlwinds are powerful, impressive, fast, and they often die down as quickly as they come on. Marriages that result from this kind of romance may seem at first to be equally powerful and impressive, but like a whirlwind, they do not usually last and may leave torn lives when they are over. Although exceptions of happy marriages can always be cited, an intense romance of a few months generally is not a firm foundation for a marriage.

In 1985, researchers at Kansas State University reported that happiness in marriage increases with the length of time that a couple courts before marriage. The happiest marriages are those in which the couples have courted for at least two years. Accordingly, the researchers found that courtships of less than six months most frequently lead to later regrets about marriage. The researchers concluded that longer acquaintance-ship enables people to sort out incompatible partners.

The Childhood Sweetheart Approach

Most of us are familiar with at least one couple who have been dating steadily since junior high or tenth grade. Sometimes childhood sweethearts go to the same college, never date anyone else, and marry as soon as possible. You may know a married couple whose relationship began this way.

This approach to courting has one clear advantage—security. People may cling to their first love out of fear that another love like it will never be found. Unfortunately, though, the *childhood sweetheart approach* can be very limiting, restricting the individuals' experiences of other people and preventing them from growing in ways that they might have grown. Eventually one of the two people may begin to realize how much she or he has missed, perhaps at the point when she or he is struggling to reach a new level of maturity.

The "I Want It All" Approach

Sometimes one member of a dating couple wants to have an exclusive, often sexually active, relationship—but without any commitment. The person's attitude is *"I want it all"*: an intimate, marriage-like relationship but no permanent ties. In his Pulitzer prize-winning memoir *Growing Up,* Russell Baker, a columnist for the *New York Times,* described himself humorously as having had such an approach:

> I had no thought of marrying Mimi and no intention of giving her up. I was only twenty-one, poor, without exciting prospects. . . . Naturally I would marry later, when I was old and stuffy, and when I did I would naturally choose "a good woman," the sort my mother would approve. In the meantime I refused to spoil the joy of youth by parting with Mimi, the only woman with whom I felt happy. . . .
>
> In this spirit I let the months go [merrily] by, and

Answer these questions in writing:
- Why do some people easily get caught up in whirlwind romances?
- Would you be vulnerable to this type of romance?

gradually months turned into years. . . . Mimi was not entirely content, to be sure. It was annoying when, as she occasionally did, Mimi suggested that she was looking forward to marriage. It was this annoying suggestion that I'd first tried to squelch by telling her, "It's not in the cards." With the passing months, though, she continued to talk rather dreamily about marriage, and, having grown fond of the phrase, I repeated it several times a year.

"Not in the cards," I said. "It's just not in the cards." (Page 253)

Eventually Baker did marry Mimi, but not until she had first left him and moved on with her life. Only then did Baker realize how much he loved Mimi, and he became quite frantic to have her agree to marry him.

Courting persons need to be honest with each other about their intentions in the relationship. A long courtship can be wonderful, but not if its length means that one person is actually "stringing along" the other.

The Late-blooming Approach

Everyone is unique, so it stands to reason that each person has her or his own schedule for exploring close relationships with the other sex. Some people do not begin dating until they are in college or even much later. With years of maturing and searching for what they want in life, these individuals may be very successful at finding a lifelong marriage partner in a *late-blooming approach* to courtship. One of the exciting aspects of high school reunions is the discovery that people who did not have dates in high school and who at the time seemed unlikely to marry are now happily married. They simply took their time.

The Open Exploration Approach

The approach to finding a lifelong partner that perhaps promises the best chance of a happy marriage is that of open exploration. Avoiding the pitfalls of the whirlwind romance and childhood sweetheart approaches, the individual who pursues this path to marriage sees dating as a way of getting to know and appreciate a variety of persons. Dating is an exploration that helps the individual to sort out what she or he wants and does *not* want in a partner. It is also an opportunity to discover how to grow and change in response to the needs of other people.

Put yourself first in Baker's situation and then in Mimi's. Reflect on these questions in writing:
- How would you feel if you were Baker? Mimi?
- Was Mimi right in leaving Baker and moving on with her life?
- How long should someone expect another person to wait for a serious commitment?

Eventually, one person may stand out from the other good friends as someone whom this individual might like to marry. The two persons may date steadily for some time. Maybe the relationship will point toward marriage, but maybe it will not. The *open exploration approach* implies a willingness to let go of a relationship that once looked promising but later does not. An individual recognizes that such experiences of loving and then letting go, painful though they can be, are opportunities to learn and grow.

When two persons who have been exploring different relationships honestly for several years begin courting and later decide that they do want to marry each other, their decision is based on more than gut feelings. Their marriage will be grounded on a solid foundation of knowledge gained through experience.

Challenging Questions: Is This the Person I Will Marry?

Imagine that it is the future and that you have been courting someone for about a year. The two of you get along well; indeed, you spend all of your free time together. You are comfortable with each other. Most of all, you love each other—at least your hearts tell you so. You are both wondering if you want to marry. This feels like, and is, an enormously important decision.

Many marriage counselors would suggest that two people who have been dating seriously ask themselves these questions:

1. Do we agree about the roles that men and women play in marriage? If a wife wants to work and the husband refuses to take equal responsibility for household chores, trouble is likely. The couple must know what each person expects about roles in the marriage. Compromise is always necessary; that means give-and-take on both sides. In addition, men and women are not static. Changing roles will require adjustments. For instance, a wife may be offered a promotion that requires a move. This change in status will require a commitment to mutual decision-making. If the couple has not worked out some understanding before marriage, the relationship could rupture.

In writing, answer each of the eighteen questions posed in this chapter as they apply only to you, not to a partner. For example, Can I tolerate genuine intimacy?

Can each of us accept change in the other?

2. **Is either of us trying to escape a bad family situation?** If either person has grown up in a conflict-ridden, abusive, or overly strict home, that person may desire marriage as an escape, especially because she or he is experiencing genuine affection for the first time. Marriage should not be used as an escape.

3. **Are we too young?** Less than one in four teenage marriages lasts. If two teenagers do not have a strong sense of their own identities, marriage between them means that two immature, impressionable persons have entered into a situation demanding maturity, responsibility, and competence. The strain can be too much for the relationship. Furthermore, people who marry before they have had a chance to study, work, travel, or date several people may eventually resent the loss of their young adulthood. This resentment can also cripple a marriage.

4. **Can we both tolerate genuine intimacy?** Intimacy is essential for a lasting marriage. Marriage demands emotional, sexual, and intellectual intimacy at the very least. However, some people cannot tolerate very much closeness. One who is seriously dating another person should ask these additional questions:
- Does she or he seem to avoid dates that include just the two of us together?
- Do we share significant experiences?
- Can we talk comfortably for long periods of time?
- Can we relax together and not have to talk or do something?
- Are our needs for closeness somewhat similar?

5. **Can each of us accept change in the other?** Change is inevitable. If one person changes and the other cannot accept that change, the relationship is in jeopardy. One should consider how the other person reacts to a change of mind or a new interest.

6. **Can each of us stand psychologically on our own two feet?** Marriages have been destroyed when one of the partners remained more committed to his or her parents than to the spouse. So a person needs to look carefully at the family of a potential spouse:
- How do my partner's parents relate to their other married children?
- Do my partner's parents seek control?

Marriage counselors report that the problem of being psychologically tied to parents in an unhealthy way is more common than people admit it to be.

7. **Do we give each other time and space to be on our own—alone or with our own friends?** Marriage or any healthy relationship relies on each person's retaining his or her own identity. In fact, good relationships enhance each person's identity. Two full persons share themselves in marriage. Some further questions can help to address this larger issue:

- Do we encourage each other to pursue our respective interests, or are my interests always secondary?
- Are my needs and ideas considered important by my partner?
- Is my partner jealous or possessive?
- Do I resent the demands placed on me by my partner and feel smothered at times?
- Do I feel like I am nothing when the two of us are apart? If you cannot live without your partner, you should seriously reconsider the relationship; you may not have explored sufficiently the fullness of the person that you are. Marriage is not the absorption of one person's life by another person.

8. **What part would children play in our marriage?** Children are an important consideration before marriage. Parenthood is intensely demanding. Both persons must be willing to assume such a responsibility. To further clarify this important question, one should ask these additional questions:

- Do we both want to have children?
- How many children would we want?
- Do we agree about child-rearing issues?
- Do we both have the same attitudes about birth control?
- How would we deal with an unplanned pregnancy?

9. **What role will sexual expression have for us?** Sexual desire varies from person to person. For most of us, passion is not a machine that we can switch on at any time. A man and a woman who are considering marriage must discuss their expectations about sex.

10. **Can both of us confront our problems head-on and then let bygones be bygones?** Problems that are allowed to fester can cause havoc in a relationship. If two persons have the ability to air problems, even little ones, as they arise, the relationship will be much better. Once problems have been talked through, it is important to let the anger and frustration end forever.

11. **Does either of us have an alcohol or drug problem?** One of the worst mistakes that people can make is thinking that marriage will reform an alcoholic or a drug addict. Marriage

Can both of us confront our problems head-on and then let bygones be bygones?

usually does not change habitual patterns of behavior, especially substance abuse. These questions must be considered: Does my partner

- have to drink to relax?
- drink when problems arise?
- become irritated when alcohol is not served?
- have to have several drinks each evening?
- get drunk a lot?
- insist that I drink?
- find it impossible to stop at one drink?
- drink quickly?
- drive under the influence of alcohol?

If the answer is yes to any of these questions, your partner may have a problem.

Does either of us have an alcohol or drug problem?

12. **Does one of us have to be the boss all of the time?** Marriage should be a commitment between equals. Each partner should ask these questions:

- Does my partner insist on having his or her way all of the time?
- Do I feel that my partner gives me orders?
- Does either of us become furious when losing at sports, cards, and so on?

Consider, too, that someone who likes to be bossed around may have a problem with self-respect.

13. Do we have similar religious beliefs? Many young adults do not consider this issue sufficiently, but when they begin raising children, it can become a major source of disagreement. These questions need to be answered:
- How far will I compromise my beliefs, if at all?
- How will religious differences affect our relationship?
- How will differences in religion affect our families?

14. Do we have enough in common upon which to build intimacy? Initially, divergent interests can be fascinating, but lasting relationships are characterized by common interests rather than differences. Answering this question requires a lot of honesty because during courtship, two persons may try to be involved in each other's interests without truly wanting to be. Only later does the gap in their interests show up.

15. Can both of us articulate our feelings for each other? Sometimes we need to hear, "I love you." It needs to be said. Some people find that expressing their feelings is very difficult. Before marriage, it is important that each partner knows his or her own need for hearing expressions of feelings and the ability of the other person to express them.

16. What are our expectations about money? One person may see no problem in buying on credit, but her or his partner may insist on the principle, If I cannot pay for it, I do not buy it. Two persons may also have differences about what constitutes a dignified standard of living and how much money and possessions are necessary.

17. How dependable is my partner in his or her work? People who cut corners, procrastinate, and are lazy in school are likely to be that way at work. They do not suddenly change old habits. As a spouse, a person with such qualities is not likely to carry his or her weight in the relationship.

18. Do I like my partner's friends? The types of friendships that a person develops say a great deal about her or him. They tend to indicate what the person is like and what her or his values are. Take a good look at your partner's friends, and pay attention to your feelings of being comfortable or uncomfortable with them.

The questions above cover some of the main issues of marriage. Many more questions need to be asked before two people become engaged or married. Naturally, individuals considering marriage will not be able to answer all of the questions in

Do we have enough in common upon which to build intimacy?

Dating and courting move persons out of themselves, anticipating a time when their dream will be united with the dream of someone whom they want to cherish forever.

favorable ways because no relationship is perfect. However, if a large number of the questions seem to have unfavorable responses, the individuals may need to conclude that marriage is not the right decision for them.

On the Way to Sharing Dreams

Whether or not we eventually marry, dating and courting are worthwhile experiences that teach us about ourselves and expand our skills and experiences. For most people, these experiences point ultimately toward marriage—when the separate dreams of two persons are joined to form a common vision of a life together. Dating and especially courting give both persons in a relationship an opportunity to share what their dreams mean to them. In this way, dating and courting move persons out of themselves, anticipating a time when their dream will be united with the dream of someone whom they want to cherish forever.

Review Questions

1. What is the difference between dating and courting?

2. List and explain the eight motives for dating that are given in this chapter.

3. How can dating put pressure on us?

4. What is the difference between hope and expectation? How do expectations put pressure on the dating situation?

5. How does the concern about being attractive cause pressure in dating? What characteristics of a spouse were found to be most valued in a study of married couples?

6. What are some helpful questions to ask yourself when thinking about what to do and where to go on a date?

7. List five of the reasons that young people sometimes give for having premarital sex.

8. Describe three negative consequences of premarital sex.

9. Explain the church's three reasons for its stand against premarital sex.

10. Why is courting a helpful step toward marriage?

11. Courting is a recent tradition. How is this so?

12. Explain the five approaches to courting that are given in this chapter.

13. List the eighteen questions that should be considered during the courting period of a relationship.

12 Marrying: A Covenant of Faithful Love

WEDDINGS rank high among life's most moving and joyful occasions for celebration. The pledge of faithful love between a husband and a wife strikes a deep chord in people's hearts, a need to see love made visible in the world. Weddings remind people that love—the kind of love that lasts forever—is the central human reality worth celebrating. It is not surprising that people often are moved to tears at weddings.

The intensity of love and joy between two persons who are marrying is expressed in the Bible's Song of Songs:

Beloved:
My love is mine and I am his. . . .

. . . I found my sweetheart.
I caught him, would not let him go,
not till I had brought him
to my mother's house,
to the room where she conceived me!

Lover:
How beautiful you are, my beloved,
how beautiful you are! . . .

.   .   .   .
You ravish my heart,
. . . my promised bride,
you ravish my heart
with a single one of your glances,
with a single link of your necklace.
What spells lie in your love. . . .
How delicious is your love, more delicious than wine! . . .
(Song of Songs 2:16; 3:4; 4:1,9–10)

Weddings remind people that love is the central human reality worth celebrating.

The delight in each other that lovers experience when they marry is part of what touches people at a wedding. Beyond that, the act of marrying evokes strong feelings in the family and friends of the couple because it anticipates with hope the reality of a love that endures through the test of time—the struggles and crises as well as the stresses of routine that mark every marriage.

"A Marriage Prayer" by John Shea speaks of this covenantal love—the faithful, year-in and year-out love that is hoped for and pledged in the act of marrying:

"He said he would never go away and she said she would always be there."

Write about your reactions to John Shea's prayer. How do you feel about the image of married love that he conveys?

He said he would never go away
and she said she would always be there
so they got an apartment
with a bedroom set that cost too much
and ate spaghetti and Chianti
with breadsticks and butter.
His sky-the-limit potential
ceilinged at forty
and she got pregnant
a respectable three times.
The best was
when she would park the kids at her mother's
and meet him after work
for drinks and dinner.
They would find out
who they were living with
and then go on as always.
The night of their first daughter's wedding
they wondered about it all
and got weeping drunk.
Once
when they were going to see
her mother in the nursing home,
she knew she loved him
and cried.
He told her not to worry.
On the dresser in their bedroom
they have photos of their grandchildren
holding hands with Mickey Mouse at Disney World.
They never thought their love a fire
so it did not burn out,
this man who would never go away
and this woman who would always be there.
     (*The God Who Fell from Heaven,* page 97)

Especially in this era of temporary relationships, a pledge of faithful love requires maturity, realism, and preparation. Living out that pledge over a lifetime is possible with the immensely graced love of the Sacrament of Marriage.

Marriage as a Covenant

A **covenant** is a deeply personal, solemn promise made between persons. The church has always viewed marriage as a covenantal relationship that mirrors God's covenant with God's people.

A Symbol of God's Faithful Love

The whole of the Jewish Scriptures is an account of God's covenant with the Jewish people. God made a covenant with them freely, out of love. But the special people chosen by God went through their ups and downs in history: They alternately clung to God and wandered from God. The Jewish people endured hardship, slavery, and exile from their land; at other times, they experienced triumph, liberation, and prosperity. Over centuries, the people of God have come to an ever-deeper understanding that God has always been faithful to them, giving them more than they could have ever expected through the good times and the bad. They have come to realize that they are not a perfect people and that at times God has been angry with them, just as they have been angry with God when life disappointed them. Nevertheless, God's people know that they are a people cherished forever by a God who will never abandon them. God will "never go away" and will "always be there."

The reality of God's faithful, covenantal love for people finds a powerful symbol in the Sacrament of Marriage, when two Christians freely give their love to each other forever. The words from the marriage vows, "in good times and in bad, in sickness and in health," echo the kind of love that God pledged to the Jewish people.

In the Sacrament of Marriage, two Christians freely give their love to each other forever.

Do you know any married couples whose love for each other could be seen as a sign of God's love? Write about your reflections, giving an example about one of these couples to illustrate your point.

As Christ Loves the Church

Giving the marriage covenant a specifically Christian meaning, Saint Paul compared the love of marriage to Christ's love for the community that is called the Church:

> Husbands should love their wives, just as Christ loved the Church and sacrificed himself for [it]. . . . Husbands must

love their wives as they love their own bodies; for a man to love his wife is for him to love himself. . . . This is why a man leaves his father and mother and becomes attached to his wife, and the two become one flesh. This mystery has great significance, but I am applying it to Christ and the Church. To sum up: you also, each one of you, must love his wife as he loves himself; and let every wife respect her husband. (Ephesians 5:25–33)

Jesus gave his whole being, his very life, for the people of God, the Church. Likewise, in marriage, the wife and the husband are called to give their energies, talents, affection, faith, hope, and love—their lives—for each other. The wonder of marriage is that as long as a woman and a man love each other, they show to the world something of the love that God has for all of us. The God who is love is made visible in the love of the couple.

The Sacrament of Marriage is not the wedding ceremony itself; rather, the sacrament is the couple's sharing of their whole life together, the living out of the covenant. The wedding ceremony celebrates and affirms the sacrament that encompasses a lifetime.

The sacrament is the couple's sharing of their whole life together, the living out of the covenant.

Why Marry?

Most but not all of us choose to marry. Those persons who do marry have decided that at least some of the following purposes of marriage are important to them:
- sharing life with a loving companion
- creating new life
- strengthening individual identities
- calling forth the best in each person
- enabling the couple to reach out beyond themselves in hospitality and compassion
- supporting the journey in faith

Sharing Life with a Loving Companion

The first and most obvious purpose of marriage is the loving companionship of another person. As research (such as that described on page 249) makes clear, people primarily look for companionship in a mate. When interviewed for a study published in *Psychology Today,* one man described the companionship of his wife:

> "Jen is the best friend I have. . . . I would rather spend time with her, talk with her, be with her than with anyone else."

A woman in the same study said this about her long and successful marriage:

> "I feel marriages can survive and flourish without today's emphasis on sex. I had a much stronger sex drive than my husband and it was a point of weakness in our marriage. However, it was not as important as friendship, understanding and respect. That we had lots of, and still do."

One of the great values and purposes of marriage is its support for two people who wish to be best friends with each other.

Creating New Life

Another purpose of marriage is the creation of new life. Conceiving children is the most obvious way of creating new life, and becoming parents traditionally has been one of the chief aims of marriage. As Pope John Paul II said,

> . . . The fundamental task of the family is to serve life, to actualize in history the original blessing of the creator— that of transmitting by procreation the divine image from person to person. (*On the Family,* no. 28)

By bringing children into the world, a wife and a husband co-create with God, the source of all life.

Strengthening Individual Identities

One of the most damaging myths about marriage is that once two persons marry, they must give up their separate, unique identities. On the contrary, marriage is intended to strengthen the individuals' identities, not to merge them or, worse, to repress them. Rather than giving up their identities when they marry, the partners should nourish one another's particular gifts. In her poem "Two-Trees," Janet Miles pictured the union of two unique and separate persons:

> A portion of your soul has been
>   entwined with mine.

Interview your parents or some other married couple to learn about their perceptions of the following:
- the purposes of their marriage at the time they married
- the purposes of their marriage now
- how they have changed for the better because of their marriage

"A gentle kind of togetherness, while separately we stand."

Make a list of reasons that some people feel pressured to marry in their teenage years. Write down your thoughts about the impact that early marriage has on young persons' futures and on the development of their identities.

A gentle kind of togetherness, while
    separately we stand.
As two trees deeply rooted in
    separate plots of ground,
While their topmost branches
    come together,
Forming a miracle of lace
    against the heavens.

If two persons have had too little time to set their roots into the ground—that is, to develop their individual identities—before they are married, they probably will experience serious problems in their relationship. The situation of Norma and Greg is an example of this problem. Norma described their three-year marriage:

> We were just out of high school, and here we were supposed to be raising our own kids! I think one of the worst things for us was that besides the kids, there was nothing to talk about. And we had so much trouble with the kids anyway that talking about them was usually depressing.
>
> We never had a chance to each become somebody before we got married. We were trying to grow up together, and it wasn't working. For one thing, Greg was always getting in arguments with people because he was threatened by how much more they knew, or maybe they had a better job. He didn't feel good about himself. And I would go along with everything Greg said or did just to please him and make peace. I didn't know any better. Life was lousy for both of us.

Marriage can strengthen and nourish the roots of our identities, but those roots first must be planted firmly.

Calling Forth the Best in Each Person

As with all loving relationships, marriage has the potential to draw out the best of each partner. If they care for each other, gradually the wife and the husband can put aside masks that they previously hid behind; they can honestly be themselves. Revealing our true selves is liberating.

For instance, a man who has a sensitive and gentle side that has been tucked away because other people might think it unmanly can offer this gift to his wife as she helps him to accept himself. A woman whose ambition has always been to enter a triathlon but who has kept this desire a secret because other people might not support her may now give full rein to her ambition with the encouragement of her husband.

In the *Psychology Today* study, a man married for thirty years summarized the excitement that a spouse can feel in the growth of a loved one:

> "I have watched her grow and have shared with her both the pain and the exhilaration of her journey. I find her more fascinating now than when we were first married."

Marriage can help spouses to tap into reservoirs of generosity that they never knew they had. Spouses who have never dealt with the sickness of other people find themselves nursing each other back to health. Wives and husbands open their hearts and homes and make special meals and careful preparations for in-laws because they know that such service will please their spouses. This man, married for many years and interviewed in the *Psychology Today* study, declared:

> "Sometimes I give far more than I receive, and sometimes I receive far more than I give. But my wife does the same. If we weren't willing to do that, we would have broken up long ago."

The give-and-take of marriage constantly calls forth gifts and personality traits that renew the partners.

Can you remember times when your own parents or another married couple tapped into their reservoirs of generosity or energy in order to serve each other? Describe in writing one example of how marriage brought out the best in these spouses.

Enabling the Couple to Reach Out

Secure in the love that they have for each other, marriage partners are in a position to love beyond the bounds of their relationship. The husband and the wife are freed by their love to reach out to other people in hospitality and compassion. One reason that the church encourages public rather than private weddings is that in the Sacrament of Marriage, the couple affirms that the community is present in their marriage, that the relationship goes beyond the two persons to welcome all of the people who enter their lives.

Kathy and Al have such a vision of their marriage; for them, life together means openness to all people in their community:

> In spite of the rigors of raising several young children, Kathy and Al seem to be very peaceful people—not simply calm but spiritually at peace.
>
> They live in an inner-city neighborhood that has a lot

of problems. Kids on the street are hungry and unsupervised, and violent crime is common. So Kathy and Al's small home has become an island of peace for kids or adults who need to put down their burdens for a while.

While talking with Kathy and eating some of her homemade bread, a troubled, restless child relaxes. A mother who feels overwhelmed by pressures finds in Kathy some gentle encouragement and a sense of hope. Al is a solid person, a man who loves carpentry and fixing things. He has been behind the move to clean up and rehabilitate some abandoned homes in the neighborhood, and Kathy has begun an after-school program for kids that offers food, fun, and lots of love.

Kathy and Al's life isn't easy; it is full of stress. But the sense of community that they foster with everyone they touch is unforgettable. Kathy and Al are intensely prayerful people. Perhaps that is why they seem to quietly bring God's presence into broken and hurting situations.

Writer Antoine de Saint-Exupéry could have been speaking of Kathy and Al, who share a vision of reaching out beyond themselves, when he wrote, "Love does not consist in gazing at each other but in looking outward together in the same direction."

Supporting the Journey in Faith

For Christians, marriage becomes a means of support for their journey in faith. In their love for each other and for those who enter their lives, the married persons experience the love that is God. They may not even be aware that in their human love, they are touching the divine. Whether the two persons are conscious of it or not, God is located in the depths of such human experiences.

When a wife and a husband consciously seek a life together with God, the marriage relationship itself is blessed. Research has shown that couples who share and develop a common faith are more satisfied in their marriages than couples who lack this dimension in their relationship.

The journey in faith cannot be traveled alone; it needs to be supported and nurtured by a community of common beliefs and values. In marriage and family life, two persons who share their faith find such a community. Ideally, their own family is

"Love does not consist in gazing at each other but in looking outward together in the same direction."

Talk with a married person who shares and develops a common faith with his or her spouse. Write about what role their faith plays in their marriage.

the core of a wider faith community that supports them in their journey. This is another reason that the Sacrament of Marriage is intended as a community celebration, not a private affair; the journey of the couple in love and faith is a challenge that is meant to be shared by other Christians who will be with them in their struggles and joys.

The Engagement: A Season of Anticipation

A period of engagement anticipates some of the purposes of marriage. It gives a couple the opportunity to begin a relationship of mutual commitment, even though that commitment has not yet been made permanent in marriage. Thus, engagement prepares the two persons for a lifetime together.

The word *engagement* implies involvement or activity. Indeed, engagement to marry needs to be a period of active involvement by the man and the woman. Numerous issues must be settled. Many important questions, which the engaged persons already should have considered while courting, were outlined on pages 259–263. These questions take on more urgency and magnitude as the time to make the marriage commitment nears. Trust needs to be deepened; mutual self-disclosure needs to become more profound. Consequently, an engagement period that adequately prepares a couple for marriage might last for months.

Engagement is also a time of trial; the couple might conclude that they really do not want to marry each other. Engagement serves a valuable purpose if it helps two persons to avoid a marriage that would not be good for them.

Engaged people need to discuss and negotiate many areas of their future life before they marry. List some problems that can arise in a marriage because of fundamental differences in any three of the following areas:
- money
- recreation
- intimacy
- sexual expression
- in-laws
- independence
- friends
- children
- alcohol
- decision-making

Sharing and Negotiating Dreams

In this course, a great deal of attention has been focused on discovering the dream of your future and making choices toward that dream. During engagement, two persons must share their dreams with each other so that they can see how their dreams coincide and conflict. Also, they need to be sure that any notions they have about their dream marriage coincide with the reality that they are about to face. A dream is an ideal, and an engagement period gives a taste of the real world ahead. For example, Tom and Nancy had to negotiate their individual dreams to meet their needs and desires as a couple:

> Nancy had always assumed that once she married Tom, she would cease working at the store for which she was a buyer. She loved children. Nancy came from a large family in which her mother stayed home to care for the children, and she wanted to do the same. Bringing in a second income was not part of her dream.

> But Tom was concerned about the expenses that they were facing. An important element of his dream was to be free of debt as soon as possible so that they could live relatively unpressured by financial worries. As Tom said, "Looking at the loans from college that we still had to pay off, the rent for an apartment, the car payment, and so on, we realized that there was no way that we could make it on my salary alone for at least three or four years."

> Nancy recalled her reaction, "I was shocked. I don't know why, but I just didn't imagine some of the expenses. Part of the problem was that I had lived at home since I graduated from college. It was easy to ignore the real costs of a household. As a business major and a buyer, I should have been more realistic, but I just didn't think about it. So I'll have to work at least until the birth of the first baby."

Another couple might find that even though they love each other intensely, his passion for the outdoors, sun, and physical exercise is in direct conflict with her preference for quiet activities in cozy, indoor places and her concern about her fair skin that burns easily. They will need to reconcile these lifestyle differences over a lifetime, but during their engagement, they can begin to think about and negotiate these aspects of their dreams. How they deal with each other over these differences is a fairly good indicator of how they will solve problems when they are married. Life is full of such compromises and adjustments that couples agree to work on because they believe that their relationship is worth the effort.

On a practical level, engagement is a good time to work through financial issues.

Practical Matters

On a practical level, engagement is a time to work through financial issues:

- life-insurance plans

- debt payments
- mortgages
- property titles
- investments
- credit-card use
- spending habits

Performing an inventory of each person's property or deciding which credit cards to use may not be romantic, but bitter arguments over such matters often can occur later in marriage. Again, if the two persons can work through these practicalities, it indicates that they can handle a basic level of joint decision-making. If they cannot settle these basic issues, they probably will not successfully manage more complex dilemmas.

Physical and mental health considerations also need to be addressed. During engagement, both persons should have thorough physical examinations. Each person should know about the medical history of his or her partner and whether hereditary medical problems exist in his or her partner's family, for example, diabetes, congenital defects, Alzheimer's disease, or sickle-cell anemia. The couple also needs to know of any physical or psychological impediment to sexual relations in either person. Genuine love is not blind, and certainly two engaged persons who are about to marry must not be blind to each other's medical history.

Do you agree that thorough knowledge of each person's medical history is important before marriage? Why or why not? Write your reflections in a brief paragraph.

Becoming Part of Two Families

When two persons marry, they become part of each other's family. Engagement is a time to get to know future in-laws, to build solid, healthy relationships with them, and to anticipate what it will be like to be part of an extended family. Any concerns about disliking future in-laws, finding them too demanding, or feeling judged by them need plenty of discussion and resolution by the couple because the rest of their lives will be bound with their in-laws' lives to some degree.

Stereotypes about interfering in-laws, especially mothers-in-law, do a grave disservice to them. In-laws can be wonderful, even essential, support for a married couple. For instance, when Mary Ann and Phil got married, they never realized the significant role that Mary Ann's parents would play in their lives:

List some TV shows that often portray in-laws. Next to the name of each show, summarize in writing how the in-laws are portrayed and why you think that the show has pictured them in this way.

- Mary Ann and Phil's fifth child, Judy, barely survived birth, but they did not realize at that time that the baby was mentally retarded. Over the months, though, Judy's handicaps became obvious. With four other children to raise, Mary Ann and Phil wondered how they could cope. But Mary Ann's parents, Charlie and Lucille, began to show up regularly at the house. They visited frequently, not only because they loved Judy and their other grandchildren but also because they knew that Mary Ann and Phil needed time alone together. Taking care of their grandchildren, especially Judy, gave Charlie and Lucille a new enthusiasm for life, too.

When Mary Ann and Phil pledged their love in marriage, they married into each other's families. The engagement period can be a valuable time to understand and appreciate future in-laws.

Once the issues outlined above have been sufficiently considered, the engaged couple must consider these major questions:

- Can I freely, responsibly, and lovingly commit myself to this person for the rest of my life?
- Do I wholeheartedly want to make this commitment?
- Will both of us, our families, and humankind be best served if we marry?

Unfortunately, no easy formula or procedure can help the couple to answer these questions. Time, prayer, reflection, and honest sharing are needed before the couple can answer them.

The Church's Program of Marriage Preparation

The engagement period varies in length, and engaged couples use the time in vastly different ways. To ensure that couples are ready to make the serious and deeply important commitment of marriage, those couples who wish to be married in the Catholic church are required to attend a marriage preparation course offered by the parish or the diocese.

Marriage in the Church or a Church Wedding?

A church wedding is just that—a ceremony performed in a church building. Most couples, even those who are not actively involved in a parish, want this kind of wedding. People who marry in the church building but who have no involvement with the worshiping community may have wonderful, permanent

By celebrating their love before the community, the married couple in effect says, "Look, love is here and now. The God who is love is present."

marriages, but a church wedding is not the same as *a marriage in the church.*

A marriage preparation course is required so that a couple realizes that marriage is a sacrament in union with the whole church and specifically with their church community; they are not merely holding their wedding in a church building. A marriage in the church implies that the persons know what the sacrament means and wish to declare before the gathered community that their marriage is a blessed event in which they commit themselves to live out their love, together and forever. By celebrating their love before the community, the married couple in effect says, "Look, love is here and now. The God who is love is present." The church, in the form of this community, acts as witness and support to the marriage.

"What God Has United . . ."

A marriage preparation course helps a couple to think through the permanent commitment that they are about to make. In the past, when the church required little preparation by marrying couples, many marriages were entered into without sufficient reflection. The Catholic Christian tradition has always taken the permanence of marriage seriously. So today, when for every two marriages taking place in the United States there is one divorce, marriage preparation is seen as essential.

The church's belief in the permanence of marriage is based on Jesus' response to a crowd that asked him about divorce: " '[In marriage] the two become one flesh. They are no longer two, therefore, but one flesh. So then, what God has united, human beings must not divide' " (Mark 10:8–9).

Permanence in marriage is necessary for the good of all society, which is ultimately the good of individual persons. If marriages end easily, society suffers from instability. To a large extent, we can see this instability in our society today. Broken marriages cause emotional, financial, spiritual, and interpersonal pain and dislocation.

The prevailing idea that divorce is usually the best solution to a difficult, unhappy marriage recently has been found to be a myth. In fact, researchers have found that only about 10 percent of divorced couples think that both of their lives have improved since their divorce. Furthermore, increasing evidence is pointing to the long-term detrimental effects of divorce on children.

The church is not oblivious to the pain of many marriages;

Complete this statement, and then write your reflections about it:
• I believe that divorce is . . .

it does not want people to live with intolerable marital conditions. But the church's emphasis is on preventing such marriages through adequate preparation and on encouraging married couples who are having difficulties to work with all their strength to resolve their problems, relying also on the support and love of the church community. With the support of the church community, a couple is not alone; this is why the Sacrament of Marriage is a reality for the community as well as for the couple.

Ensuring the Validity of the Vows

In keeping with the church's concern that marriages be healthy and life-giving, marriage preparation is a time to ensure that the vows of a couple will be valid. Marriage promises must be given freely and knowledgeably in order to be binding. In fact, the church will grant an annulment for a marriage that has ended legally in divorce if a church tribunal determines that the marriage vows were invalid from the beginning. Consequently, before the promises are given, both persons must possess the following:

Freedom from pressures: Many internal and external pressures can weaken a person's ability to consent freely to marriage, making the vows invalid. The pressure may be as blatant as a demand by the parents of a pregnant teenage girl that the baby's father marry their daughter. Or the pressure may be felt in a home where quarreling or alcoholism pushes a desperate son or daughter to escape through marriage.

Knowledge and willingness: For marriage vows to be considered valid by the church, both persons also must know what marriage, especially the marriage promises, really means; they must have the capacity and the willingness to fulfill their promises. For example, if either person decides before the marriage that she or he does not want children and will not have them but fails to tell the other person, the vows could be considered invalid because of lack of knowledge by one partner and lack of willingness to fulfill the marriage promises by the other partner.

Without sufficient time to discern the essential dynamics of their relationship, a couple may actually say the words of the marriage promises but not really be free enough from internal and external forces or knowledgeable enough to make

For marriage vows to be considered valid by the church, both persons must have the capacity and the willingness to fulfill their promises.

a valid promise. The church wants to prevent this unfortunate situation through adequate preparation. In cases where the church does grant an annulment sometime after a marriage has ended, it concludes that at the time of the wedding ceremony, one or both of the persons were not able to take a valid vow. Therefore, the marriage was never a valid sacrament in the eyes of the church.

Annulment is not divorce. A divorce dissolves the legal contract of marriage, whereas an annulment acknowledges that as a sacrament, the marriage never existed. Some people confuse these terms, but they actually describe two distinct realities.

What the Preparation Courses Cover

Although they vary from diocese to diocese, all of the church's marriage preparation courses are designed to assist couples in fulfilling their mutual commitments. The courses may be given by the parish or by the diocese. Many courses give instruction about such topics as these:

- the sacramental nature of marriage
- communication skills
- goal setting and goal sharing
- decision-making
- development of intimacy
- conflict resolution
- practical adjustments to married life
- sexuality
- children

Each couple is expected to complete a course several weeks before their wedding ceremony. In some dioceses, the date of the ceremony cannot be scheduled until the course is finished. In cases where the persons have serious obstacles to confront before they can be married, a priest may ask that the couple be counseled by a competent person.

Athletes prepare themselves for years before they can enter the professional leagues. Lawyers and doctors spend years of education and preparation for their careers. Even so, many people mistakenly believe that they can enter marriage and succeed simply by going through the most minimal preparation—a few months of dating, blood tests, an application for a marriage license, and so on. Marriage requires far more of us as total persons than do careers in professional athletics, law, or medicine.

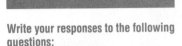

Write your responses to the following questions:
- Do you think that divorces should be easily granted?
- Do you think that annulments should be easily granted?

Reflect on this question in writing:
- Is it fair to say that marriage requires much more of an individual as a total person than do careers in professional athletics, law, or medicine?

The preparation program of the church is an attempt to prepare a couple for a lifetime together.

The Wedding Celebration

In marriage, two persons keep a solemn covenant with the awareness that hardships and struggles inevitably will be part of their life together. But on the occasion of their wedding, their joy in making the commitment is so full that they want to share that joy with their families and friends. A wedding is a community's celebration of the love of two of its members and the formal beginning of a shared, committed life that is the Sacrament of Marriage.

The Rite of Marriage

In the margin:

Interview a couple who were married recently. Ask them about their preparations for their wedding and the wedding day itself. If they had a chance to prepare the wedding over again, would they do things differently? Write about the results of the interview.

If you were planning your own wedding, what one biblical passage would you want read at the service? (For help, you can check the suggested readings for weddings given in the church's lectionary, which is available from your campus ministry office, school chaplain, or parish priest.) Write down the passage, and outline what you would want the priest to say in his homily.

In the midst of the wedding celebration, which may be elaborate or simple according to the customs and desires of the couple, is the ceremony itself—the rite of marriage. Although the church encourages a couple to have their wedding ceremony in the context of the Mass, if for some reason that is inappropriate, the ceremony can be held within a shorter religious service.

When the ceremony takes place during Mass, it comes after the liturgy of the Word, or the readings from the Bible and the homily. Some of the prayers of the rite have alternate forms, and the readings can vary as well. Any variations can be decided by a couple and their priest. At the heart of the ceremony are the following questions by the priest and vows by the couple. Addressing the couple, the priest says:

Have you come here freely and without reservation to give yourselves to each other in marriage?

Will you love and honor each other as husband and wife for the rest of your lives?

Will you accept children lovingly from God and bring them up according to the law of Christ and his church?

After responding to each question, the man and the woman each in turn vow their commitment with these words:

I promise to be true to you in good times and in bad, in sickness and in health. I will love you and honor you all the days of my life.

The ceremony highlights the public commitment of the couple to each other because the Christian community needs to hear people say that love is possible, that love exists. The promises that the couple makes before the congregation tell all who are present that two people have a goal of permanent commitment to foster each other's good and thus the good of society as a whole. Consequently, public weddings are occasions of tremendous optimism for the entire assembled community.

Celebration of a Promise, a Contract, and a Covenant

Marriage is all of the following:

- a promise
- a contract
- a covenant

The wedding ceremony celebrates all three of these dimensions.

Marriage is a promise, a contract, and a covenant.

Promise: Marriage is a promise, a declaration that the wife and the husband will do something for each other. The language of the Roman Catholic rite is given above. Most major Christian denominations use similar words, and they all include the concept of promise. Each rite specifies obligations to love and to share until death. For a marriage to be valid, the nature and implications of the promise must be understood fully, and each person must be able to fulfill it. The marriage promise indicates that each spouse will be faithful to the other and that the marriage is permanent. Being faithful means more than sexual fidelity, however. It implies that the couple will have faith in their marriage and that they will work at making their relationship flourish. Faithfulness means that loving each other is of primary importance to both the husband and the wife.

Contract: Marriage is also a legal and binding contract. The priest and the congregation are witnesses that two people have freely and responsibly assumed a partnership with legal obligations.

Covenant: As discussed at the beginning of this chapter, marriage is a covenant modeled on the solemn, binding agreement that God made with the Israelites. By that covenant, God and Israel promised to belong to each other forever. Israel would be God's people, and Yahweh would be their God. Like all covenants, both parties had obligations, and their covenant was permanent. In Christian tradition, marriage is a covenant like the

The love between married partners is a kind of miracle: its origins are a mystery, and its results are wonderful and amazing.

one made between God and Israel and like the love of Christ for the Church.

The Miracle of Marriage

At a wedding, the love of two persons is celebrated, blessed, and supported in a public way. Their love is a kind of miracle: its origins are a mystery, and its results are wonderful and amazing. A marriage gives the community hope in the miracle of human love and reminds people of a tender and ever-faithful God—a God who will never go away and who will always be there.

Review Questions

1. What is a covenant? How is marriage a covenantal act?
2. How can the marriage partners' love for each other be compared to Christ's love for the Church?
3. Explain these two purposes of marriage:
   • sharing life with a loving companion
   • creating new life
4. How is marriage intended to affect the individual identities of the partners?
5. How can marriage call forth the best in each person? How can it enable the couple to reach out to others?
6. In what ways can marriage support the faith of the couple?
7. Why is the sharing and negotiating of dreams an important part of engagement?
8. List some practical matters that need to be worked out during the engagement period.
9. Why is it important to get to know one's future in-laws before marriage?
10. What three major questions must be answered during the engagement period?
11. Explain the difference between a church wedding and a marriage in the church.
12. Why does the church support the belief in the permanence of marriage? How does this belief explain the extensive marriage preparation required by most dioceses?
13. Under what conditions could marriage vows later be considered invalid?
14. How do divorce and annulment differ?
15. What topics might be covered in a diocese's marriage preparation course?
16. What questions does a priest ask a couple in the rite of marriage? With what words do the woman and the man vow their commitment?
17. Explain marriage as a promise, a contract, and a covenant.

13 Growth in Marriage: The Blessing of Family Life

A wedding marks the formal beginning of a lifetime together—a life that promises its share of joy, profound intimacy, and fulfillment as well as disappointment, rough times, and dull routine. The rich sense of peace that often can be detected in a couple who has been married for many years is the fruit of years spent sharing and supporting each other through the high points and the low points of existence.

This mature love of married life is pictured well in Willa Cather's story "Neighbour Rosicky":

> Mary sat watching him intently, trying to find any change in his face. It is hard to see anyone who has become like your own body to you. Yes, his hair had got thin, and his high forehead had deep lines running from left to right. . . . He was shorter and broader than when she married him; his back had grown broad and curved, a good deal like the shell of an old turtle. . . .
>
> He was fifteen years older than Mary, but she hardly ever thought about it before. He was her man, and the kind of man she liked. . . . They had been shipmates on a rough voyage and had stood by each other in trying times. Life had gone well with them because, at bottom, they had the same ideas about life. . . . It was as if they had thought the same thought together. . . . Though he had married a rough farm girl, he had never touched her without gentleness.

For most couples, married life becomes family life. Through the challenges and rewards of sharing life not only with a partner but also with children, married persons can come to a deep sense of the goodness of life and the tenderness of God's love for them.

Recall any elderly couples whom you know. Pick one couple and interview them to find out how they have sustained their long marriage, that is, some of the secrets of their success. Write about the results of your interview.

The Seven Seasons of a Marriage

In any marriage, especially those that involve children, a great deal of development goes on throughout the years. The couple's development can be seen in at least three areas:
- their relationship as spouses
- their roles as parents
- their individual lives as persons and professionals

These three areas tend to overlap; development in one area affects the other areas.

Furthermore, a developmental pattern seems to emerge in most marriages that involve children, a pattern that can be thought of as the seven seasons of a marriage. Naturally the length of the seasons and the issues of each season vary from family to family because of the number and spacing of births and many other factors. Nevertheless, a fairly typical pattern can be observed.

The Blissful Beginnings: Years One to Two

Most couples report satisfaction in the first two years of marriage. Much of the bliss experienced on the honeymoon remains with them, and the couple feels a great deal of hope. The husband and the wife now become each other's primary source of support and affection; in an effort to build an "ideal" marriage, they may even be overly conscious of protecting and fulfilling the needs of each other. The couple tries to learn to live with each other's possibly annoying habits.

The spirit of hope and attentiveness smooths over some of the adjustments and compromises that need to be made on a wide variety of issues:
- who does the laundry
- who cleans the house
- whose job takes precedence if a move is required
- how much time is to be spent together
- how much time is to be spent alone or with friends
- with whose family the Christmas holidays will be spent

Although these types of compromises are required throughout life, they are particularly obvious during the first two years of marriage.

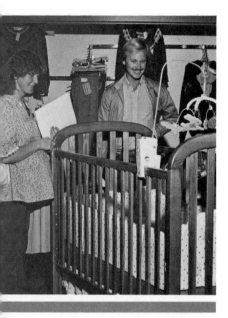

The miracle of creating new life and loving a child draws the couple together.

Make a list of habits you have right now that you will probably need to change or at least compromise if you marry. Place a check mark next to the habits that you would like to change before you marry. Describe in writing how you might alter these habits.

Any compromises that mark a loss of personal independence are often compensated by the rewards of deeper interdependence. The wife and the husband forego some independence, but they gain daily support, affection, and encouragement. They gain a companion and partner to share their worries and fears with and to help in planning and decision-making. In the first two years of marriage, the couple can learn to appreciate their new interdependence.

Becoming Domesticated: Years Three to Five

The next season, the third to fifth years of marriage, has an intensely domestic focus as the husband and the wife settle into the joys and needs of being parents and making a home. The miracle of creating new life and loving a child draws the couple together. Many couples who cannot conceive a child eventually may choose to adopt one or more children. With their innocence, affection, and openness to life, children renew their parents' sense of wonder and hope. Having children can be one of life's greatest joys.

Babies and small children are also very needy creatures who require a great deal from their parents. Along with joy and wonder, pregnancy and parenthood bring physical and emotional fatigue. Once a child is born, a round-the-clock routine of feeding, changing, and comforting sets in. Babies turn into toddlers and then into small children, who continue to need a great deal of nurturing and attention.

After the birth of their first child, the couple is no longer alone; life has to be lived around the needs of another human being. This represents a revolution in the couple's lifestyle. For some individuals, the new domestic focus of their lives is very settling, and they adjust to it easily. For others, who are used to a high degree of independence, it can be very unsettling.

Another element of this season of marriage is the redefining of role expectations. For example:

- Will both partners be involved in the physical aspects of child care?
- Will the father or the mother cease working to care for children?
- Will one income be sufficient for family needs?

These and many other questions challenge the couple to grow in new ways.

Answer these questions in writing, and explain your answers:
- Would you be willing to temporarily give up your future career to be a full-time parent?
- Would you expect your spouse to give up her or his career to stay at home with your children?

A Time of Decision: Years Six to Twelve

The sixth through the twelfth years of marriage may be the most difficult years for the couple, particularly years seven through ten. At the same time that the partners are growing—professionally, personally, and parentally—the busyness of their lives may be causing them to lose touch with each other. Their growth may be in different directions, or one person may grow while the other stagnates. Some of the sexual attraction of the early years has usually faded by this time.

Careers during this period often are at a pivotal phase. If the wife or the husband has been with a company for seven or eight years, she or he may be at the threshold of a big promotion or a disappointing plateau. A large percentage of workers change jobs during this phase of marriage.

In addition, being parents of school-age children can be fun and creative but also demanding. Children become less dependent than they were as babies but more active and involved in the world beyond the family and less subject to the parents' control. The hectic pace of keeping up with a household and the busy schedules of family members can seem like an oppressive daily grind. Sharon Addy described that sense of drudgery and its effects on her marriage in her poem "Life After Marriage":

The hectic pace of keeping up with a household can seem like an oppressive daily grind.

List as many of your parents' daily activities as you can think of, from the time they rise in the morning until bedtime. Then write your reactions to this question:
• Do you think that your parents ever ask Sharon Addy's question, "Will all our life be scheduled?"

When I said "I do" I didn't mean
I would pick up everything
any of us would ever own
or be a hash-slinging,
baby-sitting chauffeur
who runs with the vacuum
between washer loads.

What happened to the soft summer
of our life together
when our twoness
became a oneness
with an eternity of time?

Our oneness became a moreness
and the schedules began
and they race on
chopping life into fragments
leaving me with ragged edges.

Will all our life be scheduled?

Given the strains described above, it is not surprising that for many couples, this period is one of decision-making about their relationship. The honeymoon is long over. The wonder of childbirth is fading. Many of the routines so well described in Addy's poem can feel oppressive. Pressures are more complex—personally, professionally, and parentally. Individuals may find themselves asking, Is this what I want? Do I want to hang in there? Most couples make the transition into the next stage of their marriage, but frequently not without some serious soul-searching that strengthens their relationship in the end.

A Renewal: Years Thirteen to Eighteen

The thirteenth through eighteenth years of marriage are free of some of the pressures and strains of the previous season. Frequently a renewal of the marriage is experienced during these years. In a way, the partners become reacquainted. If their children have entered adolescence, the couple might have more time to spend together. Some couples also begin to socialize more. Even if they still have younger children, coping with them can be easier because the couple has had practice by raising their older children.

Being the parents of adolescents can be a tremendously positive experience. Parents learn the delicate balance between guidance and firmness on one hand and letting go and trust on the other. They learn from their adolescent children as those children develop in fascinating ways. Parents can enjoy listening to new ideas and discoveries of the young persons whose world is opening up, and they can get involved in some of the best discussions of their lives. Perhaps, too, parents fondly remember their own struggles to assert their independence twenty or so years earlier.

But being the parents of adolescents can be difficult as well. The adolescent struggle to assert independence and to establish a unique identity may cause great conflict between parents and their children. Families may argue about things like the following:

- curfews
- having an after-school job
- household responsibilities
- use of a car
- drugs and alcohol
- irritating personality traits

Interview your parents or the parents of a friend. Find out what they view as the most difficult challenges and the greatest rewards of being the parents of an adolescent. Prepare a written report of the interview.

Write an imaginary dialog between yourself and one of your parents. In the dialog, cover some unresolved issue between yourself and that parent. As your parent, try to see the issue from your parent's point of view. As yourself, say what you would like to say about the issue. Attempt to portray each of your positions as accurately as you can.

The degree of conflict makes the period more turbulent in some families than in others. But as the adolescent children grow in making increasingly important decisions and taking more responsibility for their own lives, parents generally appreciate this growth, and family relationships often improve over the course of these years.

Mid-Life Transitions: Years Nineteen to Twenty-three

When their adolescent children become young adults and leave home, parents often feel grief over the separation from these significant people who now are on their own. Usually this separation coincides with the onset of a mid-life transition for the spouses, which is trying in itself. For many people, middle age can signal feelings of physical vulnerability and inadequacy. As a person reaches forty years of age, the body cannot perform like it could at age twenty-five or even thirty-five. Individuals may begin to feel that life is passing them by.

Other mid-life pressures appear:

- A person at mid-life has been working for perhaps twenty years. Realizing that life may be half over, a person begins to ask, What has my career amounted to? Do I want to do this type of work for the rest of my life? Could I find something more interesting, challenging, and valuable to do?
- A person who has been immersed in achieving within a career may feel an urge to become more home-centered, less driven, or more attuned to relationships.
- A spouse who has not given his or her full energies to a career may long to grow in a profession.

The mid-life period often is marked by restlessness and a search for meaning. A sense that the clock of a life span is running down contributes to the urgency.

The implications of mid-life transition for a couple's relationship are enormous. One or both persons may feel restless or unfulfilled in the relationship; their search for meaning in life typically points to some shift in their way of relating or in their expectations of each other. This phase of marriage is even more difficult if the partners have ignored the building of their own relationship in order to devote themselves to their children. Developing mutual interests and other channels for communication is important, otherwise the marriage relationship might

Family relationships often improve over the course of the children's adolescence.

become plagued with boredom. As with every crisis or transition, the mid-life period presents new opportunities for the couple to deepen and broaden their love.

A Couple on Their Own Again: Years Twenty-four to Forty

In the twenty-fourth to fortieth years of marriage, once their children have left the home, the couple usually establishes new and deeper bonds. If they are creative in using their time together, the partners will use their freedom for travel, hobbies, service to their community, or other pursuits that interest them. Often the persons become grandparents; this provides opportunities to share affection with a new generation.

During this season, or even before, most couples experience the death of their own parents. When their parents die, the partners come to a fuller realization of what it means to be the older generation, taking their roles as heads of the family. Their own ability to offer wisdom and stability to the next generation is to some extent the fruit of struggling through the painful loss of their own parents and of integrating the meaning of their parents' lives into their understandings of themselves.

Growing Old Together: Years Forty-one and Beyond

The forty-first year of marriage and beyond are marked by the retirement of one or both partners. Retiring from work is frequently traumatic for people because their jobs have been a source of meaning for them. However, retirement is also an opportunity to do things that the couple may have wanted to do for a long time. With so much time to spend together, couples frequently have to learn new patterns of relating to each other. To the extent that they have developed mutual interests before retirement, the transition in their relationship will require less adjustment than previous changes.

Generally, retired couples also have to face the physical, emotional, and financial problems of aging. Because the partners are a major source of support and affirmation for each other, the terminal illness or death of a spouse is the most difficult element in this part of married life, especially if the period of disability or suffering is long. In spite of the difficulties of

Interview a couple whose children have left home. Write about their experience of seeing their children move away and about the adjustments that they had to make as a couple when this happened.

Retired couples have to face the physical, emotional, and financial problems of aging.

growing old together, spouses may come to an appreciation of each other and an integrity in their shared life far greater than they have known in earlier years.

If they have been open and flexible in their approach to life, a couple can find after years together that each season of their marriage has had its own significance and joy—even the tough seasons. For Herta Janzen, the houses that she and her family lived in over the years became symbols of the seasons of their life together:

> I began to reminisce about our various homes. Our first apartment recalled memories of the growing pains of a marriage relationship. The house on the mission complex gave us our first taste of living in another culture where we also became the proud parents of a daughter. Our older house in Canada challenged us to repair and rebuild.

However, the house in Calcutta, India, where the Janzens had been a missionary family, was, on the face of it, a terrible house. Afflicted by cockroaches, rats, bats, electrical fires, and plumbing breakdowns, the house gave them no end of headaches. For other reasons, though, the house seemed to represent the finest season of their marriage. Janzen continued with her reminiscence:

> But as a family we had our finest hours in our house in Calcutta. We played games or read. We talked, listened, learned, and sang. We had many guests. It was also in this house that we sat silent, our minds churning with whys and hows when we didn't know where to grab hold of situations that seemed hopeless—but knowing that answers were expected from us. . . .
>
> Yes . . . we did have a nice house in Calcutta. In fact, it was a fantastic house. It was our home! (Longacre, *Living More with Less,* page 123)

Ongoing Adjustments in Married Life

A couple needs to make many adjustments—to each other and to changing circumstances—as they progress through the seasons of their marriage. Over time, the choices that they make in these adjustments shape their marriage.

Watch a TV program that features a married couple, such as a soap opera or a situation comedy. Then in a brief written report, answer the following questions:
- What image of marriage and family life did this program portray?
- What behaviors in the characters contributed to that image?

From "I" to "We"

The need to move from independent action to a willingness to compromise in marriage—that is, from "I" to "we"—has already been mentioned briefly, but the topic requires more comment. Even if the couple makes compromises in the initial stage of marriage, they will have to keep making compromises throughout their life together because, as the years pass, the desires and needs of each person change and emerge. Take this situation as an example:

> For years, busy with their family's needs, Sarah and Herman did not have time to do many of the things that they wanted to do. Now that their children have left home, Sarah wants to see new places and meet new people. Herman simply wants the peace and quiet of home.
>
> One night during dinner, Sarah proposes that she and Herman take a cruise in the Caribbean. This trip has been her secret dream for years. Herman is startled because he was just about to ask Sarah if she liked his plans for landscaping the front lawn. He shares his ideas, knowing that they cannot afford to both go on the cruise and do the landscaping.

Sarah did not share her dream of traveling before because conditions would not have allowed it anyway, and Herman's ambitions for his lawn took a back seat to his commitments to raising his children. Now these desires in each person have been permitted to emerge because of a change in circumstances. Sarah and Herman need to ask themselves not simply what "I" want to do but what "we" can do that will come closest to meeting both persons' needs and desires.

Changes in Sexual Expression

Sex is only one of many elements that contribute to satisfaction in marriage, but it is an important one. Married persons have to learn to adjust to each other's changing sexual needs and desires. Sexual expression changes throughout a marriage, at times assuming more importance than at other times. These changes require sensitivity and responsiveness to each other's expectations. As in other facets of marriage, frank and open communication about sex is essential to creating and fostering intimacy.

Sexual intercourse implies an openness to new life, the life of a child that may be conceived in this act. But it also has a

Under the categories *social, financial,* and *emotional,* list all of the adjustments you can think of that you would have to make in each category if you married at the end of this school year.

Couples need to move from independent action to a willingness to compromise—from "I" to "we."

unifying function for the partners themselves; it helps to bridge the separateness of two persons. Sexual union can bring joy and renewal to two persons who have committed their lives to each other, but it does not exist apart from the rest of a marriage. Human beings are total persons, consisting of body, mind, and spirit. If spouses are to be fully loving with each other, they must be intimate in body, mind, and spirit. Sexual intimacy can deepen the affection that makes other kinds of intimacy so meaningful in a marriage—the sharing of ideas, feelings, difficulties, and fun. Those kinds of intimacy likewise complement and build sexual intimacy.

Sexual expression that is satisfying for both partners takes time to learn. It calls for a willingness to be attuned to the other person and not to be focused solely on one's own satisfaction. Sometimes this willingness requires self-control, for instance, when one partner desires sexual intimacy at a time when his or her partner is not physically or emotionally able to respond. Likewise, a partner who is always unresponsive needs to be willing to look honestly at the reasons for this and to try to discover with the other person what will make the sexual relationship more satisfying for both of them. Learning to adapt to each other's moods and needs is part of love, which seeks to foster the good of the other person.

Financial Issues

Chapter 8 of this course discussed money and possessions as part of a lifestyle. In marriage, financial issues influence the relationship in many ways.

- In a financially limited situation, a couple may have to alter their habits of eating, recreating, or shopping. They may not be able to have some of the conveniences they have hoped for or live in the area they would like.

- If a couple decides that one of the spouses will leave a job to raise their children, both persons must be willing to share in the necessary financial sacrifices that come with losing one income.

Control of money is a type of power. Consequently, a husband and a wife should thoroughly discuss who will pay bills, balance accounts, make major purchases, and so on. Ideally, both persons should have an equal role in and share responsibility for all financial decisions. Otherwise one partner may feel powerless.

Decisions that affect both persons should be made together, as equal partners.

Changing Roles

With the changes in societal expectations of female and male roles over the last few decades, women and men are faced with many conflicting values. A woman may hear the following messages from the surrounding culture:

- Be an exciting and devoted wife.
- Focus on getting to the top in a career.
- Be a great mother.
- Stay independent.

A man may hear these messages:

- Be a real man.
- Be sensitive.
- Take charge at home and at work.
- Be a nurturing partner and parent.

Responding to these conflicting messages seems to require superhuman capabilities. As formerly well-defined sex roles have begun to change, considerable pressure has been exerted on men and women to excel in all areas of life. Women are expected to be mothers, career professionals, homemakers, seductresses, and creative socializers. The pressure on men to diversify their roles does not seem to be as great, but more men are realizing that if they expect women to balance a career and child rearing, they must help. Men are also discovering new sides of themselves when they take a more active role in nurturing children and in homemaking. Even so, trying to become adept at a variety of roles can place a lot of demands on women and men.

However, while avoiding attempts at "superman" or "superwoman" status, husbands and wives do need to allow themselves and their partners the freedom to go beyond the traditional roles of our society. If a husband and a wife are to have equal dignity and a special kind of friendship, they should flexibly adjust the roles that each plays in the marriage, based on individual talents and interests. Decisions that affect both persons should be made together, as equal partners.

List ten household responsibilities or chores that must be taken care of in a family. Circle the chores that you do not know how to do well, and put an X next to any chore that you would be unwilling to do (some of these may be the same). Then answer this question:

- What would I do if my spouse and I did not agree on who would take care of the household responsibilities that neither of us wanted to do?

Coping in Crisis

- Two Teens Die in Fiery Crash
- Local Lawyer Arrested for Cocaine
- Gas Explosion Leaves Family Homeless

Headlines like these appear in newspapers all of the time.

Behind every headline is a tragic story of a family in crisis: Young people are killed on the highways, and the sudden tragedy throws their families into prolonged anguish. Spouses and parents are arrested for crimes and even go to prison, with tremendous financial and personal ramifications for their families. Freak accidents uproot families from their homes and deprive them of all of their possessions.

Other kinds of crises do not appear in the headlines:

- A parent loses a job and cannot find work.
- A family member becomes addicted to drugs or alcohol.
- A marriage exists on the verge of fracturing.
- A teenage daughter becomes pregnant.
- The mental illness of a family member requires long, perhaps lifetime, treatment.
- A baby is born severely handicapped.

Many families must cope with one or even several major crises in their life together.

Such crises obviously require major adjustments, skills, and loyalty of the family members and support from their friends. Amazingly, it seems that many marriages and families survive and become stronger through crises in spite of pressures that seem unbearable to many observers. A mystery seems at work in these situations, perhaps the same mystery that sustains other, more fortunate families through years of day-in and day-out routine and difficult adjustments. From a Christian perspective, the mystery of God's presence sustains a couple—even when they are not aware of it—as they experience the large and small deaths of marriage and family life, deaths that point ultimately toward resurrection.

In writing, briefly describe a crisis that happened to a family you know or to your own family. Tell how the family coped with the crisis, and describe what you see as the long-term effects of the crisis on the family.

Three Stances Toward Relationships

Throughout a couple's lifetime together, three basic, positive stances toward the relationships in their life are essential to their marriage:

- faithfulness to each other
- hospitality to new life
- openness to community

Faithfulness to Each Other

Faithfulness, or fidelity, is more than the avoidance of sexual involvements outside of marriage. Faithfulness means that development of the relationship is of the highest priority to both the husband and the wife. Both of them have faith that even deeper love is possible and probable. Couples who believe in each other and the possibilities for their relationship are easy to identify. Here are some indications of a couple's faithfulness:

They spend time together. They set aside time to be with each other—not necessarily to do anything in particular but simply to be present to each other.

They support and affirm each other. They take seriously their marriage promise to support each other in bad times and in good times, in sickness and in health.

They trust each other. They give each other room to make friends, even friends of the other sex, and to pursue interests that may not be shared between them.

They save their closest other-sex friendships for each other. A faithful marriage relationship implies that the partners seek out each other for sharing confidences or for support. Although each partner may have close friendships with persons of the other sex outside of the marriage, those friendships are not as intimate as the marriage relationship itself. The letting go of intimacy with friends of the other sex is a necessary step that couples take on the way to building a faithful marriage.

They see their relationship as one of constant rediscovery. People may wonder, How can I stay married faithfully without eventually becoming bored? Although some boredom is natural at times, faithful wives and husbands continue to discover a different person in their partner—if that person is growing personally, professionally, and parentally. Each "I" in the faithful "we" relationship is dynamic and changing. The partners stay together not *in spite of* boredom but *because of* interest.

One aspect of faithfulness that may be misunderstood is the importance of confronting a serious personal or marital problem:
- alcoholism or drug addiction
- physical or mental abuse

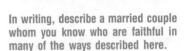

In writing, describe a married couple whom you know who are faithful in many of the ways described here.

A faithful couple sees their relationship as one of constant rediscovery.

- infidelity
- grossly irresponsible behavior

A person may be under the mistaken impression that faithfulness requires her or him to bear with these problems and not to disturb the relationship by confronting the partner.

Actually, looking the other way in the face of such problems indicates not faithfulness but *lack of faith*. Avoiding confrontation abandons responsibility for the relationship. Bringing up these problems and assisting a spouse through counseling or treatment is faithfulness. Perhaps a time will come in the marriage when the good of the family requires a separation of husband and wife. Meanwhile, faithfulness means insisting that serious problems be approached honestly.

Hospitality to New Life

Children as Honored Guests

For a married couple, hospitality to new life—that is, the sense of welcoming any children who might be born from their love—bears some resemblance to the hospitality offered to any honored guest. The welcome given to new life opens up the circle of the couple's life in order to extend to their children comfort, nourishment, shelter, respect, and the freedom to be themselves. Children are seen as honored guests, not as burdens and not as the property of their parents. Certainly the couple's hospitality comes from generosity but also from a sense of expectancy, as they ask themselves:

- What will this child be like?
- How will this child change our life and help us grow?
- What discoveries and dreams are ahead for this child?

As with hospitality extended to other visitors, the welcoming of children as honored guests means that the couple is willing to let their perhaps very comfortable life be unsettled for a while. They may even have to endure financial or emotional hardship or give up certain freedoms.

Children as Blessings

Children inevitably cause disruption in an established routine and require sacrifice of their parents, but every child is worth the disruption and sacrifice because every child is a blessing. Couples who adopt children are particularly aware of what a blessing they are receiving. And as a father said of his eleven-year-old daughter, whose birth was unplanned:

Hospitality to new life means that children are seen as honored guests, not as burdens and not as the property of their parents.

- Lisa came later in our marriage, as a "surprise." We weren't expecting to have another child, but now I can't imagine a world without Lisa in it. She's wonderful, and she's brought so much to us.

Children who are born with mental or physical handicaps are blessings just as other children are, although they may challenge a family to be generous in extraordinary ways. One man, recalling his brother who was born profoundly retarded and who had lived at home with their family into his teenage years, said:

- We all pitched in and helped out with caring for Brian. He couldn't understand what we said, and he couldn't walk or take care of himself at all. But he was the happiest, friendliest guy; he made everybody feel good just being around him. I know this sounds hard to believe, but we thought of Brian as a gift to our family.

The church has always promoted the vision of welcoming new life in marriage, and in the Jewish Scriptures, the perspective that children are blessings is expressed many times. For instance:

> . . . Happy shall you be and prosperous.
> You will be like a fruitful vine within your house,
> your children like shoots of the olive [tree] around your
> table.
>
> (Psalm 128:2-3)

> Recall a family that you know who seem to live out the description of hospitality to new life given here. Describe in writing how you have seen them welcome their children as honored guests and blessings.

The Twentieth-Century Mentality

The church's teaching that children are always blessings to be welcomed into life sometimes conflicts with the twentieth-century Western mentality. This mentality seeks more to control all of life through technology than to welcome the mystery and the spiritual riches of new life. Increasingly, many North American couples choose not simply to delay having children but to avoid having them at all. For many of these couples, it seems that their lives are too full and too busy to welcome another life.

In some cases, the choice not to have children stems from a lack of hope, a sense, as one man expressed it, that "this world is a crazy place to bring a kid into. We could all be blown up by the time the kid is a year old." But a sense of despair in the face of a dangerous world only engenders more hopelessness because it keeps a couple from imagining and working at a better future. Having a child in the midst of a hazardous world can be a sign of a couple's commitment to work toward a society and a world that are more hospitable to life.

The Church's Stand for Life

The church is concerned about the factors that motivate people not to welcome children into the world. In Pope John Paul II's document *On the Family,* he articulated why the church is opposed to artificial birth control, sterilization, and abortion, and particularly to government attempts to require these methods as measures of population control:

> . . . The church firmly believes that human life, even if weak and suffering, is always a splendid gift of God's goodness. Against the pessimism and selfishness which cast a shadow over the world, the church stands for life: In each human life [it] sees the splendor of that "yes," that "amen," who is Christ himself. To the "no" which assails and afflicts the world, [the church] replies with this living "yes," thus defending the human person and the world from all who plot against and harm life. (No. 30)

"The church firmly believes that human life, even if weak and suffering, is always a splendid gift of God's goodness."

Natural Family Planning

In recent years, an approach to regulating conception that relies on knowledge of the woman's natural rhythms of fertility and infertility has been refined by researchers to a high degree of accuracy. By charting the woman's cycle of fertility, a couple can use the method either to prevent or to achieve pregnancy. This approach, natural family planning, is affirmed by the church as consistent with its stand of openness to life. In the church's view, the respect for the natural rhythms of the woman's body make this method an acceptable way to prevent pregnancy in cases where it must be avoided for health or other compelling reasons.

To prevent pregnancy, abstinence from sexual intercourse is required during and just before the woman's fertile time of each month. Unlike artificial methods of birth control, natural family planning depends on cooperation between the spouses; it encourages dialog, shared responsibility, mutual respect, and self-control for the good of the relationship. This approach also avoids some of the health hazards of artificial methods like the intrauterine device (IUD) or the birth control pill.

Through their hospitality to any children who enter their

Research natural family planning, and prepare a brief report on how it works.

lives—whether their births are planned or unplanned—married couples widen the circle of their love.

Openness to Community

Besides widening the circle of their love to include children, married couples also are called to widen their love to include friends. A family cannot be an isolated unit, relying only on its members for support and extending love only to its own inner circle. Rather, married couples need to be open to the community of Christians and other friends. Particularly in our society, where so many couples live away from their families of origin and where traditional sources of help are often lacking, people need to have a community of friends that they can turn to for support and companionship.

On a practical level, at various times in their marriage, a couple may need financial help. If a couple has children, they might need help from friends or family in caring for the children during emergencies or while they go out together. Or a couple may need advice on insurance, buying a house, or other matters about which they could use others' expertise or opinions.

On a personal level, men and women sometimes need a listener, someone who can allow them to express sides of themselves for which their spouses may not have an understanding or an interest. In a study of friendships in marriage, a fifty-four-year-old woman, married for thirty years, summed up the importance of having friends outside of the marriage relationship:

Friends take off some of the pressure for marriage to provide all of the needs that each partner has.

> "No two people can be everything for each other, nor should they be, nor should we have such impossible expectations. Friendship is really a way to get some of the other things that you don't get from the particular person you love and married." (Quoted in Lillian Rubin, *Just Friends*, page 142)

Couples need friends who will care for them. These friends take off some of the pressure for marriage to provide all of the intellectual, emotional, spiritual, and recreational needs that each partner has.

Although many men report that they do need close friends, they find it harder to make them than women do. Part of the difficulty may be explained by the sex-role stereotype that says, Men should be able to stand on their own two feet; they don't need intimate friends. The feeling expressed by one man is typical of this problem:

> "I sometimes feel a little jealous of the ease with which [my wife], and a lot of other women I see, seem to be able to make friends. There are men I talk to—guys I have lunch with at work, or the men I play cards with, or other men I know. But it's either shop talk or horsing around, not like the things I hear [my wife] talking to her women friends about. . . .
>
> "I'd like to have that kind of ease of expressing what's inside me. And also I'd like to have a couple of friends like that who I could really talk to. But it just doesn't happen with men." (Quoted in Rubin, *Just Friends,* pages 137–138)

Close friendships can and do happen for married men. As some of the stereotypes about males being macho give way to fuller understandings of male identity, men may become more free to initiate friendships that will support and complement their marriages.

The Healthy Family

Marriage partners who are faithful to each other, welcoming to new life, and open to friendships are well on their way to building a healthy family. Living in a healthy family feels good; it is an ideal environment for an individual to grow into a happy, caring, self-respecting person. No family is perfect, but healthy families show many of the following characteristics:

Open communication: In healthy families, the members feel listened to and are able to listen. They can share feedback—both positive and negative—with everyone in the family. Independent thinking is encouraged. Television is not the centerpiece of family life because too much television crowds out more interesting ways of being together. Members of the family can reconcile conflicts in just ways. Furthermore, family problems are not pushed out of sight but are confronted openly. As one man put it, "Trying to hush up a problem is like whispering into an empty closet; it is loud and harsh and someone is bound to hear it eventually."

Affirmation: Healthy families tend to give affirmation generously to each individual. Family members take an active

Answer this question in writing:
• In what way do you either agree or disagree that men have a harder time than women sharing their emotions and convictions with male friends?

In a trusting family, the children are given the chance to grow without fear of making mistakes.

interest in what the other family members are doing. For example, if Eric is competing in a swim meet, other members of the family try to attend. If they cannot be there, they let Eric know they are interested by asking how things went. Or if the mother of the family gets a promotion at work, the family takes her to dinner or buys her a congratulatory cake. They seek some concrete way of saying, Fantastic!

Trust: In a trusting family, the husband and the wife believe in each other, and the children are given the chance to grow without fear of making mistakes. For instance, if the children attempt to bake a cake and it flops, this mistake can be treated by their parents as a chance for the children to figure out what went wrong rather than as a reason to blame someone. Trust builds self-esteem and esteem for others.

A sense of tradition: Having some family rituals or traditions is a way of binding a family together. For example, periodic family reunions reinforce a family's sense of identity. Or a family may celebrate Thanksgiving or Christmas in the same way every year: Decorations are brought out and put in the same places. The same relatives come over for dinner. Even the menu is the same. Every year Uncle Jake tells about the time that five-year-old Bobby ate all of the fudge and became ill. Bobby might groan and say to himself, "Not again!" but these stories and traditions are reminders of who the family is and where they have been. Traditions give us a sense of roots.

Shared leisure time: Shared leisure time may be one of the least common features of modern family life. Parents and children usually tend to be overscheduled with meetings, lessons, sports, and so on. But healthy families take time for leisure together. They know that leisure time spent as a family fosters talk and appreciation of one another, that being together without stress allows the members to lower their guards and be themselves. One of the best times for leisure is the shared family meal. It can be a time to talk, plan, laugh, and celebrate together. Experienced in this relaxed way, meals support health in a family.

A sense of right and wrong: Studies of moral development indicate that we acquire our sense of right and wrong primarily through our families. In healthy families, children are held responsible for their behavior. Parents teach their children why certain actions are right or wrong, and they confront wrong

Describe the following items in writing:
- one or two rituals or traditions of your family
- a story that one of your relatives always seems to tell about you or someone else in your family when your relatives get together
- one or two rituals or traditions that you would like to start if you have your own family

behavior directly. Both in the way that the members treat each other and in the way that they respond to others beyond the family, healthy families teach key values of respect for other people, honesty, and service to those in need.

A sense of responsibility: Families function best when all members take responsibility to help the family, to contribute in some way to the common good: Someone is in charge of feeding the dog. One person cooks, and another does the dishes. People do not leave the family room in a mess with the assumption that someone else will clean it up. Everyone seems to take ownership for the family's well-being. Taking responsibility enhances self-esteem, and because responsible family members feel that they have an influence on the world of their family, they are empowered for responsible participation in the world beyond their family.

List the responsibilities that you have in your family. For each one, describe your attitude toward that responsibility. Then reflect in writing on what benefits you and your family have gained from your taking on these responsibilities.

A family that shares a religious vision is united by deeply important values about the meaning of life.

A shared religious vision: A family that shares a religious vision of life is united by a common set of beliefs and religious practices and also by deeply important values about the meaning of life. Most religions, certainly Catholic Christianity, encourage families to love one another, and they help families to celebrate important passages in their members' lives, such as anniversaries, confirmations, funerals, baptisms, or marriages. Involvement in a parish community sustains families, drawing them out of themselves in generosity and enabling them to receive the support that every family needs from friends who share religious values with them. A family's shared religious vision and active participation in a worshiping community also deepen each member's faith—a faith that will strengthen them in times of crisis or suffering.

A danger of discussing the healthy family is that we might become too critical of our own families. The healthy family is an ideal. We should consider ourselves blessed if our families have even some of the characteristics of a healthy family. Parents, like their children, are limited human beings who do the best that they can with whatever talents, knowledge, and feelings they have. So the purpose of presenting the ideal is not to make us more critical of our own parents and families but to help us see ways that we ourselves can grow as potential spouses and parents.

One of life's mysteries is that vital, generous, fascinating human beings can come forth from terribly unhealthy backgrounds—abusive, alcoholic, or otherwise painfully unhappy situations. Against tremendous odds, some people not only survive but transcend their backgrounds, transforming the pain and suffering of their upbringing to some positive purpose. They carry the emotional scars of their childhood with them, perhaps causing major difficulties for them in life. But the scars ultimately do not define them. Such people remind us of the greatness of the human spirit and the power of good to triumph over evil.

In healthy families, children can grow to be self-respecting, loving, free, and responsible persons.

The Future of the Family

We would have to have our heads buried in the sand not to know that family life has undergone many changes during the last several decades. Single-parent families are more numerous. Many marriages end in divorce. Families are pulled in many directions by all kinds of pressures. A pessimist might say that the future of the family is bleak. A naive optimist might try to ignore the evidence and wish away the problems.

But young realists need to look squarely at the social and cultural trends that influence the family and, if they wish to marry, to begin thinking about how the family they create will nourish life. Our society's future depends on the existence of healthy families in which children can grow to be self-respecting, loving, free, and responsible persons. Healthy families grow from healthy couples.

Write a reflection about or a prayer for your family, focusing on each of your family members in turn and then on your family as a whole.

Review Questions

1. Describe three aspects of a couple's relationship that typically characterize the first two years of marriage.

2. What are three common adjustments in the third through fifth years of a marriage?

3. Why are the sixth through twelfth years of a marriage frequently very difficult for a couple?

4. Why are the thirteenth to eighteenth years of a marriage often a period of renewal?

5. Give three examples from this chapter of pressures on a couple during their mid-life transition.

6. Describe the challenges and opportunities for a couple who are on their own again and are growing old together.

7. What does it mean for a couple to move from "I" to "we" in their marriage?

8. Explain the need to adjust to changes in sexual expression in a marriage.

9. What are two financial issues that many couples have to deal with in their marriage?

10. What adjustments around sex roles do husbands and wives need to make?

11. Give three examples from this chapter of crises that affect families.

12. What does faithfulness in marriage mean, and what are five indicators of fidelity between a husband and a wife?

13. What is hospitality to new life? What are two ways of thinking about children that indicate hospitality to them?

14. Summarize the church's reasons for affirming and supporting new life, particularly as expressed in the quote by Pope John Paul II. With what aspect of the twentieth-century mentality does that teaching conflict?

15. Why does the church support natural family planning?

16. How should marriage widen the circle of a couple's love? In what ways is a broader circle of relationships beyond the family very important for married persons?

17. List and explain the characteristics of a healthy family.

14 Religious Life: Dedicated to God

MANY of the world's religions have members who dedicate their lives solely to the service of their deity. For example, Hindu holy men wander India, performing acts of self-sacrifice and praying, and Zen Buddhist monks and nuns gather in communities to seek enlightenment. In the Catholic Christian tradition, people who choose to live in communities where members are vowed solely to serving God are commonly called **religious.**

Certainly all Christians are called to *be religious*—that is, to live out their faith in the way that God calls them to. But within Catholicism, *religious* is also the most familiar term for sisters, brothers, and priests who belong to religious communities. Those communities of religious are also called congregations or orders.

Christian religious communities began a few centuries after Jesus' Resurrection. Men and women went into the deserts of northern Africa and the Middle East to pray, fast, and meditate on the word of God. Most of the time they banded together, even if somewhat loosely, and followed a rule of life formulated by one among them who was recognized for her or his holiness. From those beginnings to the present, hundreds of religious communities have been founded.

Living on a small farm in Georgia, this Dominican sister ministers to rural poor persons.

Immense Variety

Today members of religious orders are nuclear physicists and spiritual directors, administrators of facilities for emotionally disturbed youth and missionaries in Third World countries, people who spend their days in silent prayer and teachers in

Catholic schools. Coming from many different backgrounds, Catholic sisters, brothers, and priests in religious orders serve God in immensely varied ways. Sr. Bernadine Ternes, a Benedictine nun, and Fr. Gaet Frega, a Franciscan Capuchin priest, are examples of some of the variety of backgrounds and ways of serving:

A Benedictine nun: Sister Bernadine roams Seattle's downtown skid row district as a member of Operation Night Watch. She checks the men and the women who seek cover for the night in parks and in doorways, finds shelters or meals for down-and-out people, and arranges for health care for homeless sick people. Often she just listens to those who are lonely, desperate, and poor.

In a *Catholic Digest* article, passages from Sister Bernie's diary describe a typical night on the streets:

"So many hurting people wanting to talk and pray."

"I thought I should remember to carry a box of Kleenex, so many tears tonight. It must be end-of-the-month depression. . . .

"Almost every time I'm on the street at night I find the same lady with two shopping bags standing in some doorway. She says she has no home and keeps falling asleep as I talk to her."

Sister Bernie does whatever she can to help the people of skid row.

A Franciscan Capuchin priest: During his life, Gaet Frega has been the subject of some magazine articles, but most of them have been about his position as a bass player in a well-known jazz quartet that was called by one critic "the greatest musical group I've heard in the last ten years." Frega played bass with the group for several years, making records on the Decca label, appearing on national music programs, and becoming a well-known jazz artist. When Frega left the jazz quartet, he became a priest in a religious order, the Capuchins.

In an interview published in *The Dialog*, Father Frega talked about his life as a religious priest. Like explanations about why we love certain people, his explanation for entering religious life was mostly mysterious: "I don't know." Frega said that he felt a "finger pushing against the soul."

Although he still plays bass, most of Father Frega's time is spent giving retreats at a renewal center and around the country. He has worked in prison ministry and has been a chaplain

A Capuchin brother prays with his community.

in a Veterans Administration hospital. Using his musical background, Frega has also published his ideas about the use of music therapy with mentally ill persons.

Father Frega expressed the following thoughts about his former career in music:

> "I miss it, but I don't regret [leaving] it. I couldn't see myself not doing what I'm doing. I've turned the bend. . . . But when I hear music, when I play, gosh . . .
>   . . . "God is the beautiful, and good music is part of that beauty."

Spreading the Good News of Jesus Christ and promoting life and human dignity are central to the meaning of religious life, just as they are central to the vocation of all Christians. However, religious life is specific and distinct when compared with other Christian lifestyles because the religious take vows to serve God alone as they follow a rule of life unique to each religious congregation. That rule of life gives substance to the vows by specifying how an individual religious will fulfill the mission or purpose of his or her congregation.

Quickly list the names of three religious whom you know personally. After each name, write an explanation of why these individuals came to mind right away. What is noteworthy about them?

Essential Elements: Community, Prayer, and Service

A religious order's rule of life usually gives instructions about the essential elements of religious life:
- community
- prayer
- service

Community: Supporting, Challenging, and Strengthening

Support and Challenge

Community life is intended to support and to challenge each member of the religious community. Religious, like everyone else, need the support and affirmation of other people. For instance, a sister who ministers in a women's prison easily can become discouraged by the enormity of the problems that those women face. When she comes home from work, her community can provide her with concerned listening, practical advice, and words of encouragement. Just as important, the sister's community can challenge her to remember that God is present in each of the women with whom she is working. In this way, the sister is reminded of the sacredness of each prisoner's life.

Most religious congregations were founded to serve the human community and the church in specific ways. Some congregations opened hospitals, schools, or centers for prayer. But no matter what the work of the individual religious orders, their founders realized that the members would need community.

De La Salle: The Strength of a Community of Teachers

The community founders knew that the work they were inspired to undertake would profit from the strength of a community of people banded together to do it. For example, *Saint John Baptist de La Salle,* the founder of the Brothers of the Christian Schools (often called the Christian Brothers) and the patron saint of teachers, recognized the practicality of such a community:

- When John Baptist de La Salle realized that most of the poor boys who roamed the streets of seventeenth-century Reims, France, were in need of a practical education and religious instruction, he wanted to open a school. If poor and middle-class boys were being educated at all, it was by "writing masters," poor men who were only marginally literate themselves. De La Salle realized that the only way in which he could guarantee properly managed schools for poor boys would be to form the writing masters into a religious community—a community trained as teachers and motivated by the Good News. The resulting community life gave men who had been only writing masters support, discipline, a sense of purpose, and a role in the ministry of the church. In addition, it gave them the strength to continue their work. The schools that De La Salle founded were successful largely because of the brothers' life in community.

The writer of the Bible's Book of Ecclesiastes understood the strength that comes from community life:

> Better two than one alone, since thus their work is really rewarding. If one should fall, the other helps him up; but what of the person with no one to help him up when he falls? . . . Where one alone would be overcome, two will put up resistance; and a threefold cord is not quickly broken. (Ecclesiastes 4:9–10,12)

Write down what you think would be the advantages and disadvantages, for you, of living in a religious community. Then answer these questions:
- What are some organizations that give their members a sense of community but do not require the kind of commitment that religious make to community?
- Why do people band together in such organizations?

Saint John Baptist de La Salle, the founder of the Christian Brothers, is the patron saint of teachers.

Prayer:
Focusing on the Center of Life

Keeping Faith
that Love Will Lead to Good

As the mainstay of a person's faith in God and sense of mission, **prayer** is another essential element of religious life. In her book on religious women, laywoman Marcelle Bernstein wrote:

> Nuns deal with more of life's harsh realities than most lay people ever see. Alcoholics, homicides, drug addicts, deserted wives, delinquent children, prostitutes—this is the list of a hardened professional caseworker. The Daughters of Charity of Saint Vincent de Paul, for example, have operated Marillac House in Chicago for more than twenty years. From a settlement house in East Garfield Park, they have gone out day after day to serve an area with the highest crime, VD, illegitimacy, illiteracy, and poverty rates in the whole of the United States. (*The Nuns,* page 136)

A casual observer of these sisters in their work might wonder, How does a sister who works day in and day out in such a tough and depressing world keep her faith that God is present there and that love will finally lead to good? The answer is found to a large degree in prayer, which helps a sister in a trying situation to focus on God, the center of existence.

Deepening the Relationship with God

Prayer may take many forms: paraliturgical services, meditation, shared reflection, and so on. Prayer is a central life experience in religious life. According to the rule of the School Sisters of Saint Francis, "In prayer we encounter the living God. Prayer is the forming experience that nourishes and unifies every aspect of our lives. . . . We are opened to be transformed in Christ." Its various forms are "authentic to the degree [that] they assist us in making ordinary life experiences lead to deepening of relationship with the Living Presence who is the Center of Life." Prayer helps religious to renew their sense of the Holy Spirit at work in them.

Members of religious orders must stay in communication with God, who will enrich their faith and give them strength for the important work that they have undertaken. With deeper faith and strength for their mission, religious can fulfill the purpose of Christian life as described by Saint Bernard to his

Answer this question in writing:
- Is Marcelle Bernstein's statement about nuns consistent with the popular perception of them? If so, how so? If not, why not?

Write a brief description of how life experiences might become part of a person's prayer life.

fellow monks of Clairvaux more than eight hundred years ago: "Brothers, the whole object of our lives is to love and to make ourselves lovable."

Service: Meeting Needs in the Human Community

The love that Saint Bernard called "the whole object of our lives" results in **service**, the third essential element of religious life. Many types of service done by religious already have been cited in this chapter, but religious serve in countless other ways.

Founded in Response to Specific Needs

Religious communities frequently were founded to meet very specific human needs. For example, De La Salle's Christian Brothers had a particular focus—the education of poor boys. Likewise, the Trinitarians, founded by Saint John of Matha in 1198, met an urgent need of their own time, the ransoming of Christians held captive in slavery by Muslims, who considered them to be unbelievers. Some of the early Trinitarians even traded themselves into slavery to secure the freedom of others. Centuries after their founding, Trinitarians aided Thomas Jefferson in freeing more than one hundred U.S. seamen captured by Barbary pirates. Today this religious order is still working with persons who are held captive in the bondage of ignorance or injustice.

An Openness to Changing Needs

If a need exists in the human community, a religious congregation is probably trying to meet it. Accordingly, as needs in the human community change, so do the methods of serving that are used by religious orders. Many congregations allow their members a great deal of flexibility in choosing how they will serve, as long as their ministries reflect the mission of Jesus and the spirit of the congregation's founder.

Community, prayer, and service are the essential elements of religious life. If a religious neglects or ignores any one of these elements, her or his life will feel off balance. The sense of mission will be out of focus for that individual, and life will seem purposeless and drab. All three elements working together form a triangle—the strongest of all geometric figures. A supportive and challenging community, a rich and faithful prayer life, and dedicated service enliven and empower a religious to further

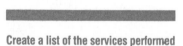

Create a list of the services performed by religious in and around the city or town in which you live.

Reflect in writing on whether you could imagine yourself performing any of the varied services that religious perform. Have you ever felt called to perform such service?

Jesus' mission to love. To help religious concentrate on their lifestyle of community, prayer, and service, they begin their special commitment by taking vows.

Religious Vows: Commitment to a Lifestyle

When two people marry, they make a solemn, public covenant with each other, vowing to be faithful in love through good and bad times, in sickness and in health. Their wedding provides a ritual to mark the end of one phase of life and the beginning of another. As tough times come along, the covenant provides an anchor for the marriage without which the two persons could drift apart.

For similar reasons, religious publicly take vows. Through these vows, men and women commit themselves to the religious lifestyle of community, prayer, and service. The vows are a public statement that says: "This is my chosen lifestyle. I am committed to be a religious and to live according to the way of Jesus as well as I can with God's help." Once the commitment is made, a religious can wholeheartedly get on with living religious life, somewhat like a newly married couple can get on with living their life together.

Traditionally, religious take three vows:

- poverty
- chastity
- obedience

The vows help to define or give shape to their lives as religious and to the ways in which they will answer the call to love that is given to all Christians. Married people answer this call to love chiefly by loving their spouses and committing themselves to each other and their families for their entire lives. The vows that religious take commit them to a more open, or less specifically focused, way of loving. They are free from concerns specific to marriage and family, but through their vows, they take on a commitment to listen for God's call to love and to follow that call no matter where it leads them during their entire lives.

The Vow of Poverty: Sharing a Simple Life

In North American culture, to say that people live in poverty implies that they are destitute or ill-nourished. But the **vow of**

With other Sisters of Saint Joseph, this sister serves poor people in Washington, D.C., through a food distribution center.

Think about the vow of poverty as it is described here. Then answer these questions in writing:
- Would any aspects of the vow be advantageous for you?
- Which aspects of the vow would you find difficult?

poverty has more to do with having little than with being destitute. In fact, the root of the word *poverty* comes from the Latin word meaning "little." Religious take a vow to have few material possessions so that they can avoid the distractions that accompany ownership. Money and possessions can make slaves of our spirits. The more that people have, the more they tend to protect and worry about their possessions. Even more important, piling up possessions is not in the spirit of Jesus' command to share with those in need. By taking the vow of poverty, religious commit themselves to live simply and to share their resources with others.

Sister Ann: Life with the Eskimos

One example of this spirit of poverty is found in the ministry of Sister Ann, a missionary deep in the Northwest Territories of Canada, just below the Arctic Circle at the Yellow-knife–Arctic Copper wasteland border. Shortly after she arrived among the Inuit, or Eskimo, people, Sister Ann realized that her ministry would include far more than teaching religion. Life in the Northwest Territories is a daily struggle to survive:

> "Sweat and grit is what it takes to work in the North Country," Sister affirms. Continuing, Sister tells of one such survival emergency. "Once while I was instructing Catechism to a group of Indian children, a distraught Eskimo mother burst into my one-room hut shrieking that her little boy had wandered off and now was lost. Most of the village men were on a trapping expedition and there was only one older white man I could turn to for help. Together we donned our snowshoes and began our trek into the snow-covered hills in search of this little one. Just as a blizzard began to stir up, we found the little boy—thanks be to God!" . . .
>
> The people of the "Nor" country never saw a Sister before Ann arrived. Her life, like her people's, is simple and brave. She lives in a hut as they do, with their hand-made snowshoes, and shares in every aspect of their rugged existence. As one Eskimo mother has put it, "Snow Sister tells about Jesus and lives like him here with us." (*Vocation Info,* pages 123–125)

Think back to some TV programs or movies that you have seen that depicted women religious. Write a reflection about how women religious typically are represented on television or in the movies and whether these representations are accurate.

Sister Ann exemplifies what the vow of poverty is about—living simply and sharing possessions, time, and talents with others. Sharing is a recognition that the goods of this earth are meant to serve everyone's needs.

Conscious Decisions About Possessions

Members of a religious order work for their daily bread in solidarity with all other workers. The congregation makes conscious decisions about how best to use the fruits of their labors, which should go to serve the human community. The vow of poverty is a reminder to religious that their lives should be like that of Jesus, who journeyed from place to place, spreading the Good News and sharing his few possessions with people in need.

The Vow of Chastity: Loving All of Humankind

All Christians are called to love God and their neighbors. But the **vow of chastity** taken by religious is a promise to love in a way that frees them to respond to all of humankind, especially those people most in need. This vow includes the pledge to be celibate, that is, to abstain from sexual intimacy that is proper to marriage. However, the meaning of the vow goes beyond this limited sense of abstaining; it is well-expressed in the rule of the School Sisters of Saint Francis:

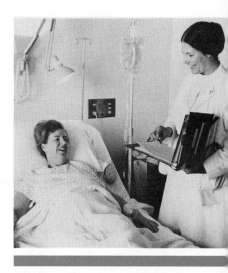

Religious, like this medical doctor, promise through the vow of chastity to love in a way that frees them to respond to all of humankind.

> Because we are "grasped by Christ Jesus" (Phil. 3:12) we consecrate all our energies to the building of the reign of God. In our celibate living we witness to the unconditional love God has for every person and to the call to love as Jesus loves. We realize that the search for, and experience of, aloneness with God opens us to the fullness of relating with others. Vowed chastity is rooted in our intimacy with God and in a deepening love and compassion for others.

The Freedom to Respond to Needs

The vow of chastity is a choice to love other people while "free of the single commitment to one person." Conversely, married couples must be committed first and foremost to love each other and their children. This arrangement has practical consequences. A married couple must provide a stable home environment, adequate education, and security for their family. They must nurture their mutual relationship so that their love will grow as the years pass. This requires work, money, time, and energy. Religious, on the other hand, need to be free to respond to needs regardless of where or when they arise. Like the Apostle Paul, who went where he was needed and faced danger to preach the word of God, religious should have the same freedom, the freedom that comes with chastity.

A Pledge to Build Community

The vow of chastity is also a pledge to build community. Religious must be loving people who are great friends, nurturers, and unifiers. They live in community and should strive to create community wherever they go and in whatever work they do. Naturally, religious need friendship and community support, too. But instead of centering their intimate personal relationships on a family of their own, religious find fulfillment in relationships within their religious communities and within the other communities to which they belong (hospital staff, close friends, parish workers, and so on).

Reliance on God

The vow of chastity also urges the religious to stay in close communication with God, who provides the strength and the courage to live celibately. A religious has to rely on the affection and affirmation of a loving God. Thus, prayer is a way of sustaining one's vow of chastity.

The Vow of Obedience: Listening to God's Will

Listening in a Loving Relationship

Any loving relationship makes demands of us. To maintain a friendship with someone, we must listen closely, seeking to find out what that friend needs or wants. Imagine this situation:

- Stephanie's friend Gail wants to go on a picnic at the local state park, but Stephanie hates picnics because of the ants in the potato salad, the lukewarm soft drinks, the flies that have to be waved away, and other annoyances. However, Stephanie knows that Gail has been under a lot of pressure and just wants some fresh air and quiet conversation. Responding to what she perceives as Gail's need and to her own desire to sustain their friendship, Stephanie willingly goes along on the picnic.

This example illustrates the process of listening and following that is the essence of the religious vow of obedience to God.

Obedience has its root in a Latin word meaning "to hear." To a religious, the **vow of obedience** pledges him or her to listen to the will of God and to follow it. Like people who respond to

Write your thoughts about whether the explanation of the vow of chastity given here matches the popular understanding of religious celibacy. Then write a dialog in which you debate with yourself about your own ability to lead a celibate lifestyle. In the dialog, have one side of yourself argue yes and the other side argue no.

Write your reactions to this statement:
- The feeling of wanting to disobey is usually linked to the feeling of not being listened to by someone.

the needs or concerns of their friends, religious try to heed the call from God that instructs them on how to love.

Learning God's Will in Human Ways

The call from God does not come through a divine voice that gives specific directions; rather, Christians—including religious—usually learn what God is calling them to in very human ways. The will of God is shown to religious through the church, through the Bible, in their constitutions and community decisions, in the signs of the times, and especially in the needs of the human family. Religious obedience requires that members of religious orders take the initiative to seek the will of God with regard to their service and lifestyle. In practice, this means that the religious members make decisions by first *listening* to the sources mentioned and then *praying* that God will lead the group to a correct decision and response. Obedience is an active, searching process, not a blindly passive mentality. This process of obedience applies both to the community as a whole and to each individual member.

For religious, obedience is an active, searching process, not a blindly passive mentality.

All members of religious congregations—whether sisters, brothers, or priests—take the vows of poverty, chastity, and obedience. In addition, religious priests, like all priests, receive the Sacrament of Holy Orders, which empowers them to lead in celebrating the sacraments. (Priests who are not members of religious congregations are called diocesan, not religious, priests.) Sisters and brothers are laypeople who have taken the religious vows.

Three Types of Religious Congregations

Over many centuries, three types of religious congregations have been founded:
- contemplatives
- mendicants
- service congregations

All of these orders have community, prayer, and service dimensions, and all take the traditional vows. Communities in each category have developed distinct manners of living religious life, although they have also adapted their lifestyles to changing needs and circumstances.

Contemplatives

The first religious orders that formed in the church were **contemplative.** As the name suggests, their way of life centered primarily on contemplation, meditation, or communion with God. Some well-known contemplative orders are the Carmelites, the Trappists, the Poor Clares, and largest of all, the Benedictines.

The Gospel of Mark tells of Jesus going into the desert or the hills to pray (for example, Mark 1:45 and 6:46). Some early Christians imitated Jesus by going into the desert to encounter God. Eventually they banded together in groups to share their faith stories, to celebrate the Eucharist, and to counsel one another. Because any group of people needs some guidelines so that their life together goes smoothly, various holy men and women composed rules for the individual communities.

Thomas Merton on Seeking God

Besides regulating communal life, the contemplatives' rules help the women and the men to focus their entire attention on

Thomas Merton, a Trappist, is perhaps the best-known modern contemplative.

God. Trappist *Thomas Merton*, perhaps the best-known modern contemplative, once wrote about the focus on God that is the key to contemplative life:

> . . . We come to the monastery to *seek God*. . . .
>
> The end which we seek is not merely something within ourselves, some personal quality added to ourselves, some new gift. It is God. . . .
>
> . . . While living by the labour of his hands, [a monk] remembers that [the] highest and most fruitful activity is the spiritual "work" of contemplation. (*The Monastic Journey*, pages 14, 37)

Merton knew well the frenzy of work and the search for power because his young adulthood had been spent in their pursuit. When he had exhausted himself, looking in vain for meaning, Merton turned at last to God. Just as he had previously poured himself into his writing and party-going, he now poured all of his energy into the work of a monk—contemplation.

Saint Benedict: Founder of Western Monasticism

Merton was hardly the first person to become a monk after having been saturated with life's illusions. Many of the sixth-century followers of *Saint Benedict*, the founder of Western monasticism, were men and women who were tired of the meaninglessness of their lives. So they joined Benedict, a man who, in imitation of Jesus, had gone into the hills to pray. He had left his life in sophisticated but corrupt Rome and the wealth that he would have inherited. Eventually Benedict wrote a rule to give guidance to the dozens of men and women—the first Benedictines—who gathered around him in the Italian mountains.

Prayer, work, and rest: The Benedictine rule orders every day so that time is given to prayer, work, and rest. The monks pray seven times each day from very early morning until night. They pray together the *Divine Office*, which is composed of psalms, special hymns, prayers, and readings from the Scriptures. In between these communal prayers, the monks are to work or study. One of Benedict's most famous sayings is *laborare est orare*—"to work is to pray." Whether a monk of Benedict's time was planting crops or copying an ancient book by hand, his work was done as a silent prayer.

"The end which we seek is not merely something within ourselves. It is God."

Contributions to Western civilization: Benedictine monasteries were like small towns. Monks were farmers, healers, librarians, carpenters, masons, cooks, and artists, so each monastery filled its own needs. Besides being islands of contemplation in a busy and often violent world, the monasteries served the human community by preserving learning in their libraries, opening schools (from which the European universities evolved), and experimenting with agricultural techniques that eventually were taught all over Europe. The Benedictines had a great impact on the progress of Western civilization.

A tradition of hospitality: Service was essential to the Benedictine way of life. In his rule, Benedict was especially careful to tell his monks that hospitality was a priority. He said: "All guests that come should be received as would the person of Christ. . . . And let them be shown every proper courtesy, especially those of the household of the faith . . . and strangers."

Contemplatives Today

Today many contemplative orders have monasteries and convents in North America. We do not hear about many of them because they continue the tradition of Benedict by living lives of prayer, quiet community, and unobtrusive service. For instance, Trappist monasteries dot the map of the United States in such places as Ava, Missouri, and Moncks Corner, South Carolina. Convents of Poor Clares are scattered throughout North America. Benedictines operate high schools or colleges, continuing the tradition of the monastery schools.

These contemplatives also try to follow the wisdom of Saint Teresa of Ávila, the sixteenth-century Spanish mystic who founded a reform movement among contemplative Carmelites:

> Let nothing disturb you,
> Nothing cause you fear;
> All things pass
> God is unchanging.
> Patience obtains all:
> Whoever has God
> Needs nothing else,
> God alone suffices.

Mendicants

Seven hundred years after Western monasticism began, two men, one in Italy and one in Spain, were inspired to initiate a

List the aspects of contemplative life that appeal to you and the aspects that do not appeal to you. Then compile a list of questions that you would ask of a monk or a contemplative sister if you had a chance to meet one.

Imagine that Teresa of Ávila has written to you, asking for your response to her poem. Write a brief letter back to her that describes your reactions to her poem, given your sense of your relationship with God right now.

new form of religious community—the mendicants. *Saint Francis of Assisi* (1181?-1226) founded the Order of Friars Minor, known today as the Franciscans, and *Saint Dominic de Guzman* (1170?-1221?) founded the Order of Friars Preachers, now named the Dominicans. Although the men had never met one another, their inspiration to found a new kind of religious community was the same.

In Francis and Dominic's time, heresy was beginning to divide the church in France and in other areas of Europe. The forces of Islam had conquered most of the Middle East and were gaining a foothold in southern Europe. Monasteries that provided stable centers of Christian faith had long been established, but combating heresy and spreading the word of God to nonbelievers required mobile preachers who would travel the countryside. Both Francis and Dominic, responding to the urgent needs of their era, were inspired to found communities of such preachers.

A Simple Life of Spreading God's Word

The new orders were called *mendicants,* a term that means "beggars." Instead of farming like the contemplative monks, the mendicants fed and clothed themselves by begging from those to whom they preached. If they were to remain mobile, they had to depend on the goodwill of people. Ownership of property such as a monastery would have tied them down. Both Francis and Dominic took seriously the words of Jesus to "go out to the whole world; proclaim the gospel to all creation" (Mark 16:15) and "take no purse with you, no [knapsack], no sandals. . . . Whatever house you enter . . . [take] what food and drink they have to offer, for the labourer deserves his wages" (Luke 10:4-5,7).

This commitment to a simple life of spreading the word of God is reflected clearly in the rule that Saint Francis gave to his brothers:

A Franciscan brother continues the ministry of Saint Francis by visiting with a woman who is blind.

> The friars are to appropriate nothing for themselves, neither a house, nor a place, nor anything else. As strangers and pilgrims (1 Peter 2:11) in this world, who serve God in poverty and humility, they should beg alms trustingly. . . .
>
> Wherever the friars meet one another, they should show that they are members of the same family. . . . A friar should certainly love and care for his spiritual brother . . . tenderly.

For the task of preaching, Francis recommended simplicity and brevity:

> ... In their preaching ... they should aim only at the ... spiritual good of their listeners, telling them briefly about vice and virtue, punishment and glory, because our Lord himself kept his words short on earth.

Prayer was to center on the Eucharist and the Divine Office, but Francis believed that a good friar also prayed throughout the day.

Franciscan and Dominican sisters, brothers, and priests continue to flourish in the many communities around the world that follow the traditions of these founders. Although most of these religious are not beggars in the same way that Francis and Dominic were, they work in ways consistent with the spirit of these two great persons. The primary purpose of the two orders has remained the same—to spread the Good News. But as times have changed, Dominicans and Franciscans have fulfilled their mission by running hospitals, schools, retreat centers, universities, and parishes.

A Dominican Sister as a Cancer Researcher

Besides being involved in the work and commitments of their religious congregations, members of mendicant communities may take on unique ministries. Because society's needs change constantly, so do the contributions made by individual religious. For instance, this member of a mendicant order has an unusual and highly skilled ministry:

> If tests on humans match the positive results from lab tests on animals, in a few years a substance called *mercenene* may be curing cancer. This substance is extracted from clams, one of the very few species that do not get cancer. The discovery of mercenene was made by Sr. Arline Schmeer, a Dominican, who has won awards and grants for her work.

To Sister Arline, being a cancer researcher with a doctorate in biomedicine harmonizes very well with her calling to religious life. In an interview for an article in *Catholic Digest*, she commented about her vocation:

> "To a Dominican, giving the fruits of your contemplation to others is very important. Truth is one. If scientists and medical researchers are searching for truth, there really can be no conflict with religious seekers of truth unless we ourselves create it."

Imagine that you are the founder of a religious community of mendicant preachers and that you have ten followers whom you are going to send out in five teams. Decide what places you want to send them to and what issues you want them to preach about. In writing, assign each team its duties, with an explanation of why you selected these assignments.

Community, she explains, is an important source of support, as are prayer and meditation: "It's a very intimate experience for me and gives me an unwinding period so that I feel refreshed when I return to the lab in the morning."

Like the thousands of Dominicans before her, Sister Arline seeks to spread God's blessings to humankind. She preaches the word of God by being a model of concern for human welfare.

Service Congregations

Many of the contemplative and mendicant orders of earlier centuries gradually evolved into orders that provide crucial human services for the church and society. But in relatively modern times—the last four hundred years—many new religious orders have been founded specifically as **service congregations**. These congregations engage in a wide variety of ministries.

For instance, the Jesuits, currently the largest men's order, run schools, colleges, and universities and serve as missionaries all over the world. The Daughters of Charity of Saint Vincent de Paul, the largest religious order of women, work in hospitals, orphanages, settlement houses, schools, and clinics. Some orders are specifically missionary in character, like the Maryknoll missionaries, the Society of the Divine Word, and the Medical Mission Sisters. Other orders work primarily in education, such as the Marianist brothers and the School Sisters of Notre Dame. Many congregations are involved in hospitals, schools, missions, and social work. The founders of these congregations were extraordinary individuals, many of whom played significant roles in shaping their own times and the eras that came after them.

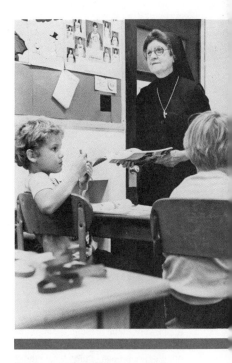

Service congregations engage in a wide variety of ministries throughout the world; some work primarily in education.

A Modern Founder: Mother Cabrini

Saint Frances Xavier Cabrini (1850–1917), known to her community as Mother Cabrini, was typical of many of the founders of religious congregations. Few people who knew her as a young person would have wagered that the frail Italian girl would do all that she did in her lifetime and later become the first U.S. citizen to be declared a saint.

While still in Italy, Cabrini heard about the hard life that Italian immigrants led when they first came to the United States. She sought to join a religious community that worked with those people. Because no such order existed, Cabrini founded one herself—the Missionary Sisters of the Sacred Heart. Her conviction to serve humankind was evident in the astounding accomplishments of her short life. She crossed the Atlantic Ocean thirty-seven times and opened orphanages, schools, hospitals, and clinics in North and South America, Spain, France, and England.

A delightful description of Mother Cabrini and her band of "daughters" appeared in a New York newspaper article in May 1889, shortly after the arrival of the missionaries in the United States:

> This week young ladies with radiant faces dressed in plain black religious hoods and robes were seen coursing the over-crowded streets of Little Italy. . . . They left no stones un-turned, climbing the dark narrow hallways of poverty to the top floors, descending murky cellar-ways into filthy basement flats. . . . They are the pioneers of a congregation called the Missionary Sisters of the Sacred Heart, and in the short period of a month have already founded a school and orphanage. . . .
>
> . . . The Directoress . . . is "Madre Francesca Cabrini," a diminutive, youthful lady with great eyes and an attractive smiling face. . . . She knows the universal language of the human spirit. (Quoted in Pietro Di Donato, *Immigrant Saint,* pages 77–78)

This simple, intelligent, courageous, loving, faith-filled woman typified many of the founders of religious congregations, who set a standard that continues to inspire the religious who follow them.

The Brother Doctor

Bro. Chester Caster is one among the thousands of contemporary religious who live the gospel spirit of service.

Growing up on a small Kentucky farm taught Chet Caster many things, but maybe his most important lesson was that people need to help one another. He had a keen awareness that health care was largely inaccessible to the people around him, either because it cost too much or because few doctors served in the hollows of eastern Kentucky's Appalachian Mountains.

Today, as a brother in the Congregation of Holy Cross, Brother Chet is a medical doctor, operating a clinic that serves the small town of Coalfield, Tennessee, and the people who inhabit the valleys and hills around it. He is the only doctor in a rural county where the coal mines have shut down, the land is hard to farm, and 60 percent of people over twenty-five years of age have not graduated from high school. For the decade that

If you were asked to found a congregation of religious to meet a pressing need in the human family, what would that need be? Describe it in writing, and explain what you would want your congregation to do in response to that need.

he has been serving the people around Coalfield, Brother Chet has, among other accomplishments, delivered five hundred babies. About being both a brother and a doctor, he comments:

> The people around here were abandoned by health care agencies. They're poor, and it's nearly impossible to attract doctors to a place like Coalfield. But for me personally, I felt I had a talent for healing. This is my ministry. And illness is a great equalizer. When people are sick, we can forget all the differences of education, gender, money. In the honesty of our humanity, we learn from each other. Besides the challenge of my healing ministry, I love nature. The mountains here are beautiful.

Brother Chet does not work alone. Several other Holy Cross brothers have joined him. One of them is a social worker, and two brothers run a thrift shop in which they sell clothes to poor residents at minimal cost. This small community of brothers is bringing—and finding—God's presence among the forgotten folks of Appalachia.

Discovering a Call to Religious Life

Positive Signs

"The people around here were abandoned by health care agencies."

- How do I know if I have a call to religious life?
- How do I know if I love someone enough to get married? What is common to both of these questions is that neither can be answered with absolute certainty. The calls to both religious life and marriage are filled with mystery, and in many ways both calls are matters of the heart. But as with thinking about a possible marriage, considering a call to religious life requires an assessment of whether several positive signs are present:
- an attraction to religious life based on proper motives
- an ability to meet the requirements of religious life
- an inner sense of being called by God to religious life

An Attraction to Religious Life

An attraction to religious life may be based on the service of a particular order: missionary projects in Third World countries, teaching, working with homeless people, and so on. Or the attraction may be to community life or prayer. Often an attraction to religious life originates in a relationship with a religious who exemplifies a lifestyle that seems to be meaningful and happy for her or him.

Proper motives that serve as a basis of attracting a person to religious life could be any of the following:

- a desire to help people who are in need
- a sense that growth in love of God and neighbor can happen in a religious community
- a belief that the vowed life has value in the modern world

On the other hand, a longing for psychological or financial security, a desire to escape loneliness, or a wish for socially recognized status are improper motives for a person to consider religious life.

An Ability to Meet the Requirements

A person who is considering religious life also needs to determine whether he or she can meet the requirements of that life. Naturally, the requirements will vary among individual religious congregations, but most requirements fall into three categories:

1. **Flexibility:** Community life can be a wonderful experience, but the members have to be flexible and tolerant. Few communities exist in total harmony; people disagree and have their quirks. So religious must be able to make allowances for other people and not be too set in their ways.

2. **Intellectual and physical qualities:** Each religious congregation has its own set of intellectual and physical requirements, depending on the work of the congregation. For instance, teaching orders would expect that their members have the potential to earn a college or perhaps advanced degree and to teach. Some medical missionary orders require that persons be professionally trained before entering and that they be healthy enough to adapt to a new, physically demanding environment.

3. **The ability to live out the vow of chastity:** To be a healthy religious, a person must be able to live out the vow of chastity fairly comfortably. People who would feel much anguish about not having a spouse and children of their own should probably follow the call to marriage rather than be continually frustrated. Or if seeking sexual gratification is frequently present in a person's consciousness, she or he will find chastity extremely difficult.

A person who is considering religious life needs to determine whether he or she can meet the requirements of that life.

An Inner Sense of Being Called by God

If an individual is aware of the previously mentioned signs toward a religious vocation, then the person needs to pray and to probe his or her heart to determine whether he or she has an inner sense of God's call to religious life.

Having an inner sense of God's call does not mean feeling spiritually superior to others; in fact, feeling superior would not be a good sign. Religious life is challenging, but congregations are composed of imperfect human beings who, with the grace of God, do the best they can to fulfill their commitments. They have not joined religious life because they feel that they are better than others but because they have recognized that in the midst of their imperfect human condition, God has invited them to a particular, vowed lifestyle of community, prayer, and service. This lifestyle is their way of responding to the Christian call to love.

Religious Formation

Before making a vowed commitment to religious life, a period of preparation is necessary and required by the church. This period is also a way of further discerning whether an individual has a permanent vocation to be a religious. Each order has its own program of formation, but usually three steps are involved:
- the novitiate
- professional training
- vows

The novitiate: A beginner at a sport or a job is called a novice. In religious life as well, beginners usually are called novices, and their one- or two-year program of training is referred to as the novitiate. (Some religious communities also offer preliminary programs of associate membership or postulancy prior to the novitiate.) A novice studies basic theology and spirituality, the history and particular rules of the order, and other facets of religious life. Novices work closely with spiritual directors, who help them to work out questions about their relationships with God and the community. At the end of the novitiate, the religious take vows (poverty, chastity, obedience, and any other vows particular to a community) by which they commit themselves to live in the community for one year.

Professional training: Religious are active in many professions—as psychiatrists, professors, social workers, nurses, carpenters, priests, catechists, and so on. If a religious has not had professional training before joining a community, he or she will receive it after the novitiate. Once professional training is completed, the religious enters into the work of the community.

Vows: After the vows taken at the end of the novitiate, religious take annual vows for several years before making the final commitment of perpetual, or lifetime, vows. Usually religious are counseled by spiritual directors and make special retreats in order to be sure that they are ready to commit themselves permanently to religious life.

Small Numbers: Big Results

Members of religious congregations make up only a tiny percentage of Catholic Christians. However, over the many centuries since the foundation of the first monasteries, religious have provided leadership for the church in learning, in education, in health care, in social service, and in forming Christian communities.

Perhaps society needs religious today more than it ever has before. We need models of community and service who help us to realize our radical dependence on God:

- In a world that seduces us to consume and to buy, we need persons vowed to poverty who can remind us that life and happiness are more than having a lot of possessions.
- In a world where people are treated like objects, we need persons vowed to chastity who can show us how to love all human beings as sisters and brothers.
- In a world that emphasizes that our personal desires are of utmost importance, we need persons vowed to obedience who can show us how to create a loving community in which the needs of the whole human family are considered.

Write your reflections about the following questions:
- After studying religious life, do you feel the need to consider further whether you have a call to that life?
- If so, what questions do you still need to ask yourself?

Review Questions

1. When and where did the first religious communities begin?

2. What are the three essential elements of religious life?

3. Using Saint John Baptist de La Salle's founding of the Brothers of the Christian Schools as an example, explain why community is so important to religious life.

4. In what ways is prayer essential for religious?

5. Name two specific ways that religious congregations have served human needs.

6. Why do religious take vows?

7. Using the example of Sister Ann, explain the meaning of the vow of poverty.

8. In what ways does the religious vow of chastity mean much more than abstaining from the sexual intimacy that is proper to marriage?

9. How is listening essential to the vow of obedience? How do religious listen to the will of God?

10. According to Thomas Merton, what is the key to contemplative life?

11. How is a Benedictine contemplative's day ordered?

12. Why were the mendicants founded, and how do they differ from the contemplatives?

13. What does the word *mendicant* mean, and how did Saint Francis expect his brothers to live?

14. List some of the accomplishments of Mother Cabrini.

15. Explain the three positive signs of a call to religious life.

16. What are the usual steps in the formation of a religious?

17. For what reasons might society need religious today more than it ever has before?

15 Ordained Ministry: Leading and Serving

MINISTRY is part of every Christian's vocation. The life-styles that have been discussed so far in this course—single life, marriage, and religious life—are full of potential for ministering to other people. Sacramentally, all Christians are called through Baptism to minister, to give witness to the love that God has for all human beings by their lives of concern and compassion. The Sacrament of Marriage adds a special call to married couples to create new life and to symbolize by their mutual love Christ's love for the church. Similarly, the **Sacrament of Ordination,** or Holy Orders, by anointing men to be bishops, deacons, and priests, calls them to a particular way of ministering that is vital to the life of the church.

An Ancient Tradition

The tradition of **ordained ministry** in the church is ancient, reaching back to Jesus' call to the Twelve Apostles. In Matthew's account of Jesus' invitation to Peter and Andrew, the first two Apostles, we read:

> As he was walking by the Lake of Galilee he saw two brothers, Simon, who was called Peter, and his brother Andrew; they were making a cast into the lake with their net, for they were fishermen. And he said to them, "Come after me and I will make you fishers of people." And at once they left their nets and followed him. (Matthew 4:18–20)

After their call, the Apostles became disciples—followers of Jesus throughout the three years of his active ministry. During this time, Jesus sent them forth to represent him and to proclaim and heal in his name. Then, at the Last Supper, Jesus indicated what the specific ministry of the ordained was to be:

The Sacrament of Ordination calls men to a particular way of ministering that is vital to the life of the church.

. . . Taking a cup, he gave thanks and said, "Take this and share it among you, because from now on, I tell you, I shall never again drink wine until the kingdom of God comes."

Then he took bread, and when he had given thanks, he broke it and gave it to them, saying, "This is my body given for you; do this in remembrance of me." He did the same with the cup after supper, and said, "This cup is the new covenant in my blood poured out for you." (Luke 22:17-20)

In the tradition of the church, it was at this first Eucharist that the specific ministry of the ordained—that is, the leadership in the sacramental life of the church—was established. The Eucharist is the central celebration of the Christian community, the sign of unity and love that draws the people of God together with one another and with God in Jesus. So, as leaders of the community, ordained ministers are called specifically to lead the Christian community in celebrating the Eucharist and the other sacraments.

The call to ordained ministry continues to be offered today. In one of his speeches, Pope John Paul II talked about the need for new ordained ministers:

. . . The Lord Jesus, in founding the Church, decided to institute particular ministries which He entrusted to those whom He freely chose from amongst His disciples.

Thus the Divine Redeemer wants many of you, more numerous than you may think, to participate in the ministerial priesthood in order to give the Eucharist to humanity, to forgive sins, to guide the community. Christ counts on you for this marvelous mission. Priests are necessary to the world because Christ is necessary. (*Message for World Day of Prayer for Vocations*, no. 3)

Single life, marriage, and religious life are all ways to serve humankind and God. The church presents a fourth option as well—ordained ministry. It would be worthwhile to take some time to consider this lifestyle.

Called as Leaders, Mediators, and Servants

The specific, unique ministry of the ordained is a sacramental one. Priests, bishops, and to some extent, deacons preside at celebrations of the sacraments. Furthermore, like all baptized

Ordained ministers are called specifically to lead the Christian community in celebrating the Eucharist and the other sacraments.

Christians, they are called to spread the Good News of Jesus Christ. But over the centuries, the ordained ministry has taken on other roles as well—the roles of leader, mediator, and servant.

Leaders:
Carrying on the Work of the Apostles

In the church's tradition, the ordained ministry carries on the work of Jesus' Apostles, the first persons called to leadership in the church. Jesus designated Peter to be the head of the new Christian community. The other Apostles were to provide leadership to the church, too, but Peter was first among them. Soon after Jesus' death and Resurrection, missionaries such as Barnabas and the Apostle Paul spread out across the Roman Empire to preach the word of God, to heal, and to form local Christian communities.

Soon many local communities were thriving—the churches of Jerusalem, Antioch, Ephesus, Philippi, and Rome, to name a few. As a local church grew in size, a leader, or bishop, was selected by one of the founding Apostles to head that Christian community. Evidence exists that some of the Apostles moved to the larger cities and exercised leadership there. For example, Peter led the community in Rome. (On the basis of Peter's residence and martyrdom there, the bishop of Rome—later called the pope—traditionally has held the central position of authority and leadership in the Roman Catholic church.)

In the earliest days of the church, the selection of a local leader was accomplished by an Apostle's working with the local church to determine who in that community was most suited for leadership. After all of the founding Apostles had died, the communities selected their own bishops, usually with the advice of a bishop from another local church.

One remarkable situation was that of the famous bishop Saint Ambrose of Milan, Italy (339–397). He was not even a Christian when the people of Milan proclaimed him bishop, but they chose him because he was an excellent Roman governor of the area and a natural leader. Another bishop came to Milan to make the appointment official, and Ambrose was baptized, confirmed, given the Eucharist, and ordained bishop—all in the space of several days. Of course, this was not the usual way that leaders were chosen for the church, but it does point to one key aspect of the ordained ministry that exists even today: bishops, deacons, and priests are expected to be leaders in the Christian community.

Over the centuries, ordained ministers have assumed the roles of leader, mediator, and servant in the church.

Mediators: Representatives of and to the Christian Community

Ordained ministers traditionally have been seen as mediators—that is, as go-betweens or representatives *of* the Christian community and *to* the Christian community. They carry the concerns *of* the Christian community to God, praying on the people's behalf and offering sacrifice to God for them. But the ordained also speak *to* the community on God's behalf, reminding the people of God's word to them in the past and challenging and helping them to discern how that word applies to their present situation.

Servants: Becoming Like Jesus

In the church's tradition, the ordained ministry has always included the expectation that leaders should follow the model of Jesus, who came "not to be served but to serve, and to give his life as a ransom for many" (Mark 10:45). Above all, bishops, deacons, and priests need to be servants, people who spend their lives and energies for others. Jesus made this very clear at the Last Supper when he performed the servant's role of washing the feet of each Apostle as an example of the loving service that his followers must give to the community (John 13:1–15). Ordained ministers, like the Apostles, are called to be servants after the model of Jesus.

Ordained ministers are called to follow the example of Jesus, who came "not to be served but to serve."

In recent decades, especially since Vatican Council II in the early 1960s, the church has renewed and broadened its understanding of priesthood, reemphasizing the meaning that it had in the early Church. Particularly in the first century, the whole Christian community was seen as sharing in Jesus' priestly function. By virtue of their baptism, all Christians were to act after the model of Jesus, the High Priest, who most clearly revealed God to human beings. But this understanding was somewhat obscured over the centuries of the church's history.

Today, however, Catholic Christians are rediscovering the sense that they, along with the clergy, are called to roles of leadership, mediation (that is, praying for the community to God and speaking of God's word to the community), and servanthood. More often, aspects of the roles that for centuries were considered exclusive to the clergy are being shared with the laity. Thus the *essential* roles of bishops, deacons, and priests—their leadership in sacramental ministry—have been able to stand out more clearly.

Bishops

Supervisors, Shepherds, and Teachers

The word *bishop* has its origin in the Greek word *episkopos,* meaning "overseer." This defines well the role of bishops. Beginning with the first century of the church, bishops were selected to head local churches, now called dioceses. Bishops have inherited the authority of the Apostles to appoint deacons and priests to serve the Christian community. **Bishops** themselves serve the church by supervising the activities of their dioceses while taking part in the roles of the ordained ministry outlined above. Perhaps you have experienced the sacramental ministry of a bishop by receiving the Sacrament of Confirmation.

These moving words from the ordination ceremony for a bishop express the union of leadership with service that is held up as an ideal for bishops:

List all of the official activities that you are aware of that are performed by the bishop of your diocese. Then summarize how your bishop provides leadership to the local Christian community.

> You, dear brother, have been chosen by the Lord. Remember that you are chosen from among men and appointed to act for men and women in relation to God. The title of bishop is one not of honor but of function, and therefore a bishop should strive to serve rather than to rule. Such is the counsel of the Master: the greater should behave as if he were the least, and the leader as if he were the one who serves. Proclaim the message whether it is welcome or unwelcome. . . . Pray and offer sacrifice for the people committed to your care and so draw every kind of grace for them from the overflowing holiness of Christ. . . .
>
> As a father and a brother, love all those whom God places in your care. Love the priests and deacons who share with you the ministry of Christ. Love the poor and infirm, strangers and the homeless. Encourage the faithful to work with you in your apostolic task; listen willingly to what they have to say. Never relax your concern for those who do not yet belong to the one fold of Christ; they too are commended to you in the Lord.

The responsibilities of bishops are complex and demanding. Bishops are to be not only administrators but also shepherds, caring tenderly about the concerns of the thousands of members of their dioceses.

In addition, because of their very public role as leaders and

Write your reaction to this statement:
- Bishops should not make official statements on subjects like apartheid, world economic imbalances, disarmament, and other social issues.

teachers in the church, bishops recently have been looking into difficult social and moral issues to try to articulate for the faithful and the world what guidance the Christian Scriptures and the tradition of the church can give for those issues.

- The U.S. Catholic bishops have issued statements on nuclear war and economic justice: *The Challenge of Peace: God's Promise and Our Response* (1983) and *Economic Justice for All: Pastoral Letter on Catholic Social Teaching and the U.S. Economy* (1986).
- The Canadian Catholic bishops have offered their perspective on the future of Canada's socioeconomic order in *Ethical Choices and Political Challenges* (1983).
- Catholic bishops in South Africa have publicly challenged apartheid, their government's official racist policy.

All over the world, Catholic bishops are stepping out courageously to offer a gospel perspective on the urgent needs of the human family.

A Bishop for Our Times: Oscar Romero

A model of a bishop's courage and loving pastoral concern can be found in *Oscar Romero,* who from 1977 until his assassination in 1980 was the Archbishop of San Salvador in the Central American country of El Salvador. (Romero was killed in the same year that North American missionary Jean Donovan, described on pages 228–229, was murdered for working with El Salvador's refugees.)

When Romero was appointed archbishop of San Salvador, the country was in the midst of a popular revolutionary movement to free the society of the oppressive rule by the rich and the military. For decades, the population had been treated as virtual slaves; the masses of peasants were landless, hungry, and uneducated. A few rich families, supported by the government, held most of the land for their own profit, using the military and paramilitary death squads to support them by terrorizing the peasants into submission.

Known as a cautious conservative, Romero nonetheless became convinced that the people had to be defended in their struggle to obtain their rights. After the murders of several priests and laypeople who were working with poor Salvadorans, Romero took an increasingly courageous stand against the torture, kidnapping, and murder of people who had shown any sympathy with the movement for justice. The peasants of El

Salvador became the archbishop's own friends, and soon he was known worldwide as "the voice of those who have no voice," a fearless advocate for the poor people of his country.

Archbishop Oscar Romero of El Salvador, assassinated in 1980, was known as "the voice of those who have no voice."

Attempts were made to silence Romero by threats against his life, but in his homilies, he continued to speak "dangerous" words of truth. At the Sunday Mass on the day before his death, he made an appeal, carried by radio across the whole country, to the army, the National Guard, and the police to end the repression:

> Brothers, each one of you is one of us. We are the same people. The peasants you kill are your own brothers and sisters. When you hear the voice of a man commanding you to kill, remember instead the voice of God: "Thou Shalt Not Kill!" God's law must prevail. No soldier is obliged to obey an order contrary to the law of God. There is still time for you to obey your own conscience, even in the face of a sinful command to kill.
>
> The Church, defender of the rights of God, of the law of God, and of the dignity of each human being, cannot remain silent in the presence of such abominations.
>
> The government must understand that reforms, steeped in so much blood, are worthless. In the name of God, in the name of our tormented people whose cries rise up to Heaven, I beseech you, I beg you, I command you, *Stop the repression!*

On the following day, 24 March 1980, Romero celebrated Mass in the chapel of a hospital for poor cancer patients. During the homily, the archbishop spoke these prophetic words:

> Whoever out of love for Christ gives himself to the service of others will live, like the grain of wheat that falls and only apparently dies. If it did not die it would remain alone. . . . Only in undoing itself does it produce the harvest.

At the end of the homily, a shot rang out; a short time later, Romero was dead, killed by an assassin. He had joined the long line of bishop-martyrs who, from the time of the Apostles, died for preaching the law of love—the word of God.

Describe in writing your reactions to the excerpts from the two homilies given by Archbishop Romero. Can you think of any issues about which you wish your bishop would speak as forcefully?

Deacons

Ministers of Charity, of the Word, and of the Liturgy

Deacons have served in the church from its earliest years. In fact, the first martyr, Saint Stephen, was a deacon. He had been elected with six other men by the Christian community of Jerusalem to help the Apostles; these deacons distributed food to widows and poor members whose needs might otherwise have been overlooked. Deacons were important in the early church's ministry because they had significant roles in preaching, in the liturgy, and in service to poor members of the community.

Over the centuries, the role of deacons declined, with the diaconate—or period of serving as a deacon—becoming only a stage in the preparation for the priesthood. Since the idea of restoring the permanent diaconate was approved by the Vatican Council II, many men have become permanent deacons. Other deacons are in the process of preparing to become priests. Men already married may become permanent deacons; in fact, most permanent deacons are married and support their families with full-time secular jobs. However, single men may not marry after they have been ordained as deacons.

Permanent deacons go through a three- to four-year training period that includes studies in theology, preaching, the Scriptures, and counseling, as well as practical experiences in ministry. After they are ordained, deacons usually attend classes to deepen their spirituality and to enhance their competencies as ministers. Today deacons serve in three areas:

- *Charity:* Like the first deacons of the early church, today's deacons are involved in serving poor people and those persons on the margins of society. For example, deacons might work with prisoners, inner-city homeless people, or sick people in nursing homes.

- *Preaching:* Deacons may read the Gospel at Mass and preach, but their responsibilities often extend to other ways of proclaiming the word, such as religious education and campus ministry.
- *Liturgy:* Deacons have official functions at liturgies. They distribute the Eucharist and may officiate at baptisms, marriages, wakes, funerals, and burial services.

One Deacon: Feeding the Hungry and Sheltering the Homeless

Jack offers an example of the possible ways of serving as a permanent deacon, especially as a minister of charity. He and his wife, Ann, operate a Catholic Worker house (one of the network of houses of hospitality started by Dorothy Day). A friend offers this account of his visit with Jack:

Interview a deacon or a priest. Ask him about the satisfactions and problems in his ministry, his views on obedience to the bishop, and any other questions of interest to you. Write a brief summary of your interview.

> Jack opens the door wide and stretches out his big, calloused hand. "Hi, I'm Jack. Welcome!"
>
> That is how everyone who comes to this Catholic Worker house is greeted. Then Jack usually asks the folks who come in if they want something to eat or drink. Once he sits down with the people, they usually start talking. Jack listens intently, asking a question now and then and nodding.
>
> "You know," Jack explains about his work at the house of hospitality, "all those years I was a plumber I met lots of people who really just wanted someone to listen to them. I'd go into a house to work on someone's bathroom, and they'd talk away about all kinds of things. I'd just keep working and listening. Now here at the house, I can be almost a full-time listener. Lots of homeless people who come here want a friendly ear about as much as they want soup and bread."
>
> Jack became a deacon at the age of sixty. He and Ann had raised their four children. Jack had done well as a plumbing contractor, but he felt there was something more that he wanted to do with his life. He heard about the permanent diaconate, was accepted for the training, and finally was ordained. After ordination, he and Ann visited

"If one word could describe the ministry of the parish priest, it would be 'diversity.'"

Write your reflections on this question:
• Why is it necessary that priests display by their actions what they preach in their words?

a Catholic Worker house in another city and were inspired to open one in their own city. Each day Jack and Ann feed a line of hungry people who gather at the house, and they give overnight shelter to eighteen homeless people.

"We work real closely with our local parish," Jack explains, "and I even give a homily now and then when they need me. Mostly, though, this is my ministry here—with the homeless folks."

Priests

Catholic Christians usually are more familiar with the work of priests than with that of bishops and deacons. However, the priesthood as it is understood today was the last of the three forms of ordained ministry to emerge in the Christian community. In the early centuries of the church, the dioceses were similar in population size to our parishes. Bishops were able to preside at the Eucharist and other liturgies. Eventually, the church spread out into small towns, and Christian communities in cities became too large for bishops to supervise effectively. With this growth came another level of ordained ministry—the presbyters, or elders. The modern word *priest* comes from *presbyter.* Organizationally, presbyters as well as deacons worked under the local bishop. The role of presbyter evolved into what we now know as the priesthood.

Diverse Roles and Functions

Like bishops and deacons, priests are to be sacramental ministers, leaders, mediators, and servants of the people of God. Most commonly, diocesan priests (priests who are not members of religious orders) work in parishes, presiding at sacramental celebrations, preaching, teaching, and coordinating the ministries done by other men and women in the parish. Diocesan priests also work in other ministries besides parishes; for example, they teach in and administer schools, work in social-service agencies, write for diocesan newspapers, and minister on college campuses.

Priests belonging to religious orders minister under the supervision of their congregations, doing the work of their own religious community. But by the Sacrament of Ordination, they also are empowered to fulfill the role of sacramental minister.

The actual functions of a priest in a local community vary greatly. In many small towns and villages throughout the world, a priest might be the only educated resident. Consequently, he may become a civic leader, an agricultural adviser, a health and welfare agent, and a judge in addition to performing his priestly duties.

Even in large cities, parish priests often assume many roles. Fr. Donald J. Winkles, a diocesan priest, described the duties of a parish priest:

> If one word could describe the ministry of the parish priest, it would be "diversity."
>
> The scope of his daily concern would include the celebration of the Eucharist, the care of the sick, administrative responsibilities, programs of sacramental preparation, meetings with parish council and committees, community concerns, spiritual direction, reconciliation and healing, teaching and homily preparation and time for prayer, study, and recreation.
>
> Over and above these concerns are the "surprises," the unscheduled needs that can emerge anytime, and can be anything from the highly unusual to the very inspiring. All are opportunities for service and often are the most effective ministry of the day. In all this, diversity is the word.

Handling such diversity is difficult. The expectations placed on priests are numerous, and sometimes people judge priests harshly when they do not possess strengths in all areas of their diverse ministry.

One important role of priests is to build up the Christian family.

Building Up the Christian Family

In fact, a pastor cannot possibly perform all of the functions of ministry that are needed in a parish. Sharing ministry with parishioners is the key not only to the priest's own sense of balance but also to building up a sense of family and nurturing the real gifts of the people in the parish. For instance, one parishioner in what was formerly a declining inner-city parish recalled how the pastor built a sense of community and shared ministry with the people:

Think of a priest whom you admire. List the qualities that make this priest admirable, and write a reflection on how this priest can be a model for your own life.

> Father Bill had the remarkable ability to get things to start happening between people. He often worked behind the scenes, encouraging a parishioner to get someone else involved in a project or to reach out to a member who needed to be brought into the community. He loved us and believed in us so much that we found ourselves wanting to pass that on. We used to say, "Father Bill has 'calling power.' When

he calls, you listen." And he passed that calling power on to his parishioners.

Pretty soon, lots of people were taking the initiative of calling others to get involved in the liturgy, offering retreats for the rest of the parish, or simply befriending the lonely or abandoned folks who usually found their way to our parish. With all of these connections between people, our lives were really being knit together. Eventually, we turned our focus outward as well; the parish took on a regular ministry to homeless people and a peace ministry.

When Father Bill celebrated Sunday Mass with us, it was not simply a ritual that we were going through. It was a celebration of our life together in Jesus, with all of its frustrations and joys. Since Father Bill was transferred, the spirit of family and of reaching out beyond our parish has stayed alive and grown.

Persons who are considering the priesthood need to examine their motives and their ability to live as a priest.

Qualifications for the Priesthood

Persons who are considering the priesthood need to examine themselves to determine whether they have the qualities necessary to become a priest. If they find that they do have the following qualities, then through prayer and discussion with a spiritual guide or counselor, they may become aware that God is calling them to the priesthood.

An Attraction to the Priesthood

First, an individual needs to have an attraction to the lifestyle of the priesthood based on proper motives. Perhaps a friendship with a priest gives a person an initial attraction to the lifestyle. Proper motives would include a desire to do any of the following:

- serve the Christian community
- preach the word of God
- enter into leadership in the sacramental ministry of the church

An Ability to Live as a Priest

Living as a priest entails promises of obedience and celibacy. Someone considering the priesthood needs to assess whether he can faithfully fulfill these promises.

Obedience: Priests place themselves at the service of the church by submitting to the authority of the diocesan bishop. Although assignments usually are made after close consultation between the bishop and the priest, a priest may be asked to assume duties for which he does not feel a great fondness. Someone who cannot promise obedience to a bishop should probably minister in a different vocation.

Celibacy: Celibacy is required of priests for many of the same reasons that it is required of religious. Celibacy allows the priest the freedom to love inclusively—that is, with a love that extends to the wider human community and without the limitations of a commitment to a wife and family—and to move when required. Celibacy can result in intense loneliness. Nevertheless, loneliness is part of every person's life—married, single, or celibate. Fr. John Reedy, writing in *Notre Dame Magazine,* remarked:

> . . . Commitments [to either marriage or celibacy] . . . do not erase the yearning for the kind of intimacy that can come from a unique sharing of one's life, with all its hopes and fears and hurts, with one other person who accepts this trust and returns it. I'm not so naive as to believe that all marriages provide such intimacy. But married or celibate, most of us feel the need for it. . . .
>
> Ideally, the [priest] should find such intimacy in his relationship with God. . . .
>
> . . . Every life has its difficulties. Mine also has had satisfactions which have enabled me, with God's support, to accept the difficulties and to find a deep, underlying happiness beneath the routine.

Priests can and should develop all types of intimacy with friends, except sexual intimacy. Like everyone else, priests rely on the support of close friends and loved ones, but they vow that no one relationship will claim their primary attention and responsibility.

Sufficient Intellectual Ability

Candidates for the priesthood must have sufficient intellectual ability to complete their course of study, which usually includes an undergraduate degree and four years of theological and ministerial training. Some priests are brilliant scholars, but brilliance certainly is not required. Indeed, the patron saint of parish priests, Saint John Vianney, was barely able to finish

Answer these questions in writing:
- What characteristics do you have that would qualify you for the ordained ministry?
- What obstacles might be standing in the way of your following a call to ordained ministry?

his studies. What made him a saintly, wonderful priest was his great love for God and other people.

Sharing the Richness of Human Life

Complete each part of the following statement in writing: If my best friend announced that he was going to be a priest,
- my greatest joy would be . . .
- my greatest concern would be . . .
- I would feel . . .

Bishops, deacons, and priests carry the dream of Jesus in a special way. In preaching, in leading, and in their sacramental ministry, these ordained ministers call to Christians to build the peaceable kingdom, create a loving community, and nourish persons to become fully alive.

The sacramental ministry especially offers ordained ministers a unique opportunity to enter into the richness of human existence in community and to help people to realize how the dream of Jesus is happening in their own lives. Fr. Bob Stamschror, a diocesan priest, summarized how ministering through the sacraments is a great blessing:

> No life is without its problems, but I'm quite happy. The priesthood has been a blessing for me, especially because people share so much of the richness of their lives with me. As a priest, I am a part of and celebrate some of the most important and touching times in people's lives: At Baptism, I wonder at the creation of new life. At the Eucharist, I share with my community the love of God. In the Mass of the Resurrection [funeral Mass], I am allowed to share in people's grieving, I try to console them, and we celebrate the new life of resurrection. Then, in Reconciliation, I share in the pain of guilt and the relief of forgiveness and healing. I can't imagine any other profession that so totally permits a person to partake of the richness of human life—its suffering and joy, despair and hope, blindness and creativity. I feel continually blessed.

In writing, summarize your beliefs and feelings about the lifestyle of the ordained ministry.

Review Questions

1. Which passage from the Christian Testament is cited in this chapter as part of the discussion about the church tradition of ordained ministry? Which passage is cited to explain the ordained's specific ministry of leadership in the sacramental life of the church?

2. Explain how the tradition of ordained ministers as leaders originated and has continued.

3. In what ways are ordained ministers to be mediators and servants?

4. What are some of the roles of bishops?

5. How was Archbishop Oscar Romero a model of courage and pastoral concern?

6. When did the ministry of deacons begin, and in what ways do they serve in the church?

7. How is Jack's ministry, described on pages 343–344, typical of the traditional work of deacons?

8. How did the role of priests evolve in the church? What word does the word *priest* come from?

9. Why is *diversity* a good word to describe the ministry of a parish priest?

10. How can a parish priest help to build up the Christian family?

11. List and explain the qualifications necessary to become a priest.

12. How can ministering through the sacraments be a great blessing for a priest?

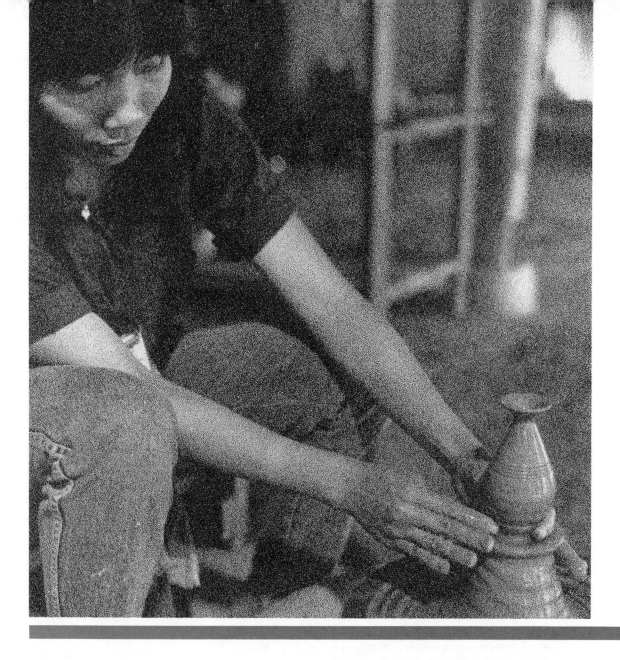

Conclusion

W E began this course by discussing dreams, and it is fitting that we end by reconsidering them. During this course, you have had opportunities to develop insights about yourself and your dream by looking at some of the major choices that will shape your life. Your dream—the vision of the future that you want to bring about for yourself and for those whose lives you touch—will give your life energy, direction, and meaning.

Uniting Our Dreams with Jesus' Dream

In this course, we have seen that Christians are called to unite their own unique dreams with Jesus' dream of building the peaceable kingdom, creating a loving community, and nourishing people to be fully alive. As Christians love one another and love God, they build a more human world:

- a peaceful world where conflicts are resolved in ways that strengthen the bonds of the human family
- a world where homeless people are sheltered, sick people are comforted, hungry people are fed, and people on the margins of society are welcomed into community
- a world where every person has the chance to grow to her or his potential

With every act of love, the dream of Jesus comes closer to fulfillment: " '. . . The kingdom of God is very near to you' " (Luke 10:9).

With every act of love, the dream of Jesus comes closer to fulfillment.

Our dreams are realized moment by moment, day by day, in the way that we take on the choices and challenges at hand.

Shaping the Dream: The Power of the Present Moment

Dreams do not magically come true. In the real world, despite the affectionate kisses of a beautiful princess, a toad does not become a handsome prince. Winners of million-dollar sweepstakes may be very lucky, but they at least had to mail in their entry forms. Our dream is realized—it "comes true"—moment by moment, day by day, in the way that we take on the choices and challenges at hand.

Focusing on our dream does not remove us from the present moment; rather, it calls us to live more deeply in the present by making choices consciously. In truth, the present moment is all that we have. Essayist and poet Ralph Waldo Emerson said, "One of the illusions of life is that the present hour is not the critical, decisive hour. Write it on your heart that every day is the best day of the year." Today is full of possibilities for choosing consciously; today is the best day of the year.

This course has given you the opportunity to consider your choices in these major areas of life:
- identity and autonomy
- love
- communication
- sexuality
- lifelong learning
- work
- money and possessions
- leisure

This course has also presented four lifestyle paths as options:
- single life
- marriage
- religious life
- ordained ministry

Each of these paths has its advantages and disadvantages, and each can be meaningful, loving, joyous, and full of opportunities to contribute to humankind.

Jesus certainly understood our need to realize our dreams in the present moment through the choices that we make, even small choices that might not seem significant at a particular time. It was Jesus who encouraged people to see a dream's potential in small, even hidden beginnings:

. . . "What can we say the kingdom is like? What parable can we find for it? It is like a mustard seed which, at the time of its sowing, is the smallest of all the seeds on earth. Yet once it is sown it grows into the biggest shrub of them all and puts out big branches so that the birds of the air can shelter in its shade." (Mark 4:30–32)

Jesus urged people to open their eyes so that they might see clearly that the dream they did not even understand was already in their midst: " '. . . Look, the kingdom of God is among you' " (Luke 17:21). Jesus, more than anyone, recognized the power and the possibility of the present moment and the significance of each person's daily choices.

You Are Important

Imagine a clear, calm pond. In your mind, toss a small stone into the water. Immediately, ripples spread out in an ever-widening circle, changing the face of the pond.

The world is large. Several billion people inhabit our planet. Nevertheless, small pebble that each of us is, you affect the world and its future. Your decisions and actions spread ripples of effects far beyond what you can see.

The value of your life cannot be measured. You are important because, in the Christian understanding of things, you are made in God's image, created to love because God is love.

> Yahweh . . .
> You created my inmost being
> and knit me together in my mother's womb.
> For all these mysteries—
> for the wonders of myself,
> for the wonder of your works—
> I thank you.
>
> (Psalm 139:1,13–14)

You are important.

Index

Acknowledgments (*continued*)

The psalms quoted in this book are from *Psalms Anew: In Inclusive Language,* by Nancy Schreck, OSF, and Maureen Leach, OSF. Copyright © 1986 by Saint Mary's Press.

All other scriptural quotations used in this book are from *The New Jerusalem Bible.* Copyright © 1985 by Darton, Longman & Todd, Ltd., and Doubleday, a division of Bantam, Doubleday, Dell Publishing Group, Inc. Reprinted by permission of the publisher.

Chapter 1

The song lyric on page 15 is from "Over the Rainbow," composed by E. Y. Harburg and Harold Arlen. Copyright © 1938, 1939 (renewed 1966, 1967) by Metro-Goldwyn-Mayer, Inc. All rights controlled and administered by Leo Feist, Inc. All rights of Leo Feist, Inc., assigned to SBK Catalog Partnership. All rights controlled and administered by SBK Feist Catalog. International copyright secured. Made in USA. All rights reserved. Used with permission.

The excerpt from a speech by Dr. Martin Luther King, Jr., on pages 15–16 is quoted in *The Days of Martin Luther King, Jr.,* by Jim Bishop (New York: G. P. Putnam's Sons, 1971), page 327. Copyright © 1971 by Jim Bishop. All rights reserved.

The excerpts from "The Death of Ivan Ilych" on page 28 are from *The Raid and Other Stories,* by Leo Tolstoy (Oxford, England: Oxford University Press, 1982), pages 235 and 276. Used with permission.

Chapter 2

The excerpt on page 45 is from *That Hideous Strength,* by C. S. Lewis (New York: Macmillan Co., 1946), pages 287–288. Used with permission of the Bodley Head, Ltd., on behalf of the Estate of C. S. Lewis.

The Hindu saying on page 45 is from *The Upanishads,* translated from the Sanskrit with an introduction by Juan Mascaró (Harmondsworth, England: Penguin Books, 1965), page 140. Copyright © 1965 by Juan Mascaró. Reproduced by permission of Penguin Books, Ltd.

The poem by Robert Frost on page 50 is from *The Poetry of Robert Frost,* edited by Edward Connery Lathem (New York: Holt, Rinehart and Winston). Copyright © 1916, 1969 by Holt, Rinehart and Winston. Copyright © 1944 by Robert Frost. Reprinted by permission of Henry Holt and Company, Inc., and by Jonathan Cape, Ltd., on behalf of the Estate of Robert Frost.

Chapter 3

The excerpt from the poem by Emily Dickinson on page 67 is from number 1732 in *The Complete Poems of Emily Dickinson,* edited by Thomas H. Johnson (Boston: Little, Brown and Co., 1960).

The passage about Michael Geilenfeld on page 68 is taken from "A Theater of Living Hope," an unpublished information sheet about the Saint Joseph's Boys Home in Haiti.

The excerpt on pages 73–74 is from *Ironweed,* by William Kennedy (New York: Viking Penguin, 1983), pages 35–36. Copyright © 1979, 1981, 1983 by William Kennedy. Reprinted by permission of Viking Penguin, Inc.

The quotation on page 78 is from *Following Jesus,* by Segundo Galilea (Maryknoll, NY: Orbis Books, 1981), page 31.

The bulleted excerpts on page 78 are from *There Is a Season,* by Eugene S. Geissler (Notre Dame, IN: Ave Maria Press, 1969), pages 118–119, 83, and 89 respectively. Used with permission.

The prayer on page 79, "Canticle to the Sun," by Saint Francis of Assisi, is quoted in *Teaching Manual for "The Catholic Church: Our Mission in History,"* by Carl Koch, FSC (Winona, MN: Saint Mary's Press, 1985), page 168.

The poem by Mary Eleanore Rice on page 86 is from *Images: Women in Transition,* compiled by Janice Grana (Winona, MN: Saint Mary's College Press, 1977), page 65. Copyright © 1976 by the Upper Room, Nashville, Tennessee.

Chapter 4

The excerpts on pages 89 and 104 are from *The Annotated Alice: Alice's Adventures in Wonderland and Through the Looking Glass,* by Lewis Carroll, with an introduction and notes by Martin Gardner (New York: Clarkson N. Potter, 1960), pages 268–269 and 94 respectively. Used with permission.

The excerpt on page 103 is from *Ordinary People,* by Judith Guest (New York: Viking Press, 1976), pages 225 and 227. Copyright © 1976 by Judith Guest. Reprinted by permission of Viking Penguin, Inc.

Chapter 5

The excerpts on pages 119, 120, and 125 are from *Love and Sexuality: A Christian Approach,* by Mary Perkins Ryan and John Julian Ryan (New York: Holt, Rinehart and Winston, 1967), pages 43, 44, and 77 respectively. Used with permission.

The excerpt on page 121 is from *Educational Guidance in Human Love,* by the Sacred Congregation for Catholic Education (Rome: Sacred Congregation for Catholic Education, 1983), number 4. Used with permission.

The poem excerpts on pages 122–123 are from "What Manner of Thing Is Love," by Jorge Manrique, in *The World's Love Poetry,* edited by M. R. Martin and S. Beckett (New York: Bantam Books, 1960), pages 166–167.

The excerpt on page 129 is from *Living More with Less,* by Doris Janzen Longacre (Scottsdale, PA: Herald Press, 1980), page 41. Copyright © 1980 by Herald Press, Scottsdale, PA 15683. Used with permission.

The first excerpt on page 130 is from *Coming Up for Air,* by George Orwell (New York: Harcourt, Brace and Co., 1950), page 75. Reprinted by permission of Harcourt Brace Jovanovich, Inc.

The excerpt on pages 130–131 is entitled "Ain't I a Woman?" by Sojourner Truth, quoted in *The Norton Anthology of Literature by Women,* edited by Sandra M. Gilbert and Susan Gubar (New York: W. W. Norton and Co., 1985), page 253.

The poem on page 132 is "For Every Woman," by Nancy R. Smith, quoted in *Images: Women in Transition,* compiled by Grana, page 52.

Chapter 6

The poem by Molly Dee Rundle on pages 139–140 is from *Images: Women in Transition,* compiled by Grana, page 65.

The excerpts on pages 143–144 and 162 are from *Self-Renewal,* revised edition, by John W. Gardner (New York: W. W. Norton and Co., 1981), pages 10–11 and 11 respectively. Copyright © 1981 by John W. Gardner. Used with permission.

The quotation on page 156 is from *The Language of the Night,* by Ursula K. Le Guin (New York: Berkley Books, 1982), page 187. Copyright © 1979 by Susan Wood. Used with permission.

The excerpt on page 157 is from R. Newmarch, *Life and Letters of Peter Illich Tchaikovsky* (John Lane, 1906), reprinted in *Creativity,* edited by P. E. Vernon (New York: Penguin Books, 1970), page 57.

Chapter 7

The excerpts on pages 165–166, 167, 169, 170, and 180 are from *Working: People Talk About What They Do All Day and How They Feel About What They Do,* by Studs Terkel (New York: Pantheon Books, a Division of Random House, Inc.), pages 422–424, 294–295, 489–493, xxiv, and 463 respectively. Copyright © 1972, 1974 by Studs Terkel. Used with permission.

The excerpt on page 172 is from *The Pastoral Constitution on the Church in the Modern World,* quoted in *On Human Work,* by Pope John Paul II, number 25.

The excerpt on page 173 is from "Resign Your Nuclear Jobs," a statement by Bishop Leroy T. Matthiesen of Amarillo, Texas, reprinted in *Center Peace: A News Journal for Alternative Living* 4, September–October 1981, page 3.

The excerpt on page 174 is from the encyclical *On Human Work,* by Pope John Paul II, 14 September 1981 (Washington, DC: United States Catholic Conference, 1981), number 8.

The excerpt on page 179 is from *Death of a Salesman,* by Arthur Miller. Copyright © 1949 by Arthur Miller, renewed 1977 by Arthur Miller. Taken from *Arthur Miller's Collected Plays,* 1957, reprinted in *The American Tradition in Literature,* sixth edition, volume 2 (New York: Random House, n.d.), page 1505. Used with permission.

The excerpt on page 181 is from *Work and Play,* by Alasdair Clayre (New York: Harper & Row, 1974), page 176.

The excerpt on page 184 is from *Economic Justice for All: Catholic Social Teaching and the U.S. Economy,* by the U.S. bishops (Washington, DC: United States Catholic Conference, 1986), numbers 136–137. Copyright © 1986 by the United States Catholic Conference. Used with permission.

Chapter 8

The excerpt on page 192 is from "The Rocking-Horse Winner," by D. H. Lawrence, reprinted from *The Complete Short Stories of D. H. Lawrence,* volume 3. Copyright © 1933 by the Estate of D. H. Lawrence. Copyright renewed 1961 by Angelo Ravagli and C. M. Weekley, Executors of the Estate of Frieda Lawrence Ravagli. Reprinted by permission of Viking Penguin, Inc., with acknowledgment to Laurence Pollinger, Ltd., London.

The quotations on pages 197 and 202 and the excerpt on page 200 are from *Economic Justice for All*, by the U.S. bishops, numbers 75, 34, 186, and 172 respectively. Used with permission.

The quotation on page 197 is from *On Human Work*, by Pope John Paul II, number 14.

The quotation from the papal address at Yankee Stadium on page 199 is from "Special Sensitivity Toward Those in Distress," by Pope John Paul II, 2 October 1979, reprinted in *Justice in the Marketplace*, edited by David M. Byers (Washington, DC: United States Catholic Conference, 1985), page 352.

The excerpt on page 201 is from "Neighbour Rosicky," taken from *Obscure Destinies*, by Willa Cather (New York: Alfred A. Knopf, Inc.). Copyright © 1932 by Willa Cather and renewed in 1960 by the Executors of the Estate of Willa Cather. Reprinted in *The American Tradition in Literature*, page 940. Reprinted by permission of Alfred A. Knopf, Inc.

Chapter 9

The excerpt on pages 209–210 is from the *Tao Teh Ching*, by Lao Tzu, quoted in *Freedom and Destiny*, by Rollo May (New York: W. W. Norton and Co.), page 165. Copyright © 1981 by Rollo May. Used with permission.

The excerpt on pages 210–211 is from *The Work Trap: Solving the Riddle of Work and Leisure*, by Martin C. Helldorfer (Winona, MN: Saint Mary's Press, 1981), page 17. Reprinted by permission of Affirmation Books.

The excerpt on page 213 is from *Living More with Less*, by Longacre, pages 220–221. Used with permission.

The excerpt from the poem by Robert Frost on page 214 is taken from *Selected Poems of Robert Frost*, with an introduction by Robert Graves (New York: Holt, Rinehart and Winston, 1963), page 78. Used with permission.

The excerpt on page 222 is from *Freedom and Destiny*, by May, page 177. Used with permission.

Chapter 10

The excerpts on pages 228–229 are from *Salvador Witness: The Life and Calling of Jean Donovan*, by Ana Carrigan (New York: Simon and Schuster, 1984), pages 67 and 96. Copyright © 1984 by Ana Carrigan. Reprinted by permission of Simon & Schuster, Inc.

The excerpt on page 232 is from *By Little and By Little: The Selected Writings of Dorothy Day*, edited and with an introduction by Robert Ellsberg (New York: Alfred A. Knopf, Inc., 1983). Copyright © 1983 by Robert Ellsberg and Tamar Hennessy. Used with permission of Alfred A. Knopf, Inc., and Dove Communications.

The excerpts on pages 234–235 are from *Flannery O'Connor: The Habit of Being*, letters edited and with an introduction by Sally Fitzgerald (New York: Farrar, Straus and Giroux, Inc., 1979), pages 163–164 and 92–93. Copyright © 1979 by Regina O'Connor.

The excerpt on pages 236–237 is from *Loneliness*, by Clark E. Moustakas (Prentice-Hall, Inc., 1961), pages 102–103. Copyright © 1961 by Clark E. Moustakas. Reprinted by permission of the publisher, Prentice-Hall, Inc., Englewood Cliffs, New Jersey.

The excerpts on pages 237 and 242 are from *Markings*, by Dag Hammarskjöld, translated by W. H. Auden and Leif Sjöberg (New York: Alfred A. Knopf, Inc., 1976), pages 85 and 53.

The excerpt on page 240 is from *Love and Lifestyles: Building Relationships in a Changing Society*, by Mary Judd (Winona, MN: Saint Mary's Press, 1981), page 88.

Chapter 11

The extract on pages 257–258 is from *Growing Up*, by Russell Baker (New York: Congdon & Weed, 1982), page 253. Copyright © 1982 by Russell Baker. Reprinted by permission of Congdon & Weed, Inc.

Chapter 12

The prayer on page 268 is from *The God Who Fell from Heaven*, by John Shea (Niles, IL: Argus Communications, 1979), page 97. Copyright © 1979 by Tabor Publishing, a division of DLM, Inc., Allen, TX 75002. Used with permission.

The first two excerpts on page 271 and the excerpts on page 273 are from "Marriages Made to Last," by Jeanette Lauer and Robert Lauer, in *Psychology Today*, June 1985, pages 24 and 26 respectively. Copyright © 1985 by the American

Psychological Association. All rights reserved. Used with permission.

The third excerpt on page 271 is from *On the Family,* by Pope John Paul II, 15 December 1981 (Washington, DC: United States Catholic Conference, 1982), number 28. Copyright © 1982 by the United States Catholic Conference. Used with permission.

The poem on pages 271–272 by Janet Miles is taken from *Images: Women in Transition,* compiled by Grana, page 70.

The quotation by Antoine de Saint-Exupéry on page 274 is quoted in *Gift from the Sea,* by Anne Morrow Lindbergh (New York: Random House, 1977), page 81.

The excerpts on page 282 are from the English translation of *Rite of Marriage.* Copyright © 1969 by the International Committee on English in the Liturgy, Inc. (ICEL), in *The Rites of the Catholic Church,* study edition (New York: Pueblo Publishing Co., 1983), pages 560–561. All rights reserved. Used with permission.

Chapter 13

The extract on page 287 is from "Neighbour Rosicky," taken from *Obscure Destinies,* by Cather, reprinted in *The American Tradition in Literature,* page 943. Reprinted by permission of Alfred A. Knopf, Inc.

The poem on page 290 by Sharon Addy appeared in "Marriage Matters," by David Mace, *Marriage and Family Living,* May 1985, page 37. Used with permission.

The excerpts on page 294 are from *Living More with Less,* by Longacre, page 123. Used with permission.

The excerpt on page 302 is from *On the Family,* by Pope John Paul II, number 30. Used with permission.

The excerpts on pages 303 and 304 are from *Just Friends,* by Lillian B. Rubin (New York: Harper & Row), pages 142 and 137–138 respectively.

The quotation on page 304 is from "Families Shouldn't Hush Up Problems," by Michael Cahill, *U.S. Catholic,* September 1984, page 17. Used with permission.

Chapter 14

The excerpt on page 312 is from "Sister of the Night," by Beverly Jeanne McBride and Dot Sten-

ning, taken from *The Catholic Digest,* January 1981, page 40.

The quotations on pages 312 and 313 are from "Melodious Monk," by Marielena Zuniga, condensed from *The Dialog,* 15 March 1985, in *The Catholic Digest,* July 1985, pages 80–81. Used with permission.

The excerpt on page 315 and the quotation by Saint Bernard on page 316 are from *The Nuns,* by Marcelle Bernstein (Philadelphia: J. B. Lippincott Co., 1976), pages 136 and 47 respectively.

The quotation on page 315 and the excerpt on page 319 are from *Response in Faith: Rule of Life,* by the School Sisters of Saint Francis, Milwaukee, Wisconsin, pages 8 and 13 respectively. Used with permission.

The excerpt on page 318 is from *Vocation Info,* edited by Jeremiah J. McGrath, MIC (Stockbridge, MA: Marian Press), pages 123–125. Copyright, n.d., by the Congregation of Marian Fathers, Inc. Used with permission.

The excerpt on page 323 is from *The Monastic Journey,* by Thomas Merton and edited by Bro. Patrick Hart (Mission, KS: Sheed Andrews and McMeel, Inc., 1977), pages 14 and 37.

The quotation on page 324 is from *The Rule of Saint Benedict,* translated by Urban J. Schnitzhofer, OSB (Canon City, CO: Holy Cross Abbey, 1967), page 226.

The excerpt by Saint Teresa of Ávila on page 324 is quoted in *Saints for All Seasons,* edited by John J. Delaney (Garden City, NY: Doubleday and Co., 1978), page 128. Used with permission.

The excerpts on pages 325 and 326 are from *St. Francis of Assisi: Writings and Early Biographies,* edited by Marion A. Habig (Chicago, IL: Franciscan Herald Press, 1973), pages 61–63. Copyright © 1973 by Franciscan Herald Press. Used with permission.

The quotations on pages 326 and 327 are from "Sister Arline Seeks a Cancer Cure from the Sea," by Nathan Alexander, condensed from *Marian Helpers Bulletin,* January–March 1985, in *The Catholic Digest,* May 1985, pages 81 and 83. Used with permission.

The excerpt from a newspaper article on page 328 is quoted in *Immigrant Saint: The Life of Mother Cabrini,* by Pietro Di Donato (New York: McGraw-Hill Book Co., 1960), pages 77–78. Copyright © 1960 by Pietro Di Donato. Used with permission.

Chapter 15

The excerpt on page 336 is from *Message from His Holiness, John Paul II, on the Occasion of the 1985 World Day of Prayer for Vocations,* 28 April 1985, number 3.

The excerpt on page 339 is from the English translation of *Ordination of Deacons, Priests, and Bishops,* copyright © 1975, International Committee on English in the Liturgy (ICEL), in *The Rites of the Catholic Church,* volume 2 (New York: Pueblo Publishing Co., 1980), page 91. All rights reserved. Used with permission.

The excerpt from Oscar Romero on page 341 is quoted in *Salvador Witness: The Life and Calling of Jean Donovan,* by Carrigan. Reprinted by permission of Simon & Schuster, Inc.

The excerpt from Oscar Romero on page 342 is quoted in "Since Death Came to the Archbishop," by Jack Wintz, OFM, condensed from the *St. Anthony Messenger,* March 1985, in *The Catholic Digest,* June 1985, page 32.

The excerpt on page 345 is from ". . . To See the Miracles of Salvation Taking Place Day by Day," by Rev. Donald J. Winkles, in *Priest: A Way of Life,* a publication of the Diocese of Winona (Winona, MN: Immaculate Heart of Mary Seminary, n.d.). Used with permission.

The excerpt on page 347 is from "Why I'm Still a Priest," by John Reedy, CSC, condensed from *Notre Dame Magazine,* July 1980, in *The Catholic Digest,* February 1981, pages 66–67. Used with permission.

Conclusion

The quotation by Ralph Waldo Emerson on page 352 is from *Great Thoughts of Thirty Centuries,* selected and arranged by Thomas Elbert Clemmons (Stuart, FL: Southeastern Press, 1970), page 53.

Photo Credits

The Image Bank: cover

Alfred A. Knopf/Bob Fitch: page 231

Bettmann Newsphotos: pages 15, 56, 242, 341

Paul Buddle: pages 31, 53, 54, 101, 103, 111, 122, 150, 153, 159, 162, 218, 219, 248, 266, 267, 272, 278, 283, 286, 353

James Carroll: page 39

Alan Cliburn: page 66

Jim Cronk: pages 32, 49, 62, 104, 119, 148 (top), 217, 241, 240, 292, 295, 300, 304, 330

Crosier Monastery: Rev. Gene Plaisted, OSC: pages 6, 11, 20, 44, 58, 59, 69, 77, 79, 88, 107, 114, 136, 145, 164, 213, 238, 268, 293, 310, 327, 334, 338, 345, 352

Gail Denham: page 298

EKM-Nepenthe: pages 3, 7, 9, 10, 12, 17, 21, 25, 29, 30, 35, 38, 48, 57, 60, 64, 70, 84, 108, 130 (both), 132, 137, 138, 148 (bottom), 156, 161, 169, 171, 172, 175, 178, 183, 186, 187, 189, 190, 192, 194, 199, 202, 204, 206, 208, 214, 216, 221, 222, 224, 225, 226, 230, 233, 235, 244, 251, 253, 263 (both), 290, 302

Mimi Forsyth: pages 50, 90, 112, 116, 120, 122, 147, 274, 350

National Catholic Photo Service: pages 311, 312, 317, 319, 322, 325, 329

St. Paul Pioneer Press: page 68

James Shaffer: pages 1, 4, 13, 14, 18, 19, 22, 27, 33, 34, 41, 42, 47, 55, 63, 74, 78, 80, 82, 83, 86, 92, 94, 96, 100, 124, 128, 129, 133, 158, 173, 174, 180, 181, 207, 250, 254, 256, 261, 264, 270, 276, 280, 284, 288, 303, 306, 307, 321, 323, 335, 336, 337, 344, 346, 351

Steve and Mary Skjold: pages 16, 73, 98, 197, 227, 236, 245, 260, 296

Smithsonian Institute: page 131

Task Force on Central America: page 228

The photo on page 314 is of Saint John Baptist De La Salle (from the painting, "The School of St. Sulpice," by Gagliardi).

The photo on page 322 is courtesy of Holy Cross Health System Corporation.

The drawings on pages 23 and 134 are by Dürer.

The drawings on pages 105 and 264 are from *The Annotated Alice,* by Lewis Carroll.